# Better Homes and Gardens®

# 1989 BEST-RECIPES
# YEARBOOK

Our seal assures you that every recipe in the *1989 Best-Recipes Yearbook* has been tested in the Better Homes and Gardens® Test Kitchen. This means that each recipe is practical and reliable, and meets our high standards of taste appeal.

# Better Homes and Gardens.

**Editor DAVID JORDAN**
**Managing Editor KATE GREER**
**Art Director BRADFORD W.S. HONG**

### Food and Nutrition
**Editor  NANCY BYAL**
*Department Head—Cook Books*  SHARYL HEIKEN
*Senior Food Editor—Magazine*  JOY TAYLOR
*Senior Food Editor—Meredith Publishing Services*
JOANNE JOHNSON
*Senior Food Editor—Special Interest Publications*
JANET FIGG
*Associate Department Heads*  SANDRA GRANSETH
ROSEMARY HUTCHINSON  ELIZABETH WOOLEVER
*Senior Food Editors*  BARBARA GOLDMAN
LINDA HENRY  BARBARA JOHNSON
MARCIA STANLEY  PAT TEBERG  JOYCE TROLLOPE
*Associate Food Editors*  JENNIFER DARLING
HEATHER HEPHNER  LISA HOLDERNESS
SHELLI McCONNELL  MARY MAJOR
MARY JO PLUTT  LOIS WHITE  DIANE YANNEY
*Editorial Assistants*
JENNIFER BRAUSEY  KAREN POLLOCK

### Graphic Design
*Managing Art Director*  GERALD PREATOR
*Associate Art Director*
JERRY J. RANK
*Senior Graphic Designer*  NANCY KLUENDER
*Graphic Designers*
KELLY BARTON  DAN BISHOP  KEVIN S. LUDGATE

### Copy and Production
*Copy Chief*  ELIZABETH HAHN BROOKS
*Makeup Editor*  LINDA R. THOMAS
*Associate Makeup Editor*  JUDY HUNSICKER
*Electronic Text Facilitator*  NANCY HALL
*Administrative Assistant*  CINDY ALBERTS

### Editorial Marketing Services
**Director  MARGARET McMAHON**
*New York-Shopping Editor*  ARLENE AVILES

### Editorial Services
**Executive Director DUANE L. GREGG**
*Director, Editorial Research*  C. RAY DEATON  *Research Associate*  SCOTT R. TOLAN
*Editorial Planning Manager*  DAVID S. JOHNSON  *Administrative Editor*  ROSE ANDERSON
*Art Business Office Manager*  DIANE BOYLE  *Test Kitchen Director*  SHARON STILWELL
*Photo Studio Manager*  DON WIPPERMAN

### Special Interest Publications
*Editor*  WILLIAM J. YATES  *Managing Editor*  LAMONT OLSON  *Art Director*  DON NICKELL
*Food Editor* JANET FIGG  *Furnishings Editor* HEATHER J. PAPER  *Traditional Home Editor* KAROL DeWULF NICKELL
*Building and Remodeling Editor* DAVID W. TOHT  *Crafts Editor* LAURA HOLTORF COLLINS

### Meredith Publishing Services
*Editor*  DOUGLAS A. HOLTHAUS  *Managing Editor*  PATRICIA POLLOCK  *Design Director*  DEETRA LEECH

### Books
*Editor*  GERALD KNOX  *Managing Editor*  DAVID A. KIRCHNER  *Art Director*  ERNEST SHELTON
*Associate Art Directors*  NEOMA THOMAS  LINDA FORD VERMIE  RANDALL YONTZ
*Editorial Project Managers*  LIZ ANDERSON  JAMES D. BLUME  MARSHA JAHNS
JENNIFER SPEER RAMUNDT  ANGELA K. RENKOSKI
*Assistant Art Directors*  LYNDA HAUPERT  HARIJS PRIEKULIS  TOM WEGNER
*Graphic Designers*  MARY SCHLUETER BENDGEN  MIKE BURNS

**Magazine Group Vice President** *Editorial Director* **DORIS M. EBY**
*Creative Director, Product Development* DAVID R. HAUPERT
*Editorial Management Associate* JOHN THOMAS

**Senior Vice President–Executive Publisher, Better Homes and Gardens**
**J. WESLEY SILK**
**Publisher DEL RUSHER**
*Publishing Services Director* TERRY UNSWORTH
*Advertising Sales Director* ROBERT M. BAXTER

**MAGAZINE GROUP PRESIDENT JAMES A. AUTRY**
**Magazine Group Vice Presidents**
Publishing Directors **ADOLPH AUERBACHER, BURTON H. BOERSMA,**
**CHRISTOPHER M. LEHMAN, MYRNA BLYTH**
**DEAN PIETERS,** Operations  **MAX RUNCIMAN,** Finance

MEREDITH CORPORATION
**Chairman of Executive Committee E. T. MEREDITH III**

CORPORATE OFFICERS: **Chairman of the Board ROBERT A. BURNETT**
**President JACK D. REHM**
**Group Presidents: JAMES A. AUTRY, Magazines**
**JERAMY LANIGAN, Books**
**W. C. McREYNOLDS, Broadcasting  ALLEN L. SABBAG, Real Estate**
**Vice Presidents: LEO R. ARMATIS, Corporate Relations**
**THOMAS G. FISHER, General Counsel and Secretary**
**NEIL KUEHNL, Product Development  FRED STINES, Special Projects**
**GERALD D. THORNTON, Administrative Services**
**JAMES F. STACK, Finance  Treasurer MICHAEL A. SELL**
**Corporate Controller and Assistant Secretary LARRY D. HARTSOOK**

# CONTENTS

In a year's time, *Better Homes and Gardens®* magazine publishes lots of wonderful recipes covering a myriad of subjects— from quick and easy cooking to upscale entertaining. In this, our seventh annual recipe yearbook, we invite you to rediscover the very best we had to offer in 1988.

# JANUARY

THE MAGAZINE FOR AMERICAN FAMILIES

JANUARY 1988
$1.50

## Better Homes and Gardens.

**Cuddle-Up Afghans**
Easy to Make!
Page 32

**Spirituality**
A New Source of
Strength for
Today's Families
Page 16

**Magic Moments**
How to Play with
a Child

**Free Butterick
Home-Sewing Pattern**
Page 78

# FAMILY FAST FAVORITES

# POT

**Y**our family will love the homey goodness. And, convenience foods make them a cinch to fix.

By Lynn Hoppe

## SLOPPY JOE PIE

*If you're sodium conscious, use low-sodium tomato sauce and corn—*

- **1½ cups packaged biscuit mix**
- **1 tablespoon parsley flakes**
- **1 17-ounce can whole kernel corn, drained**
- **1 15-ounce can tomato sauce**
- **8 ounces thinly sliced cooked beef (from deli), chopped**
- **1 1½-ounce envelope sloppy joe seasoning mix**

● **In a large bowl combine** biscuit mix and parsley. Add water; stir till moistened. Reserve ¾ *cup* of the dough. With lightly floured hands pat remaining dough onto the bottom and 1½ inches up the sides of a greased 2-quart au gratin dish or an 8x8x2-inch baking dish.

● **In a saucepan combine** the corn, tomato sauce, beef, and seasoning mix; heat through. Spoon tomato mixture over dough. Drop the reserved dough by small spoonfuls around the edge of the dish. Bake in a 400° oven for 15 to 20 minutes or till dumplings are golden. Makes 6 servings.

***Nutrition information per serving:*** *280 cal., 15 g pro., 39 g carbo., 8 g fat, 34 mg chol., 1,499 mg sodium. U.S. RDA: 16% vit. A, 16% thiamine, 15% riboflavin, 23% niacin, 19% iron, 22% phosphorus.*

## READY IN 25 MINUTES

**1. Simply pat crust into the baking dish.**

**2. Spoon in the savory sloppy joe filling.**

**3. Cap with spoonfuls of dough around the edge.**

# PIES!

## CHEDDAR AND TURKEY PIE

*Home-style, yet easy—*

- 1 9-inch folded refrigerated unbaked piecrust
- 1 pound ground raw turkey
- 2 cups loose-pack frozen mixed vegetables (such as broccoli, French-style green beans, onion, and red pepper), thawed
- 1 11-ounce can condensed cheddar cheese soup
- 1 5-ounce can (⅔ cup) evaporated milk
- ½ teaspoon dried thyme, crushed

• • •

- 1 beaten egg white
- 1 tablespoon water

Sesame seed

- ● Let plecrust stand at room temperature according to package directions.
- ● In a 3-quart saucepan brown turkey. Drain off any fat. Stir in vegetables, soup, milk, and thyme. Bring to boiling; reduce heat. Simmer 5 minutes. Spoon into an 8-inch round baking dish.
- ● Unfold crust; cut decorative cutouts or slits in crust so steam can escape. Place crust on top of dish. Turn edge under; flute. Combine egg white and water; brush over crust. Sprinkle sesame seed atop. Bake in a 400° oven for 25 to 30 minutes or till golden. Let stand 5 minutes. Makes 4 to 6 servings.

*Nutrition information per serving: 593 cal., 36 g pro., 44 g carbo., 30 g fat, 94 mg chol., 1,060 mg sodium. U.S. RDA: 89% vit. A, 12% thiamine, 30% niacin, 24% calcium, 27% riboflavin, 16% iron, 41% phosphorus.*

**READY IN 40 MINUTES**

1. **Place purchased crust over filling.**

2. **Turn under and flute the piecrust edge.**

3. **For a glistening crust, brush with egg mixture.**

SCOTT LITTLE

7

# SLIMMING DINNERS FROM YOUR MICROWAVE

278 CALORIES

By Joy Taylor

**Five great reasons for you and your family to try the main dish and dessert recipes featured here—**

1. **QUICK TO FIX**
2. **LOW CALORIE**
3. **LOW SODIUM**
4. **INEXPENSIVE**
5. **DELICIOUS**

245 CALORIES

### ▲ Cajun Chicken

● *278 CALORIES*
Health-conscious cooks rely on chicken for mealtime variety. Here, it's fired up for today's tastes with red, white, and black peppers. Whoever said low-calorie food had to be bland!

### ◀ Deep-Sea Kabobs

● *245 CALORIES*
No doubt you've discovered fish is a natural for light dining and micro-cooking. To cook marinated fish in less than 5 minutes, thread fish strips onto wooden skewers; serve with vegetable kabobs.

### Turkey Spirals with Fruit Stuffing ▶

● *259 CALORIES*
When the occasion calls for something special, don't throw nutrition to the wind. For a winning dinner, serve fruit-stuffed turkey with an orange-pineapple sauce.

Photographs: Jim Krantz
Food stylist: Janet Herwig

8

259 CALORIES

263 CALORIES

## MICROWAVE CUTS FAT

Microwave cooking is a moist cooking method similar to steaming on the rangetop. That means most foods micro-cook without added oil, margarine, or butter. Plus, the speed of the microwave oven lets you spend less time in the kitchen—and that means less temptation to nibble!

### ▲Polenta with Chunky Meat Sauce

● *263 CALORIES*

To make polenta, an Italian staple that's eaten in place of bread or noodles, stir together cornmeal and water and micro-cook it for 6 to 8 minutes. Spoon the mixture into a loaf pan to set. When you're ready to eat, reheat the polenta and serve slices along with a ground beef, corn, and pepper sauce.

### Lamb Dinner For One▶

● *414 CALORIES*

Here's a special treat for the lamb lover in your family. The lean lamb chop, couscous, and baby squash cook tender in fewer than 15 minutes. It's all made and eaten from one dish, so you're out of the kitchen in a flash.

### Beef Cherry-Yaki▶

● *345 CALORIES*

By stir-frying on a microwave-safe browning dish, you can use half the oil of the conventional wok method! To keep this dish on the lean side, use fat-trimmed sirloin steak and stretch it with a sweet surprise (cherries), plus carrots, onions, and water chestnuts. Limit rice to ½ cup per serving.

414 CALORIES

### Fettuccine with Broccoli Cheese Sauce▶

● *403 CALORIES*

Go ahead—enjoy a plateful of high-carb pasta, but keep the calories in check by fixing a low-fat sauce. Here, Neufchâtel cheese produces a creamy sauce accented with bits of Canadian bacon for the range-top pasta. It's all ready in 25 minutes.

345 CALORIES

175 CALORIES

188 CALORIES

# SLIMMING DESSERTS

A New Year's resolution to eat right is easy to keep with these two dessert recipes in your file. Both rely on naturally sweet fruits and a minimum of fat and sugar.

## ◄ Poached Apples With Banana Cream

● *175 CALORIES*

4 cooking apples
½ cup cranberry juice cocktail
2 tablespoons honey
1 ⅛-inch slice gingerroot
1 recipe Banana Cream

● **Core apples.** Slice each apple *crosswise* into thirds. Arrange apples in a 12x7½x2-inch microwave-safe dish.

● **Combine** juice, honey, and gingerroot; pour over apples. Micro-cook, covered, on 100% power (high) 5 to 7 minutes or till tender; turn dish, rearrange apples, and spoon liquid over apples once during cooking. Serve immediately with Banana Cream. Makes 4 servings.

*Banana Cream:* One hour or less before serving, in a small mixer bowl beat 1 *egg white* till frothy. Gradually add 1 tablespoon *honey,* beating till well combined. Mash 1 large *banana* to make ½ cup; stir in 3 tablespoons *lemon juice.* Add to egg-white mixture. Beat to stiff peaks. Serve immediately.

*Nutrition information per serving:* 175 cal., 2 g pro., 45 g carbo., 1 g fat, 0 mg chol., 15 mg sodium, and 3 g fiber. U.S. RDA: 33% vit. C.

## ▼ Light Lemon Cake

● *188 CALORIES*

1 cup all-purpose flour
2 teaspoons finely shredded lemon peel
½ teaspoon baking powder
¼ cup margarine
¾ cup sugar
2 egg yolks
1 tablespoon lemon juice
½ cup reconstituted nonfat dry milk
2 egg whites
Cinnamon-sugar
Strawberries (optional)

● **Stir together** flour, lemon peel, and baking powder. In a small mixer bowl beat margarine with an electric mixer on medium speed for ½ minute. Add sugar; beat till fluffy. Add yolks and lemon juice. Beat till combined. Add flour mixture and milk alternately to beaten mixture, beating on low speed after each addition just till combined.

● **Using clean beaters, beat** egg whites on high speed till stiff peaks form. Fold egg whites into batter. Transfer batter to an 8x8x2-inch microwave-safe baking dish.

● **Micro-cook,** uncovered, on 100% power (high) for 4 to 6 minutes or till done, giving the dish a quarter-turn every 2 minutes. (To check doneness, scratch the surface slightly with a wooden toothpick. If done, a cooked texture appears underneath.) Sprinkle cake lightly with cinnamon-sugar. Serve warm with berries. Makes 9 servings.

*Nutrition information per serving:* 188 cal., 3 g pro., 30 g carbo., 7 g fat, 56 mg chol., 97 mg sodium.

## CAJUN CHICKEN

*Some like it hot! If you use the ⅛ teaspoon ground pepper, add an extra ½ teaspoon paprika—*

- 2 **medium (1 pound) yams** *or* **sweet potatoes, sliced ¼ inch thick (about 3 cups)**
- 1 **2½- to 3-pound broiler-fryer chicken, cut up**
- ½ **teaspoon onion powder**
- ¼ **teaspoon garlic salt**
- ⅛ **to ¼ teaspoon** *each* **ground red, black, and white pepper**
- ½ **teaspoon dried thyme, crushed**
- ¾ **teaspoon paprika**

**Milk**
**Lime** *or* **lemon juice**
**Lime** *or* **lemon wedges (optional)**
**Parsley sprigs (optional)**
**Salsa (optional)**

In a 1-quart microwave-safe casserole combine yams or sweet potatoes and 2 tablespoons *water*. Micro-cook, covered, on 100% power (high) for 5 to 7 minutes or just till tender, stirring once. Cover and set aside.

Rinse chicken and pat dry; remove skin. In a bowl combine onion powder, garlic salt, red pepper, black pepper, white pepper, thyme, and paprika.

In a 12x7½x2-inch microwave-safe baking dish arrange chicken pieces, meaty side up, with meatier portions toward edges. Brush chicken pieces with milk. Sprinkle seasoning mixture evenly over top side of all the chicken pieces. Cover with waxed paper.

Cook on high for 11 to 14 minutes or till tender and no pink remains, giving the dish a half-turn and rearranging chicken pieces after 6 minutes. Remove the chicken from the oven.

Return yams to oven and reheat on high for 1 minute.

To serve, sprinkle lime juice over the yams. Arrange the chicken and yams on a serving platter. Garnish with lime or lemon wedges and parsley sprigs, if desired. Serve with salsa, if desired. Makes 6 servings.

**NOTE:** This recipe is not recommended for low-wattage ovens.

**Conventional directions:** Rinse chicken and pat dry; remove skin. Set aside. Stir together seasonings. In a lightly greased 13x9x2-inch baking pan arrange chicken, meaty side up. Brush chicken pieces with milk. Sprinkle seasoning mixture over tops of chicken pieces. Bake in a 375° oven for 45 to 55 minutes or till tender.

Meanwhile, place yams or sweet potatoes in a medium saucepan with ¼ cup *water*. Bring to boiling; reduce heat. Simmer, covered, for 15 minutes or till tender. Serve as directed.

*Nutrition information per serving:* 278 cal., 23 g pro., 23 g carbo., 7 g fat, 84 mg chol., 176 mg sodium, 869 mg potassium, 3 g dietary fiber. U.S. RDA: 22% vit. C, 10% thiamine, 12% riboflavin, 46% niacin, 10% iron.

## DEEP-SEA KABOBS

*Soak the wooden skewers before threading the food to prevent sticking—*

- 6 **ounces fresh** *or* **frozen skinless, boneless swordfish, salmon,** *or* **halibut steaks** *or* **fillets, cut ½ inch thick**
- 1 **large pink grapefruit**
- 1 **8-ounce can pineapple chunks (juice pack)**
- ½ **teaspoon dried dillweed**
- ¼ **teaspoon salt**
- ⅛ **teaspoon pepper**
- 1 **small green pepper, cut into ¾-inch squares**
- ½ **of a 10-ounce package (¾ cup) frozen Parisienne carrots, thawed**

Thaw fish, if frozen. Cut into ½-inch-wide strips (low-wattage ovens: cut fish into 1-inch cubes).

Finely shred grapefruit to obtain *1 teaspoon* peel. Remove remaining peel from grapefruit; discard peel. Section grapefuit over a bowl to catch juices. Reserve and chill grapefruit sections.

Drain pineapple, reserving juice. Cover and chill pineapple chunks.

In a shallow bowl combine grapefruit and pineapple juices, the 1 teaspoon peel, dillweed, salt, and pepper. Add fish. Cover; marinate in the refrigerator 2 hours, stirring occasionally.

At serving time, drain fish, reserving the marinade. In a 1-quart microwave-safe casserole micro-cook the green pepper and carrots with 2 tablespoons *water*, covered, on 100% power (high) for 4 to 5 minutes or till peppers are crisp-tender. Drain.

On four 12-inch wooden skewers thread the fish accordion-style. On four more wooden skewers thread the green pepper and carrots (low-wattage ovens: alternate fish cubes and vegetables on *four* wooden skewers).

Place kabobs in a 12x7½x2-inch microwave-safe baking dish (low-wattage ovens: use a 10x6x2-inch microwave-safe dish). Pour the reserved marinade over the kabobs. Cover with vented clear plastic wrap.

Cook on high for 3 to 5 minutes (low-wattage ovens: 5 to 7 minutes) or till fish flakes easily with a fork, giving the dish a half-turn after 2 minutes and brushing juices over kabobs.

To serve, arrange reserved grapefruit sections, pineapple, and kabobs on 2 lettuce-lined dinner plates. Serves 2.

**Conventional directions:** Marinate fish strips as directed.

In a 1-quart saucepan cook green pepper and carrots in a small amount of boiling water about 5 minutes or till crisp-tender. Drain.

On four 12-inch metal skewers thread the fish accordion-style. On 4 more metal skewers thread the green pepper and carrots. Place kabobs on an unheated rack of a broiler pan. Brush with some of the reserved marinade. Broil 4 inches from the heat for 5 minutes. Turn kabobs over. Brush with marinade. Broil about 4 minutes more or till the fish flakes easily with a fork. Serve as directed.

*Nutrition information per serving:* 245 cal., 19 g pro., 36 g carbo., 4 g fat, 47 mg chol., 623 mg sodium, 900 mg potassium, 5 g dietary fiber. U.S. RDA: 336% vit. A, 120% vit. C, 16% thiamine, 40% niacin, 12% iron.

## TURKEY SPIRALS WITH FRUIT STUFFING

*If you don't have a meat mallet to pound the turkey, try the back of a metal ice-cream scoop—*

- ½ teaspoon instant chicken bouillon granules
- ⅓ cup hot water
- 2 tablespoons mixed dried fruit bits *or* raisins
- 2 turkey breast tenderloin steaks (about 8 ounces total)
- ¼ teaspoon onion salt
- ¼ teaspoon paprika
- Dash ground cinnamon
- 1 cup dry raisin bread cubes (2 slices)
- ½ cup orange-pineapple juice
- 1¼ teaspoons cornstarch
- 1 teaspoon honey
- 1 carrot (optional)
- 1 zucchini (optional)

For stuffing, dissolve the bouillon granules in the hot water; pour over dried fruit. Let stand for 5 minutes.

Meanwhile, halve the turkey steaks lengthwise. If necessary, with a meat mallet pound each turkey piece between 2 sheets of clear plastic wrap till ¼ inch thick.

Stir the onion salt, paprika, and cinnamon into fruit mixture, then toss with the dry bread cubes.

Spread *one-fourth* of the stuffing on 1 side of *each* turkey piece. Loosely roll up the turkey steaks around the stuffing. Secure each roll-up with a toothpick, if necessary.

Arrange the roll-ups, spiral side up, in an 8x4x2-inch microwave-safe loaf dish. Cover the dish with vented clear plastic wrap.

Micro-cook on 100% power (high) for 3 to 4½ minutes (low-wattage ovens: 5 to 6 minutes, giving the dish a quarter-turn after 3 minutes) or till turkey is tender and no pink remains. Cover to keep warm.

In a 1-cup glass measure combine the orange-pineapple juice, cornstarch, and honey. Cook on high for 1 to 2 minutes or till thickened and bubbly, stirring every 30 seconds.

To serve, transfer 2 turkey rolls to each dinner plate. Spoon sauce over rolls. Serve with steamed carrot and zucchini that have been sliced lengthwise with a vegetable peeler. Serves 2.

**Conventional directions:** Loosely roll up the turkey pieces around stuffing as directed in recipe at left. Arrange the roll-ups, spiral side up, in a greased 8x4x2-inch loaf pan. Cover the pan with foil and bake in a 325° oven for 35 to 40 minutes or till the turkey is tender and no pink remains. Meanwhile, in a small saucepan stir together the orange-pineapple juice, cornstarch, and honey. Bring mixture to boiling; reduce heat. Cook and stir over medium heat till mixture is thickened and bubbly. Cook for 2 minutes more. Remove pan from heat. Serve as directed.

*Nutrition information per serving:* *259 cal., 30 g pro., 30 g carbo., 2 g fat, 71 mg chol., 441 mg sodium, 566 mg pot., 2 g dietary fiber. U.S. RDA: 18% vit. C, 12% thiamine, 12% riboflavin, 39% niacin, 13% iron.*

## POLENTA WITH CHUNKY MEAT SAUCE

*For a quick meal, make the polenta a day ahead—*

- 3 cups water
- 1 cup yellow cornmeal
- 1 cup cold water
- 1 teaspoon salt
- 1 pound lean ground beef *or* Italian seasoned ground turkey sausage
- 2 green onions, sliced
- 1 17-ounce can cream-style corn
- 1 small green pepper, cut into thin strips
- 1 teaspoon Italian seasoning
- Dash pepper
- 1 2-ounce jar diced pimiento, drained

In a 4-cup microwave-safe measure micro-cook the 3 cups water on 100% power (high) for 4 to 6 minutes or till boiling. Meanwhile, in a 2-quart microwave-safe casserole stir together the cornmeal, cold water, and salt.

Slowly pour the boiling water into cornmeal mixture, stirring constantly till well combined. Cook, uncovered, on high for 6 to 8 minutes or till mixture is very thick, stirring every minute.

Spread mixture in a greased 12x7½x2-inch baking dish or 8x4x2-inch loaf pan. Set aside to cool for 45 minutes till firm, or chill overnight.

At serving time, for sauce, crumble meat into a 2-quart microwave-safe casserole. Add green onions. Cook, covered, on high for 5 to 7 minutes (low-wattage ovens: 8 to 10 minutes) or till no pink remains, stirring once. Drain meat in a colander; set aside. Wipe casserole with paper towels.

Combine corn, green pepper, Italian seasoning, and pepper in casserole.

Cook, covered, on high for 5 to 6 minutes (low-wattage ovens: 7 to 8 minutes) or till green pepper is crisp-tender. Stir in the meat and pimiento. Set aside.

Cut the chilled polenta into 24 squares, or into slices if using loaf pan; arrange on a microwave-safe platter. Cover polenta with waxed paper, and cook on 70% power (medium-high) (low-wattage ovens: high) for 4 to 5 minutes or till heated through.

Cook sauce, covered, on 100% power for 1½ to 2½ minutes (low-wattage ovens: 3 to 4 minutes) or till hot. Serve sauce with polenta slices. Serves 6.

**Conventional directions:** In a small saucepan bring the 3 cups water to boiling. Meanwhile, in a medium saucepan combine the cornmeal, cold water, and salt. Slowly pour boiling water into cornmeal mixture, stirring constantly till well blended. Cook and stir over medium heat until very thick, about 5 minutes. Spread mixture in a greased 12x7½x2-inch baking dish or 8x4x2-inch loaf pan. Set aside; cool 45 minutes till firm, or chill overnight.

For sauce, crumble meat into medium saucepan. Add the green onions. Cook meat over medium-high heat till no pink remains, stirring occasionally. Drain off fat. Add corn, green pepper, Italian seasoning, and pepper. Simmer, uncovered, about 5 minutes or till heated through and green pepper is crisp-tender. Stir in pimiento. Meanwhile, cut polenta into 24 squares, or into slices if using a loaf pan, and arrange on baking sheet. Cover with foil and heat in a 300° oven for 10 to 12 minutes. Serve sauce with polenta slices.

*Nutrition information per serving:* *263 cal., 19 g pro., 31 g carbo., 8 g fat, 53 mg chol., 625 mg sodium, 381 mg potassium, 4 g dietary fiber. U.S. RDA: 28% vit. C, 10% thiamine, 11% riboflavin, 23% niacin, 17% iron.*

## LAMB DINNER FOR ONE

¼ **cup water**
¼ **cup quick-cooking couscous**
 2 **tablespoons sliced green onion**
   **or ¼ teaspoon onion powder**
½ **teaspoon instant chicken**
   **bouillon granules**
 1 **lamb leg sirloin chop, cut ¾ inch**
   **thick (about 5 ounces) and**
   **trimmed of fat**
 2 **tablespoons orange marmalade**
 2 **teaspoons prepared mustard**
 1 **baby golden nugget squash or**
   **½ of a medium acorn squash**
   **(about 5 ounces)**
½ **teaspoon margarine or butter**

In a 1-cup glass measure micro-cook the water on 100% power (high) for 45 to 60 seconds or till boiling. Stir in couscous, green onion, and bouillon granules. Let stand for 2 minutes.

Spread couscous mixture over the bottom of an individual au gratin dish. Place the lamb chop in the center of the dish, atop the couscous.

Combine the marmalade and mustard. Brush a little over the chop.

Halve squash and remove seeds. Cut squash into ½-inch-thick slices. Place squash in dish alongside chop. Dot squash with margarine or butter. Cover dish with waxed paper.

Cook on high for 2 minutes (low-wattage ovens: 3 to 4 minutes). Turn chop over. Brush with more of the marmalade mixture. Cook for 3 to 5 minutes more (low-wattage ovens: 5 to 6 minutes, giving dish a quarter-turn after 3 minutes) or till chop and squash are done. Brush with the remaining marmalade mixture before serving. Makes 1 serving.

**Conventional directions:** In a medium saucepan bring the water to boiling. Stir in the couscous, onion, and bouillon granules. Spread the couscous mixture over the bottom of a greased individual au gratin dish. Place chop in center over couscous. Stir together the marmalade and mustard. Brush some of the mixture over chop. Halve and seed squash. Cut squash into ½-inch-thick slices. Place in dish alongside chop. Dot squash with margarine. Cover dish with foil. Bake in a 350° oven for 35 to 40 minutes or till squash is tender and chop is done. Brush with remaining marmalade mixture before serving.

*Nutrition information per serving:* *414 cal., 23 g pro., 67 g carbo., 7 g fat, 61 mg chol., 386 mg sodium, 706 mg potassium, 7 g dietary fiber. U.S. RDA: 201% vit. A, 36% vit. C, 17% thiamine, 12% riboflavin, 29% niacin, 10% calcium, 16% iron.*

## BEEF CHERRY-YAKI

*Partially freezing the meat makes it much easier to slice—*

¾ **pound boneless beef sirloin**
   **steak, trimmed of fat**
1½ **cups frozen unsweetened pitted**
   **dark sweet cherries**
 2 **tablespoons dry sherry**
 2 **tablespoons soy sauce**
 1 **tablespoon lemon juice**
 3 **¼-inch slices gingerroot**
 1 **tablespoon cooking oil**
 2 **medium carrots, thinly bias**
   **sliced**
 6 **green onions, bias-sliced into**
   **1-inch pieces**
 1 **tablespoon cornstarch**
½ **of an 8-ounce can sliced water**
   **chestnuts, drained**
 2 **cups hot cooked rice**

Partially freeze the meat. Thinly slice across the grain into bite-size strips; set aside. Thaw the cherries; drain, reserving juices.

For marinade, in a small deep bowl combine the sherry, soy sauce, lemon juice, and gingerroot slices. Add beef. Cover; chill for 1 hour, stirring once. Drain meat, reserving marinade. Discard gingerroot slices.

Heat a 10-inch browning dish on 100% power (high) for 5 minutes. Add oil; swirl to coat dish. Add meat.

Micro-cook, uncovered, on high for 2 to 3 minutes or till meat is brown, stirring after every minute. Use a slotted spoon to remove meat from dish; leave juices in dish. Set meat aside.

Add reserved marinade to juices in dish. Stir in carrots. Cook, covered, for 1 minute. Add green onions. Cook, covered, for 1 to 2 minutes more or till vegetables are tender.

Add enough water to the reserved cherry juice to make ¼ cup. Stir in cornstarch. Stir the cornstarch mixture into vegetable mixture.

Cook, uncovered, on high for 2 to 4 minutes or till mixture is thickened and bubbly, stirring every minute.

Stir in cooked meat, cherries, and water chestnuts. Cook, covered, on high for 2 to 3 minutes or till mixture is heated through.

Serve over rice. Makes 4 servings.

**NOTE:** Because most browning dishes won't fit in low-wattage ovens, this recipe is not recommended for these small ovens.

**Conventional directions:** Slice and marinate meat as directed. Drain the meat, reserving the marinade. Discard gingerroot. Drain cherries, reserving juice. Add water to cherry juice to make ¼ cup. Stir into cornstarch.

Heat a wok over high heat for 2 to 3 minutes. Add oil to hot wok. Stir-fry carrots and green onions for 1 to 2 minutes or till crisp-tender. Remove vegetables from wok. (Add more oil, if necessary.) Stir-fry meat for 2 to 3 minutes or till brown. Push meat away from center of wok. Stir cornstarch mixture and add to wok. Cook and stir till thickened and bubbly. Stir in cooked meat, vegetables, cherries, and water chestnuts. Heat through. Serve over hot cooked rice.

*Nutrition information per serving:* *345 cal., 17 g pro., 50 g carbo., 8 g fat, 37 mg chol., 562 mg sodium, 524 mg potassium, 3 g dietary fiber. U.S. RDA: 205% vit. A, 11% vit. C, 14% thiamine, 10% riboflavin, 22% niacin, 19% iron.*

## FETTUCCINE WITH BROCCOLI CHEESE SAUCE

*Use a 1½-quart casserole if the 2-quart casserole won't fit in your low-wattage oven—*

- **8 ounces uncooked fettuccine**
- **1 parsnip, cut into matchstick pieces (3 cups)**
- **2 cups broccoli flowerets**
- **1 small onion, sliced and separated into rings**
- **½ cup sliced celery**
- **2 tablespoons water**
- **¾ cup skim milk**
- **2 teaspoons cornstarch**
- **⅛ teaspoon ground nutmeg**
- **4 ounces Neufchâtel cheese, softened**
- **6 ounces thinly sliced Canadian-style bacon, chopped**
- **1 4-ounce jar sliced mushrooms, drained**
- **4 teaspoons grated Parmesan cheese**

Cook fettuccine on the range top according to package directions.

Meanwhile, in a 2-quart microwave-safe casserole combine parsnip, broccoli, onion, and celery. Add water.

Micro-cook, covered, on 100% power (high) for 5 to 7 minutes (low-wattage ovens: 8 to 9 minutes, stirring once) or till vegetables are just tender. Transfer vegetables and liquid to a bowl.

In same dish combine milk, cornstarch, and nutmeg. Cook, uncovered, on high for 2 to 3 minutes (low-wattage ovens: 5 to 7 minutes) or till thickened and bubbly, stirring every minute.

Stir in the Neufchâtel cheese till combined. Add cooked vegetables, bacon, and mushrooms. Cook, covered, for 4 to 6 minutes more (low-wattage ovens: 6 to 8 minutes) or till heated through, stirring twice.

Serve sauce over drained pasta. Sprinkle *each* serving with *1 teaspoon* Parmesan cheese. Makes 4 servings.

**Conventional directions:** Cook fettuccine on range top according to package directions. Drain; keep warm.

In a medium saucepan cook parsnips, broccoli, onion, and celery in a small amount of boiling water, covered, for 7 to 9 minutes or till crisp-tender. Drain vegetables into a colander.

In the same saucepan combine milk and cornstarch. Stir in Neufchâtel cheese. Cook and stir till thickened and bubbly. Stir in vegetables, bacon, mushrooms, and nutmeg. Cook and stir for 2 minutes more. Serve as above.

*Nutrition information per serving:* *403 cal., 22 g pro., 55 g carbo., 11 g fat, 44 mg chol., 863 mg sodium, 637 mg potassium, 4 g dietary fiber. U.S. RDA: 21% vit. A, 63% vit. C, 60% thiamine, 26% riboflavin, 35% niacin, 12% calcium, 16% iron.*

## POACHED APPLES WITH BANANA CREAM

*High-wattage directions for this recipe on page 12—*

- **4 cooking apples**
- **½ cup cranberry juice cocktail**
- **2 tablespoons honey**
- **1 ⅛-inch slice gingerroot**
- **1 recipe Banana Cream (see page 12)**

Low-wattage microwave oven directions: Core apples. Slice each apple *crosswise* into thirds. Place in an 8x8x2-inch microwave-safe dish.

Combine cranberry juice, honey, and gingerroot. Pour mixture over apples. Micro-cook, covered with vented clear plastic wrap, on 100% power (high) for 6 to 9 minutes or till the apples are tender. Turn, rearrange apples, and spoon the cranberry juice mixture over once during cooking time. To serve, transfer 3 pieces of apple to each plate. Serve immediately with Banana Cream spooned atop. Serves 4.

**Conventional directions:** Core apples. Slice each apple *crosswise* into thirds. In a greased 12x7½x2-inch baking dish arrange the apples. Stir together the cranberry juice, honey, and gingerroot. Pour over the apples. Bake, uncovered, in a 350° oven for 15 to 20 minutes or till apples are tender, basting occasionally with the juice mixture.

To serve, transfer 3 pieces of apple to each plate. Serve immediately with Banana Cream spooned atop.

## LIGHT LEMON CAKE

*A microwave cake's test for doneness is different from a conventional cake's. The microwave cake will look moist on top, even though it's done—*

- **1 cup all-purpose flour**
- **2 teaspoons finely shredded lemon peel**
- **½ teaspoon baking powder**
- **¼ cup margarine *or* butter**
- **¾ cup sugar**
- **2 egg yolks**
- **1 tablespoon lemon juice**
- **½ cup reconstituted nonfat dry milk *or* skim milk**
- **2 egg whites**
- **Cinnamon-sugar**
- **Fresh strawberries (optional)**

Low-wattage microwave oven directions: In a small mixing bowl stir together the flour, lemon peel, and baking powder.

In a small mixer bowl beat margarine or butter with an electric mixer on medium speed for ½ minute. Add the sugar; beat till fluffy. Add the egg yolks and lemon juice. Beat till well combined. Add flour mixture and milk alternately to beaten mixture, beating on low speed after each addition just till combined.

Wash beaters thoroughly. In another small mixer bowl beat the egg whites with an electric mixer on high speed till stiff peaks form (tips stand straight). Fold egg whites into batter. Transfer batter to an 8x8x2-inch microwave-safe baking dish.

Micro-cook, uncovered, on 100% power (high) for 7 to 10 minutes or till done, giving the dish a quarter-turn every 2 minutes. (To check doneness, scratch the surface slightly with a wooden toothpick. If done, a cooked texture will have formed underneath.) Sprinkle the top lightly with the cinnamon-sugar. Serve warm with strawberries, if desired. Makes 9 servings.

**NOTE:** This recipe was developed for microwave ovens only, and is not recommended for conventional ovens. High-wattage directions can be found on page 12.

# FEBRUARY

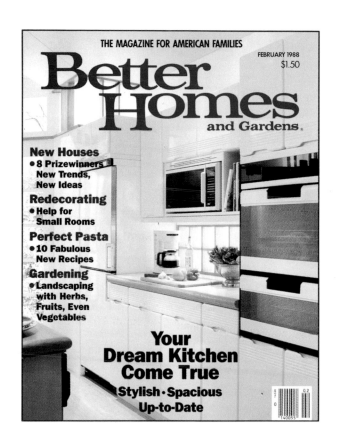

THE MAGAZINE FOR AMERICAN FAMILIES

FEBRUARY 1988
$1.50

## Better Homes
and Gardens.

**New Houses**
- 8 Prizewinners
  New Trends,
  New Ideas

**Redecorating**
- Help for
  Small Rooms

**Perfect Pasta**
- 10 Fabulous
  New Recipes

**Gardening**
- Landscaping
  with Herbs,
  Fruits, Even
  Vegetables

**Your
Dream Kitchen
Come True**
Stylish · Spacious
Up-to-Date

# ORIENTAL

By Barbara Johnson

### SWEET-AND-SOUR CHICKEN CHUNKS

*Five ingredients and fast! Heat the chicken in your microwave oven while you stir up the vegetable sauce, and you will have this colorful, enticing dinner on the table in 15 minutes—*

- 1 cup water
- 1 cup quick-cooking rice

• • •

- 1 12-ounce package frozen, breaded chicken chunks

• • •

- 1 16-ounce can unpeeled apricot halves, drained
- 1 6-ounce package frozen pea pods
- ¾ cup bottled sweet and sour sauce

● **In a medium saucepan bring** the 1 cup water to boiling. Stir in the rice. Remove the pan from the heat. Cover and let stand for 5 minutes.

● **Micro-cook or bake chicken chunks** according to package directions.

● **Meanwhile,** in a medium saucepan stir together the apricots, pea pods, and sweet and sour sauce; heat through (see photo, *right*).

● **To serve, spoon rice** around edge of platter. Stir chicken chunks into apricot mixture; spoon into center of rice. Makes 4 servings.

Chicken in a tangy sauce: a real family pleaser!

*Nutrition information per serving:*
*378 cal., 16 g pro., 53 g carbo., 12 g fat, 60 mg chol., 579 mg sodium, 471 mg potassium, 4 g dietary fiber. U.S. RDA: 46% vit. A, 22% vit. C, 19% thiamine, 12% riboflavin, 21% niacin, 18% iron.*

● **Heat apricot halves and pea pods in the sweet-and-sour sauce just till peas are tender, but crisp.**

# DINNERS!

"*Fast and easy, yet home cooked and wholesome. That's my favorite kind of after-work cooking.*"

—Barbara Johnson

## PEANUT BUTTER AND PORK STIR-FRY

*Start with cut-up vegetables from your grocer's salad bar, and you can have dinner on the table in 20 minutes—*

- 2 **tablespoons cooking oil**
- ¾ **pound lean boneless pork, thinly sliced**
- 2 **carrots, thinly bias sliced (1 cup)**
- 1 **medium red *or* green sweet pepper, cut into 1-inch pieces (1 cup)**
- 1 **stalk celery, thinly bias sliced (½ cup)**
- 1 **medium onion, sliced and separated into rings (½ cup)**
- 1 **15-ounce can garbanzo beans, drained**
- 1 **recipe Peanut Butter Sauce**

● **In a wok or large skillet heat** *1 tablespoon* oil over high heat. Stir-fry pork 3 minutes or till no pink remains (see photo, *right below*). Remove the pork from the wok.

● **Add** remaining oil, carrots, pepper, celery, and onion to the wok; stir-fry for 3 minutes. Add beans; stir-fry for 1 minute or till vegetables are crisp-tender. Return the pork to the wok.

● **Stir** Peanut Butter Sauce; add to the wok. Cook and stir till mixture is thickened and bubbly. Serve at once. Makes 4 servings.

**Peanut Butter Sauce:** Stir together 3 tablespoons *water*, 2 tablespoons *creamy peanut butter*, 2 tablespoons *soy sauce*, and 1 teaspoon *cornstarch*.

Pork and vegetables in creamy peanut sauce.

*Nutrition information per serving:* *371 cal., 22 g pro., 27 g carbo., 20 g fat, 43 mg chol., 1,032 mg sodium, 742 mg potassium, 9 g dietary fiber. U.S. RDA: 215% vit. A, 96% vit. C, 34% thiamine, 14% riboflavin, 23% niacin, 23% iron.*

● **To evenly cook pork, use a long-handled spatula to lift and turn the strips constantly to avoid sticking.**

# PASTA PERFECT!
## FAST TO FANCY, 10 FABULOUS RECIPES

By Barbara Johnson

Everybody seems to love pasta—and no wonder! It's quick, nutritious, and delicious. Try these super pasta recipes—there's something here for everyone!

### ◀ FAST!
#### 20-MINUTE CARBONARA
Give carbonara (pasta with a creamy cheese sauce and meat) a face-lift: Use both egg and spinach linguine, dot with strips of pimiento, and serve the meat (thin slices of prosciutto) on the side. Looks great in no time!

### ▶ ELEGANT!
#### SAFFRON ROTOLO IN RED PEPPER SAUCE
Roll up a rich, triple-nut filling in a sheet of homemade pasta that's delicately flavored with saffron. Heat through. Then, slice at an angle and serve pooled in an enticing sweet-pepper sauce for an exquisite first course.

### ◀ HEALTHFUL!
#### FUSILLI WITH LOW-FAT PESTO
Classic pesto is a puree of oil, herbs, nuts, and Parmesan. To make this version, skip the nuts, and reduce both oil and cheese. Toss with pasta for a light side dish.

**▲ COOK THE PASTA SHEET**
Carefully immerse your pasta into the pot of boiling water. Use a light touch to avoid tearing the pasta.

**▲ ROLL PASTA AND FILLING**
Start rolling up the pasta sheet from one of the short sides. Use the towel to help lift and roll along the way.

### HOW TO TELL WHEN YOUR PASTA IS DONE

Some folks tell you to throw your cooked pasta against the wall; if it sticks, it's done. But, we say there's a better way: taste it. Only your teeth can tell when those golden strands are tender, but still slightly firm—the perfect stage for eating.

**Tasting is the only way to tell when pasta is done.**

21

# PASTA PERFECT!

### ▼ FIX 'N' FORGET!
### 24-HOUR
### GREEK PASTA SALAD

Try a twist on classic 24-hour salad: use pasta in place of lettuce. Slather a tangy yogurt-garlic dressing atop layers of cut ziti, vegetables, and feta cheese.

### ▼ NO BOILING!
### SKIP-A-STEP
### LASAGNA ROLL-UPS

Soak, don't cook, no-boil lasagna noodles—a new time-saving pasta now available. Roll them around a robust filling of tomato sauce, sausage, and eggplant; bake.

### ▶ DISTINGUISHED!
### OVERSTUFFED
### SEAFOOD RAVIOLI

Transform lasagna noodles into giant ravioli by criss-crossing and filling to overflowing with an irresistible teriyaki-flavored stir-fry. It's perfect for entertaining.

### ▲ MICROWAVE! VEGETARIAN VERMICELLI

Boil vermicelli (fine spaghetti) on the stove top while you cook a peppy vegetable sauce in your microwave oven. The entire meatless meal takes less than 30 minutes to make!

### ▲ HOME STYLE! SALMON NOODLE CHOWDER

Here's a nourishing soup with rich, homemade taste. Because you start with a convenient packaged noodle mix, you can ladle the soup up in a mere 15 minutes.

## ▲ SHRED BOK CHOY
Loosely roll up the leaves and cut crosswise into strips. Bok choy is a crisp contrast to tender pasta.

## ▲ FILL THE NOODLES
Crisscross two noodles on the plate. Spoon on the stir-fried filling. Then, fold over the ends of the noodles.

## HOW TO EAT PASTA
The debate rages! Do you twirl pasta on a fork against a large spoon, or just against the plate? You'll find folks who will stand by one method or the other as the only real way to eat pasta. Our advice? Any way you get the noodles to stay on a fork is OK!

There's an easier way to eat pasta: twirl it on a fork.

23

# PASTA PERFECT!

### ◄ DOWN-HOME GOOD!
### SAUSAGE AND TORTELLINI TOSS

Cook cheese-filled tortellini (stuffed pasta rings) just till tender. Combine with slices of Polish sausage and crisp-tender broccoli flowerets. Then, smother the entire dish in a creamy Swiss and caraway sauce. You've just created a hearty one-dish meal that we bet tops your family's list of favorites!

### ◄ LIGHT 'N' LUSCIOUS!
### RUFFLED PASTA IN WILTED GREENS

Tuck tender pasta ruffles (known as *radiatore* in Italy) in with your favorite greens. Toss with a hot sesame-soy dressing for a warm, ever-so-slightly-wilted salad.

### IT'S OK FOR DIETS!

Some folks think pasta is high in calories. Actually, ½ cup cooked noodles has about 100 calories. But, go easy on the sauce!

## 20-MINUTE CARBONARA

*To help your pasta stay hot, warm your plates in hot water or a warm oven—*

- 1 beaten egg
- ½ cup grated Parmesan *or* Romano cheese
- 2 tablespoons whipping cream *or* light cream
- 1 tablespoon sliced pimiento
- 4 ounces egg *and/or* spinach linguine
- 1 8-ounce package frozen sugar snap peas *or* one 6-ounce package frozen pea pods
- 2 ounces thinly sliced prosciutto *or* fully cooked ham

Combine the egg, cheese, cream, and pimiento. Set aside.

In a large kettle or Dutch oven cook pasta, uncovered, in boiling water for 8 to 10 minutes or till tender but still slightly firm, stirring occasionally.

Meanwhile, prepare snap peas according to package directions. Drain.

On each of 2 dinner plates, fan *half* of the prosciutto on 1 side of plate. Fan snap peas on other side of plate. In a large colander drain pasta; return to hot kettle. Add egg mixture; toss gently till well coated. Serve immediately in center of plates. Makes 2 main-dish servings.

*Nutrition information per serving: 509 cal., 30 g pro., 52 g carbo., 20 g fat, 246 mg chol., 860 mg sodium, 385 mg potassium, 5 g dietary fiber. U.S. RDA: 21% vit. A, 57% vit. C, 61% thiamine, 32% riboflavin, 28% niacin, 45% calcium, 22% iron.*

## SAFFRON ROTOLO IN RED PEPPER SAUCE

*Instead of making your own pasta, you can purchase a sheet of pasta from your local gourmet pasta shop to use in this elegant recipe. Just trim the pasta sheet to the size specified in the recipe directions below—*

- ½ cup all-purpose flour
- ¼ teaspoon salt
- ⅛ teaspoon ground saffron *or* ground turmeric
- 1 egg
- 1 teaspoon olive oil *or* cooking oil
- 3 tablespoons all-purpose flour
- 1 recipe Cheese and Nut Filling (see recipe, right)
- 1 tablespoon margarine *or* butter, melted
- 1 recipe Red Pepper Sauce (see recipe, page 26)

For pasta dough, in a small mixing bowl stir together the ½ cup flour, salt, and saffron. Make a well in the center. In a small bowl or a custard cup stir together egg and oil; add to flour mixture. Mix well.

Sprinkle the kneading surface with the remaining 3 tablespoons flour. Turn pasta dough out onto the floured surface. Knead till the pasta dough is smooth and elastic (about 8 minutes). Cover and let rest for 10 minutes.

On a lightly floured surface roll pasta dough into a 12-inch square. Cover; let stand for 15 minutes.

In a 4½-quart kettle bring a large amount of water to boiling. Carefully immerse the pasta sheet into the boiling water (see photo, page 21). Return water to boiling. Cook, uncovered, for 1 to 2 minutes or just till pasta is tender but still slightly firm. (Pasta will expand during cooking.) Carefully drain pasta sheet in a large colander. Rinse with cold water and drain well.

To assemble rotolo, lay pasta sheet flat on a damp cloth. Let stand, uncovered, for 15 to 20 minutes to dry slightly. Trim to a 13x12-inch rectangle. Spread pasta sheet with Cheese and Nut Filling to within ½ inch of edges. Roll up from 1 of the short sides, using the towel to aid in rolling (see photo, page 21).

Place the rotolo, seam side down, in a greased 13x9x2-inch baking pan. Brush roll with the melted margarine or butter. If desired, cover and chill for several hours or overnight.

To serve, cover and bake the rotolo in a 375° oven for 20 to 30 minutes or till the pasta and filling are heated through. Meanwhile, cook and puree the Red Pepper Sauce. To serve, cut the rotolo diagonally into 12 slices. Spoon *some* of the Red Pepper Sauce on each individual dinner or appetizer plate; place the rotolo slices on top. Makes 4 main-dish or 12 appetizer servings.

*Nutrition information per main-dish serving: 461 cal., 13 g pro., 30 g carbo., 34 g fat, 117 mg chol., 607 mg sodium, 570 mg potassium, and 4 g dietary fiber. U.S. RDA: 190% vit. A, 320% vit. C, 26% thiamine, 23% riboflavin, 13% niacin, 13% calcium, and 27% iron.*

## CHEESE AND NUT FILLING

- 2 3-ounce packages cream cheese with chives
- ⅛ teaspoon salt
- ¼ cup milk
- ½ cup snipped watercress *or* parsley
- ¼ cup pine nuts *or* slivered almonds
- ¼ cup chopped almonds
- ¼ cup chopped hazelnuts (filberts)

In a small mixer bowl beat cheese and salt with an electric mixer on medium speed for 30 seconds or till softened. Beat in milk. Stir in watercress or parsley and nuts. Makes about 1½ cups.

## RED PEPPER SAUCE

*Trim the plate with sweet pepper strips, ripe olives, and nasturtium leaves\**—

- ½ cup water
- 1 teaspoon instant chicken bouillon granules
- ¼ teaspoon salt
- 3 medium (1¼ pounds) red sweet peppers, seeded and cut into chunks (3½ cups)
- ⅓ cup watercress *or* parsley leaves

In a medium saucepan bring water, bouillon granules, and salt to boiling; add peppers. Cook about 5 minutes or till tender. Remove from heat. Add watercress or parsley. Cool slightly.

In a food processor bowl or blender container process or blend pepper mixture, covered, till peppers are pureed. Serve warm, reheating if necessary. Makes about 2¼ cups sauce.

*\*Note:* Use nasturtium leaves grown specifically for eating purposes.

## FUSILLI WITH LOW-FAT PESTO

- 1 10-ounce package frozen chopped spinach
- 4 ounces rippled fine noodles (fusilli) *or* spaghetti
- ½ of a 20-ounce package (2½ cups) frozen crinkle-cut carrots
- 1 egg white
- 2 tablespoons dried basil, crushed
- 1 tablespoon olive *or* cooking oil
- 2 cloves garlic *or* 1 teaspoon bottled minced garlic
- ¼ cup shredded *or* grated Parmesan cheese

Thaw spinach, but do not drain. Cook pasta, uncovered, in boiling water for 7 minutes for fusilli or 2 minutes for spaghetti, stirring occasionally. Add the carrots and cook for 8 minutes more or till the pasta is tender but still slightly firm, stirring occasionally.

For pesto, in a blender container or food processor bowl, combine the *undrained* spinach, egg white, basil, oil, and garlic. Cover; blend till smooth, stopping occasionally to scrape sides.

In a large colander drain pasta and carrots. Return to hot pan. Add *half* of the pesto to hot pasta and carrots. Toss over low heat till pasta is well coated and heated through. Season to taste with salt and pepper. Serve topped with cheese. Makes 4 side-dish servings.

**Note:** Place remaining pesto in a moisture- and vaporproof freezer container. Seal, label, and freeze for up to 3 months for another use. To use, thaw overnight in the refrigerator.

*Nutrition information per serving: 195 cal., 9 g pro., 29 g carbo., 5 g fat, 31 mg chol., 193 mg sodium, 333 mg potassium, 3 g dietary fiber. U.S. RDA: 360% vit. A, 14% vit. C, 20% thiamine, 13% riboflavin, 12% niacin, 18% calcium, 14% iron.*

## SKIP-A-STEP LASAGNA ROLL-UPS

*Look for no-boil lasagna noodles on the shelf next to dry pasta. If you can't find them, use regular lasagna noodles. Boil 8 minutes; drain, assemble, and bake—*

- 8 no-boil lasagna noodles *or* regular lasagna noodles
- 1 small eggplant, peeled
- 1 pound bulk Italian sausage *or* Italian seasoned ground turkey sausage
- ½ cup sliced celery
- 2½ cups meatless spaghetti sauce
- Fresh oregano, chives, and parsley (optional)

Soak no-boil lasagna noodles in warm water for 10 minutes.

Meanwhile, cut twelve ¼-inch-thick slices crosswise from the bottom of the eggplant; halve each slice cross-

wise, forming semicircles. Set aside. Chop the remaining eggplant. (You should have about 1 cup.)

In a 10-inch skillet cook the chopped eggplant, sausage, and celery about 5 minutes or till sausage is done and vegetables are tender. Drain well. Stir in *1 cup* of the spaghetti sauce.

Drain lasagna noodles well. In the bottom of a 1½- to 2-quart au gratin dish spread ½ *cup* of the spaghetti sauce. Spread about ⅓ cup of the sausage mixture on *each* noodle. Roll up noodles from 1 of the short ends. Place, seam side down, in the dish. Arrange the halved eggplant slices around the edge of the dish, rounded edge up, overlapping slightly. Spoon the remaining sauce over the roll-ups.

Cover and bake in a 375° oven for 35 minutes or till filling is heated through and pasta is tender. Garnish with fresh oregano, chives, and parsley, if desired. Makes 4 main-dish servings.

*Microwave directions:* Soak no-boil lasagna noodles, and slice and chop eggplant as directed above. In a 1½-quart microwave-safe casserole crumble sausage. Add chopped eggplant and celery. Micro-cook, covered, on 100% power (high) for 5 to 7 minutes or till no pink remains in meat and vegetables are tender, stirring once. Drain well. Stir in *1 cup* of the spaghetti sauce.

Drain no-boil noodles and assemble in a 1½- to 2-quart microwave-safe au gratin dish or 10x6x2-inch baking dish as directed. Cover with vented clear plastic wrap. Cook on high for 10 to 12 minutes or till heated through and pasta is tender, giving dish a half-turn once. Serve as directed.

*Nutrition information per serving: 433 cal., 19 g pro., 51 g carbo., 16 g fat, 42 mg chol., 1,375 mg sodium, 396 mg potassium, 6 g dietary fiber. U.S. RDA: 21% vit. A, 20% vit. C, 54% thiamine, 24% riboflavin, 35% niacin, 20% iron.*

## 24-HOUR GREEK PASTA SALAD

     6 ounces cut ziti (about 2 cups)
    ½ cup plain yogurt
    ½ cup creamy garlic salad dressing
    ½ teaspoon dried oregano,
       crushed
     1 small cucumber, halved length-
       wise and thinly sliced (1¼ cups)
    ½ cup sliced pitted ripe olives
     1 cup crumbled feta cheese
    12 cherry tomatoes, quartered
     1 cup alfalfa sprouts
       Onion and garlic croutons

In a large saucepan cook pasta, uncovered, in boiling water about 14 minutes
or till tender but still slightly firm, stirring occasionally. Immediately drain in
a large colander. Rinse with cold water;
drain well. Transfer to a large bowl.

For dressing, in a small bowl combine yogurt, dressing, and oregano.

Stir ⅓ cup of the dressing into
drained pasta. Place in bottom of a 2-
quart straight-sided clear bowl. Layer
the cucumber slices, olives, and cheese
on top. Spread the remaining dressing
over top. Top with tomatoes and
sprouts. Cover tightly; chill for up to 24
hours. To serve, top with croutons.
Makes 4 to 6 side-dish servings.

*Nutrition information per serving:*
*449 cal., 13 g pro., 41 g carbo., 26 g fat, 27*
*mg chol., 734 mg sodium, 364 mg potas-*
*sium, 3 g dietary fiber. U.S. RDA: 13%*
*vit. A, 12% vit. C, 32% thiamine, 31%*
*riboflavin, 16% niacin, 26% calcium,*
*12% iron.*

## OVERSTUFFED SEAFOOD RAVIOLI

     1 small bunch bok choy
     6 lasagna noodles
    ¼ cup teriyaki sauce
     2 tablespoons dry sherry
     2 tablespoons Dijon-style mustard
     2 teaspoons cornstarch
     3 tablespoons cooking oil
     1 clove garlic, minced
     1 9-ounce package frozen French-
       style green beans, thawed and
       drained
    ½ cup shredded carrot
     2 green onions, thinly sliced
     1 cup sliced fresh mushrooms
     1 6-ounce package frozen
       crabmeat and shrimp

Remove bok choy leaves from bunch.
To shred leaves, loosely roll up and cut
crosswise into strips (see photo, page
23). You should have about 2½ cups.
Thinly slice bok choy stems. You
should have about 2 cups. Set aside.

Cook lasagna noodles, uncovered,
in boiling water for 12 to 15 minutes or
till tender but still slightly firm, stirring occasionally. Immediately drain
well in a large colander.

Meanwhile, for sauce, in a bowl
stir together teriyaki sauce, sherry,
mustard, and cornstarch; set aside.

Preheat a large skillet or wok over
high heat; add cooking oil. Stir-fry garlic in hot oil for 15 seconds; push from
center of skillet. Add bok choy stems;
stir-fry for 1½ minutes. Add green
beans, carrot, and green onions; stir-fry
for 30 seconds. Add mushrooms; stir-fry
for 1 minute or till vegetables are crisp-
tender. Push mixture away from center
of skillet. Stir sauce; add to center of
skillet. Cook and stir till thickened and
bubbly. Add seafood; cook and stir for 1
minute or till seafood is heated. Stir to
coat entire mixture.

Arrange *two* hot lasagna noodles
so they form an X on *each* of 3 warm
dinner plates. Spoon *one-third* (about
1⅓ cups) of the filling into center of
each X (see photo, page 23). Fold edges
of noodles over filling into center of X.
Top each with 2 cooked, peeled, and de-
veined *shrimp*, if desired. Serve at once
with shredded bok choy; top with lemon slice, if desired. Pass additional teriyaki sauce for bok choy, if desired.
Makes 3 main-dish servings.

*Nutrition information per serving:*
*422 cal., 19 g pro., 48 g carbo., 16 g fat, 57*
*mg chol., 805 mg sodium, 707 mg potas-*
*sium, 6 g dietary fiber. U.S. RDA: 175%*
*vit. A, 53% vit. C, 40% thiamine, 25%*
*riboflavin, 30% niacin, 16% calcium,*
*20% iron.*

## VEGETARIAN VERMICELLI

     6 ounces vermicelli, broken up
     1 medium red sweet pepper,
       seeded and cut into thin strips
     1 medium green sweet pepper,
       seeded and cut into thin strips
     1 8-ounce jar cheese spread with
       jalapeño peppers
     1 16-ounce can golden hominy,
       drained
     1 8-ounce can red kidney beans,
       drained
     1 8-ounce carton dairy sour cream
     2 tablespoons pumpkin seeds *or*
       peanuts

In a large kettle or Dutch oven cook
pasta, uncovered, in boiling water for 5
to 7 minutes or till tender but still
slightly firm, stirring occasionally.

Meanwhile, in a 2-quart microwave-safe casserole micro-cook peppers
and 2 tablespoons *water*, covered, on
100% power (high) for 2 to 4 minutes or
till tender. Drain. Stir in cheese spread
till melted. Stir in hominy and beans.
Cook, covered, on high for 3 to 4 minutes or till heated through, stirring after every minute. Stir in sour cream.
Cook, covered, on high for 3 to 5 minutes or till heated through, stirring
once or twice.

Drain pasta. Transfer to a platter;
top with cheese mixture. Sprinkle with
seeds or nuts. Toss and serve immediately. Makes 4 main-dish servings.

*Conventional directions:* Cook
the pasta as directed. Meanwhile, in a
large saucepan cook peppers, uncovered, in a small amount of boiling water for 3 to 5 minutes or till tender.
Drain well.

In the same saucepan combine
peppers, cheese spread, hominy, and
beans. Cook and stir over medium heat
for 3 to 4 minutes or till cheese is melted and mixture is heated through. Stir
in the sour cream. Cook and stir over
low heat for 3 to 5 minutes more or just
till mixture is heated through. (*Do not
boil.*) Serve as directed above.

*Nutrition information per serving:*
*626 cal., 25 g pro., 59 g carbo., 33 g fat, 79*
*mg chol., 1,049 mg sodium, 548 mg po-*
*tassium, 6 g dietary fiber. U.S. RDA:*
*62% vit. A, 112% vit. C, 39% thiamine,*
*32% riboflavin, 20% niacin, 44% calci-*
*um, 24% iron.*

## SALMON-NOODLE CHOWDER

2¼ cups water
2 tablespoons margarine *or* butter
1 4½-ounce package noodles with sour cream and chive sauce
1½ cups loose-pack frozen broccoli, corn, and peppers
½ teaspoon dried dillweed
1 7½-ounce can red salmon
2 cups milk

In a large saucepan bring water and margarine or butter to boiling. Stir in noodles with sour cream and chive sauce, frozen vegetables, and dillweed. Return to boiling; reduce heat. Simmer, uncovered, for 5 minutes.

Meanwhile, drain salmon; remove skin and bones. Break salmon into chunks. Stir milk into noodle mixture. Return to boiling; add salmon. Cook and stir for 1 minute more. Serve at once. Makes 3 main-dish servings.

***Microwave directions:*** In a 3-quart microwave-safe casserole microcook *2 cups* water and margarine or butter on 100% power (high) for 6 to 8 minutes or till boiling. Stir in noodles with sour cream and chive sauce, vegetables, and dillweed. Cook, uncovered, on high for 10 to 12 minutes or till noodles and vegetables are tender. Drain salmon; break up as directed. Stir in salmon and milk. Cook, uncovered, on high for 4 to 6 minutes more or till heated through. Serve at once.

***Nutrition information per serving:*** *478 cal., 26 g pro., 43 g carbo., 23 g fat, 33 mg chol., 703 mg sodium, 616 mg potassium, 3 g dietary fiber. U.S. RDA: 39% vit. A, 45% vit. C, 19% thiamine, 25% riboflavin, 25% niacin, 31% calcium.*

## SAUSAGE AND TORTELLINI TOSS

½ of a 7-ounce package rainbow-colored *or* plain dried cheese-filled tortellini (about 1 cup)
2 cups broccoli flowerets
½ pound fully cooked smoked Polish sausage, halved lengthwise and thinly bias sliced
1 tablespoon margarine *or* butter
1 tablespoon all-purpose flour
1 teaspoon caraway seed
¾ cup milk
1 cup shredded process Swiss cheese (4 ounces)
1 tablespoon coarse-grain brown mustard

In a large saucepan cook tortellini, uncovered, in boiling water for 15 minutes; stir occasionally. Add broccoli flowerets and Polish sausage to water. Return to boiling; reduce heat. Simmer, uncovered, for 5 to 10 minutes more or till tortellini is tender but still slightly firm; stir occasionally.

Meanwhile, in a medium saucepan melt margarine or butter. Stir in flour and caraway seed. Add milk all at once. Cook and stir till thickened and bubbly. Stir in cheese and mustard till cheese melts. Remove from heat.

Drain tortellini mixture; return to hot pan. Add cheese mixture; toss till coated. Serve at once. Makes 4 main-dish servings.

***Nutrition information per serving:*** *412 cal., 22 g pro., 15 g carbo., 29 g fat, 97 mg chol., 1,092 mg sodium, 449 mg potassium, 2 g dietary fiber. U.S. RDA: 35% vit. A, 47% vit. C, 26% thiamine, 21% riboflavin, 16% niacin, 35% calcium, 12% iron.*

## RUFFLED PASTA IN WILTED GREENS

*Cook the pasta according to the directions on your package; it varies from brand to brand—*

4 ounces pasta ruffles *or* corkscrew macaroni (2 cups)
2 tablespoons water
2 tablespoons dry sherry
2 tablespoons soy sauce
1 tablespoon honey
1 tablespoon lemon juice
1 large red onion, thinly sliced and separated into rings
1 tablespoon sesame seed
2 tablespoons sesame oil *or* cooking oil
6 cups torn mixed greens

In a large saucepan cook pasta, uncovered, in boiling water according to package directions till tender but still slightly firm, stirring occasionally. Immediately drain in a colander. Rinse with cold water; drain. Set aside.

Meanwhile, in a small bowl combine water, sherry, soy sauce, honey, and lemon juice. Set aside.

In a large skillet cook onion and sesame seed in hot oil about 5 minutes or just till onion is tender and seeds are toasted. Stir in soy mixture; bring to boiling. Remove from heat. Add pasta. Toss till coated.

Place greens in a large bowl. Pour pasta mixture over greens. Toss; serve at once. Makes 8 side-dish servings.

***Nutrition information per serving:*** *118 cal., 3 g pro., 16 g carbo., 4 g fat, 0 mg chol., 261 mg sodium, 200 mg potassium, 1 g dietary fiber.*

# MARCH

SUSAN SCHELLING

# GOOD·FOR·YOU MEALS...
# FAST!
## (30 MINUTES OR LESS)

By Lynn Phelps

- **GREAT TASTING!**
- **LOW IN FAT AND CHOLESTEROL!**
- **LOW IN CALORIES AND SODIUM!**
- **LOADED WITH FIBER, VITAMINS, AND MINERALS!**

PHOTOGRAPHS: GARRICK PETERSON; FOOD STYLIST: PAT GODSTED

**Choose lean cuts of meat and trim away any fat you can. For each chop, trimming fat saves about 20 g fat.**

## MUSTARD-ORANGE PORK CHOPS WITH STIR-FRIED ONIONS

● Classy and only four ingredients! The marmalade-glazed pork chops quick-cook in 15 minutes under the broiler. Watch the excess fat drip away! Serve them with crisp stir-fried green onions.

### NUTRITION INFORMATION

| Per serving | | |
|---|---|---|
| Calories.................316 | Fat..........................10 g |
| Cholesterol........83 mg | Sodium............ 292 mg |
| Carbohydrate.......28 g | Fiber ........................2 g |
| Protein..................29 g | |

RECIPES BEGIN ON PAGE 37

## MICROWAVE SPINACH-STUFFED SOLE

● The tasty stuffing made from frozen chopped spinach, cottage cheese, and a hint of cocktail sauce goes together in a jiff. Tuck it inside the sole fillets; then micro-cook. Your meal-in-a-cup is done in 25 minutes.

Cook fish without added fat by using your microwave oven. For evenly done fish, center the sole-filled custard cups in your oven.

## TEX-MEX TURKEY TENDERLOINS

● More than ever, turkey cuts fill butchers' counters. They cost a little more compared to some meats but are good for you and cook quickly. Just season the turkey, sauté in a dab of margarine, and serve.

Rely on spicy flavors instead of salt to season food. Sprinkle a cumin-pepper blend onto the turkey tenderloins for sit-up-and-take-notice flavor.

### NUTRITION INFORMATION

| Per serving | |
|---|---|
| Calories............178 | Fat...............4 g |
| Cholesterol........41 mg | Sodium............475 mg |
| Carbohydrate......12 g | Fiber..............2 g |
| Protein..................23 g | |

### NUTRITION INFORMATION

| Per serving | |
|---|---|
| Calories............180 | Fat...............4 g |
| Cholesterol........71 mg | Sodium..............82 mg |
| Carbohydrate......10 g | Fiber..............1 g |
| Protein..................27 g | |

## PEPPERED BEEF AND ASPARAGUS

Stir-fry the low-fat way by spraying a cold wok with nonstick spray coating. During cooking, add a scant tablespoon of cooking oil as needed to prevent the food from sticking.

● Sodium-reduced soy sauce, plenty of fresh vegetables, and thinly sliced lean beef—they all add up to a good-for-your-family, one-dish meal that's ready in 25 minutes! Make it a weekly favorite at your house!

## VEAL CHOPS WITH VEGETABLE SAUCE

Vegetables add fiber and vitamins to your family's diet, especially if they're cooked just till crisp-tender in a minimum of water. And, use the nutrient-rich cooking liquid to make a sauce.

● Frozen already-chopped vegetables and bottled minced garlic streamline preparation time in this skillet meal. Serve with sliced crusty bread to soak up the savory juices.

### NUTRITION INFORMATION

| Per serving | | |
|---|---|---|
| Calories..............196 | Fat.....................9 g | |
| Cholesterol........52 mg | Sodium...........880 mg | |
| Carbohydrate.......8 g | Fiber...................2 g | |
| Protein.................21 g | | |

### NUTRITION INFORMATION

| Per serving | | |
|---|---|---|
| Calories..............272 | Fat.....................14 g | |
| Cholesterol........85 mg | Sodium...........236 mg | |
| Carbohydrate.....10 g | Fiber...................4 g | |
| Protein.................25 g | | |

RECIPES BEGIN ON PAGE 38.

## CHICKEN WITH WALDORF SAUCE

Instead of frying in oil, poach poultry in broth or fruit juices. The chicken breasts take up lots of flavor, not fat (alias unwanted calories).

● Your butcher does part of the work when you buy chicken breasts with the skin and bones removed. He'll save you at least 10 minutes, which you can put to good use cutting up the apples and celery for the fresh-tasting sauce.

## SCALLOP AND ARTICHOKE STIR-FRY

Stir-fry the cholesterol-fighting scallops just till opaque. (Scallops as well as certain other fish and seafood contain omega-3 fatty acids, which appear to lower blood cholesterol levels.)

● Dinnertime can be a hectic, stressful time, so do some of the work ahead. When you prepare a stir-fried meal, most of the ingredients can be cut up in the morning or the night before.

### NUTRITION INFORMATION

| Per serving | | |
|---|---|---|
| Calories.................223 | Fat.........................7 g | |
| Cholesterol........76 mg | Sodium............128 mg | |
| Carbohydrate......15 g | Fiber........................1 g | |
| Protein..................25 g | | |

### NUTRITION INFORMATION

| Per serving | | |
|---|---|---|
| Calories.................269 | Fat.........................4 g | |
| Cholesterol........40 mg | Sodium............413 mg | |
| Carbohydrate......36 g | Fiber........................6 g | |
| Protein..................23 g | | |

## BROILED PARMESAN POTATOES

● Love fried potatoes? Mimic their goodness in the broiler to save cooking time, cleanup time, and calories. Fix a batch alongside your next broiled burger.

To avoid deep-frying, simply brush potato slices with a single stroke of seasoned margarine for crispy results. Then cook them under the broiler for just 12 minutes.

## ITALIAN TOMATO AND RICE SOUP

● Surprise! This hearty hodgepodge of vegetables, salsa, and rice requires no chopping! All you do is dump everything into a saucepan and cook till the vegetables are nice and tender.

Quick-thaw frozen vegetables by running water over them in a colander. Add the vegetables near the end of cooking so they retain their texture and nutrients.

### NUTRITION INFORMATION

| Per serving | | |
|---|---|---|
| Calories..............142 | Fat......................8 g | |
| Cholesterol..........5 mg | Sodium............188 mg | |
| Carbohydrate......14 g | Fiber ..................2 g | |
| Protein..................4 g | | |

### NUTRITION INFORMATION

| Per serving | | |
|---|---|---|
| Calories..............86 | Fat......................1 g | |
| Cholesterol..........0 mg | Sodium............628 mg | |
| Carbohydrate......15 g | Fiber ..................4 g | |
| Protein..................3 g | | |

RECIPES BEGIN ON PAGE 40.

## PEAS AND ONIONS AU GRATIN

● In 10 minutes you can have this vegetable side dish piping hot on your table. Just start with five ingredients plus seasonings and let your microwave do the work. Each time you make this dish, try a different blend of vegetables.

**Instead of a high-fat sauce, flavor your favorite vegetables with reduced-calorie cream cheese. Blend the low-fat cheese into hot micro-cooked vegetables till smooth.**

## CREAMY PASTA AND CABBAGE SALAD

● How you grocery shop can save time at home. For salad fixings, cruise the produce section for an already-shredded cabbage and carrot mixture. Buy cucumbers and chopped tomato at the supermarket salad bar.

**Be smart: Include high-fiber salads in your meals several times a week. And, of course, use a healthful dressing! Start with a reduced-calorie salad dressing and stir in plain yogurt.**

### NUTRITION INFORMATION

| Per serving | |
|---|---|
| Calories.................124 | Fat.........................6 g |
| Cholesterol...........1 mg | Sodium............169 mg |
| Carbohydrate.......13 g | Fiber.......................3 g |
| Protein....................5 g | |

### NUTRITION INFORMATION

| Per serving | |
|---|---|
| Calories.................131 | Fat.........................3 g |
| Cholesterol..........2 mg | Sodium............155 mg |
| Carbohydrate.......21 g | Fiber.......................2 g |
| Protein....................5 g | |

35

# GOOD-FOR-YOU DESSERTS... *FAST!*

Gently warm peaches and bananas in the honey-lime mixture so the fruits don't overcook and get mushy. Serve over frozen yogurt.

## HONEY-LIME FRUIT WITH FROZEN YOGURT

● Yield to temptation without regret. Instead of hot fudge, hot fruit! Instead of ice cream, frozen yogurt! In less than 20 minutes you can make this gorgeous dessert for family or health-conscious friends.

### NUTRITION INFORMATION

| Per serving | | |
|---|---|---|
| Calories..................334 | Fat............................14 g | |
| Cholesterol..........8 mg | Sodium............ 173 mg | |
| Carbohydrate.......51 g | Fiber ........................5 g | |
| Protein.....................5 g | | |

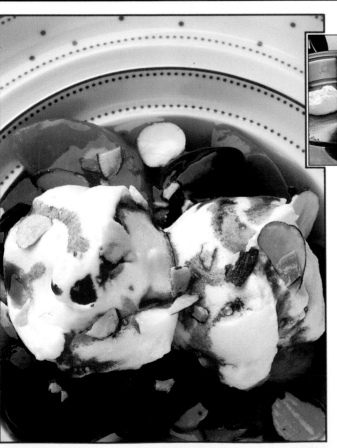

Drop mounds of egg-white meringue into boiling water; cook in water till firm. The cholesterol-free fluffy meringues take just 5 minutes to cook.

## FRUITED FLOATING ISLANDS

● Nutrition-conscious cooks know that the best dessert around is fruit. Frozen mixed fruits, simmered into a warm sauce, make a quick addition to the sweet poached meringue.

### NUTRITION INFORMATION

| Per serving | | |
|---|---|---|
| Calories..................161 | Fat............................1 g | |
| Cholesterol..........0 mg | Sodium...............28 mg | |
| Carbohydrate.......36 g | Fiber ........................1 g | |
| Protein.....................3 g | | |

## MUSTARD-ORANGE PORK CHOPS WITH STIR-FRIED ONIONS

*Serve with cooked green beans and cherry tomatoes. For a special look (as shown on page 30), select long Chinese beans and tie them in a knot after cooking—*

- ⅓ cup orange marmalade *or* apricot preserves
- 2 tablespoons Dijon-style mustard
- 4 pork rib chops, cut ½ inch thick (1 to 1¼ pounds total)
- Nonstick spray coating
- 24 green onions, bias-sliced into 1-inch pieces (3 cups)

Preheat the broiler. Meanwhile, for glaze, in a small saucepan stir together marmalade or preserves and mustard. Cook and stir over medium heat about 2 minutes or till marmalade or preserves are melted. Set mixture aside.

Trim excess fat from chops. Place the chops on the unheated rack of a broiler pan. Broil about 4 inches from the heat for 6 minutes. Turn the chops. Broil for 2 minutes. Brush *half* of the glaze over the chops. Broil for 4 to 5 minutes more or till the pork chops are no longer pink.

Spray a medium skillet with nonstick spray coating. Cook over high heat. Stir-fry onions for 2 to 3 minutes or till crisp-tender. Stir in remaining glaze; heat through. Serve mixture with chops. Makes 4 servings.

*Nutrition information per serving:* *316 cal., 29 g pro., 28 g carbo., 10 g fat, 83 mg chol., 292 mg sodium, 570 mg potassium, and 2 g dietary fiber. U.S. RDA: 15% vit. C, 70% thiamine, 16% riboflavin, 24% niacin.*

## MICROWAVE SPINACH-STUFFED SOLE

*To serve, slide a fish portion from a cup onto a carrot- and pea-pod-lined plate—*

- 4 fresh *or* frozen sole, flounder, catfish, *or* other thin fish fillets (about ¾ pound total)
- 1 10-ounce package frozen chopped spinach
- 1 beaten egg white
- 1 cup herb-seasoned croutons
- ½ cup cream-style, low-fat cottage cheese, drained
- 1 small carrot, shredded (about ¼ cup)
- 2 tablespoons cocktail sauce
- Nonstick spray coating

To thaw frozen fish, micro-cook, uncovered, on 50% power (medium) for 4 to 5 minutes or till nearly thawed, separating and rearranging fillets once. Set aside. To thaw frozen spinach, microcook, uncovered, on 100% power (high) for 3 to 4 minutes or till thawed, breaking up with a fork after 2 minutes. Drain the spinach well, pressing out the excess liquid.

For stuffing, in a mixing bowl stir together egg white, croutons, cottage cheese, carrot, and cocktail sauce; stir in spinach.

Spray four 10-ounce microwave-safe custard cups with nonstick spray coating. Line insides of cups with fillets, trimming and piecing as necessary. Spoon stuffing into the center of the fish-lined cups. Loosely cover custard cups with waxed paper. Microcook on high for 5 to 6 minutes or just till fish flakes with a fork and stuffing is heated through, rotating and rearranging the cups once during cooking. Slide the fish and stuffing out of the cups onto plates. Makes 4 servings.

*Nutrition information per serving:* *178 cal., 23 g pro., 12 g carbo., 4 g fat, 41 mg chol., 475 mg sodium, 715 mg potassium, and 2 g dietary fiber. U.S. RDA: 133% vit. A, 14% riboflavin, 10% niacin, 12% calcium, 14% iron.*

## VEAL CHOPS WITH VEGETABLE SAUCE

*The skillet drippings left from cooking the veal chops produce a richly flavored sauce to spoon over the cooked meat—*

- 4 veal top loin chops, cut ½ to ¾ inch thick (1¼ to 1½ pounds total)
- 1 tablespoon margarine *or* butter
- 1 16-ounce package loose-pack frozen broccoli, baby carrots, and water chestnuts
- ½ cup chicken broth
- 1 clove garlic, minced, *or* ⅛ teaspoon bottled minced garlic
- 2 tablespoons white-wine Worcestershire sauce
- 2 teaspoons cornstarch

Trim excess fat from veal chops. In a 10-inch skillet cook chops over medium heat in hot margarine or butter for 4 to 6 minutes or till veal is done, turning once. Transfer the cooked chops to a serving platter. Cover hot chops with foil to keep warm.

Stir the frozen vegetables, chicken broth, and garlic into skillet drippings. Bring the mixture to boiling. Reduce heat. Cover and simmer for 2 minutes.

Stir together Worcestershire sauce and cornstarch; add to skillet. Cook and stir till thickened and bubbly. Cook and stir for 2 minutes more. Spoon over the veal. Makes 4 servings.

*Nutrition information per serving:* *272 cal., 25 g pro., 10 g carbo., 14 g fat, 85 mg chol., 236 mg sodium, 533 mg potassium, and 4 g dietary fiber. U.S. RDA: 84% vit. A, 73% vit. C, 18% riboflavin, 28% niacin, 19% iron.*

## TEX-MEX TURKEY TENDERLOINS

*For a colorful dinner accompaniment, season rice with a pinch of ground turmeric before cooking—*

- 1 **pound turkey tenderloin slices, cut about ½ inch thick**
- 1 **teaspoon ground cumin**
- ⅛ **teaspoon pepper**
- 1 **tablespoon margarine** *or* **butter**
- 1 **large tomato, seeded and chopped**
- 1 **small zucchini, chopped (about 1 cup)**
- 2 **green onions, sliced (¼ cup)**
- 1 **4-ounce can diced green chili peppers, drained**
- 2 **tablespoons vinegar**
- 1 **tablespoon sugar**
- 1½ **teaspoons cornstarch**
- **Hot cooked rice (optional)**

Rinse turkey; pat dry. Stir together cumin and pepper; sprinkle on both sides of the tenderloins.

In a large skillet cook tenderloins in hot margarine or butter for 8 to 10 minutes or till tender and no longer pink, turning once. Transfer tenderloins to a serving platter. Cover the platter with foil to keep the turkey tenderloins warm.

Stir the tomato, zucchini, green onions, and chili peppers into the drippings in the skillet. In a small bowl stir together the vinegar, sugar, and cornstarch. Stir into the mixture in the skillet. Cook and stir for 1 to 2 minutes or till the onion is tender and the mixture is thickened and bubbly. Cook and stir for 2 minutes more. Spoon the mixture over tenderloins. Serve with rice, if desired. Makes 4 servings.

**Microwave directions:** Rinse turkey; pat dry. Coat turkey tenderloins with the cumin and pepper mixture as directed. *Omit* the margarine or butter.

In a 12x7½x2-inch microwave-safe dish arrange the tenderloins. Cover with vented microwave-safe clear plastic wrap. Cook on 100% power (high) for 6 to 7 minutes or till turkey tenderloins are tender and no longer pink, rearranging once. Cover turkey with foil to keep warm.

For sauce, in a microwave-safe 4-cup measure stir together vinegar, sugar, and cornstarch. Stir in tomato, zucchini, green onions, and chili peppers. Cook, uncovered, on high for 5 to 7 minutes or till mixture is thickened and bubbly, stirring every minute. Cook on high for 1 minute more. Spoon over turkey.

*Nutrition information per serving:* *180 cal., 27 g pro., 10 g carbo., 4 g fat, 71 mg chol., 82 mg sodium, 410 mg potassium, and 1 g dietary fiber. U.S. RDA: 15% vit. A, 70% vit. C, 35% niacin, and 12% iron.*

## PEPPERED BEEF AND ASPARAGUS

*When cutting the pepper fan, cover your hands with a plastic bag or rubber gloves to protect your skin from the oils in the fresh hot pepper. Avoid direct contact with your eyes. When finished, wash your hands thoroughly—*

- ½ **cup water**
- ¼ **cup sodium-reduced soy sauce**
- 1 **tablespoon cornstarch**
- ¼ **teaspoon pepper**
- ⅛ **teaspoon dried minced garlic**
- ⅛ **teaspoon ground red pepper**
- **Nonstick spray coating**
- ½ **pound fresh asparagus spears, bias-sliced into 1-inch pieces,** *or* **one 10-ounce package frozen cut asparagus, thawed**
- 1 **tablespoon cooking oil**
- ¾ **pound lean boneless beef, cut into thin bite-size strips**
- ½ **of a 16-ounce can straw mushrooms, drained**
- 2 **cups hot cooked cellophane noodles** *or* **hot cooked brown rice (optional)**
- **Red Anaheim pepper fan (optional)**

In a small bowl stir together water, soy sauce, cornstarch, pepper, garlic, and ground red pepper. Set aside.

Spray a cold wok or large skillet with nonstick spray coating. Heat over high heat. Add asparagus and stir-fry for 3 to 5 minutes or till crisp-tender. Remove asparagus from wok.

Add oil to the wok. Stir-fry beef in hot oil for 2 to 3 minutes. Push beef to the side of the wok.

Stir cornstarch mixture. Pour into center of wok. Cook and stir till thickened and bubbly. Cook and stir for 2 minutes more. Add the asparagus and mushrooms. Cook and stir till heated through. Serve over cellophane noodles or brown rice. Garnish with a pepper fan, if desired. Makes 4 servings.

*Nutrition information per serving:* *196 cal., 21 g pro., 8 g carbo., 9 g fat, 52 mg chol., 880 mg sodium, 410 mg potassium, and 2 g dietary fiber. U.S. RDA: 11% vit. A, 22% vit. C, 12% riboflavin, 20% niacin, 16% iron.*

## CHICKEN WITH WALDORF SAUCE

*The sauce for the light 'n' lean poultry is chock-full of crisp apples, fresh celery, and naturally sweet raisins, which makes it taste just like a hot variation of Waldorf salad—*

- 4 **skinless, boneless chicken breast halves (about 1 pound)**
- 1 **6-ounce can apple juice**
- ½ **teaspoon instant chicken bouillon granules**
- 2 **small red apples, cored and sliced**
- ¼ **cup sliced celery**
- 2 **green onions, sliced (¼ cup)**
- 2 **tablespoons raisins**
- 2 **tablespoons cold water**
- 1 **tablespoon cornstarch**
- ¼ **teaspoon ground nutmeg**
- 1 **tablespoon brandy (optional)**

Rinse chicken; pat dry. Season chicken lightly with salt and pepper. In a 10-inch skillet combine apple juice and bouillon granules. Bring to boiling. Add chicken to skillet. Reduce heat. Cover and simmer the chicken for 5 minutes. Turn chicken over.

Add apples, celery, onions, and raisins. Cover and simmer for 5 minutes more or till chicken is tender. Use a slotted spoon to transfer chicken to plates. Cut chicken into ¼-inch-thick slices. Top with apple mixture. Cover and keep the chicken and apple mixture warm.

For sauce, combine water, cornstarch, and nutmeg. Stir into juices in skillet. Cook and stir till thickened and bubbly. Cook and stir for 2 minutes more. Stir in brandy, if desired. Spoon sauce over each serving. Serves 4.

**Microwave directions:** Rinse, dry, and season chicken as directed. In a microwave-safe 10x6x2-inch baking dish arrange chicken. Cover with microwave-safe vented clear plastic wrap. Cook on 100% power (high) for 1½ minutes; rearrange chicken, turning less-cooked portions toward outside. Cook on high for 1½ minutes more. Turn chicken over; top with apples, celery, onions, and raisins. Cover with vented microwave-safe clear plastic wrap. Cook on high for 3 to 5 minutes more or till no longer pink. Cover chicken and apple mixture to keep warm.

For sauce, in a microwave-safe 2-cup measure stir together apple juice, bouillon granules, cornstarch, and nutmeg. *Omit* the water. Cook on high for 2 to 4 minutes or till thickened and bubbly, stirring after every minute. Cook on high for 30 seconds more. Stir in brandy, if desired. Use a slotted spoon to transfer chicken to dinner plates. Cut into ¼-inch-thick slices. Top with the apple mixture. Spoon sauce over each serving.

***Nutrition information per serving:*** *223 cal., 25 g pro., 15 g carbo., 7 g fat, 76 mg chol., 128 mg sodium, 359 mg potassium, and 1 g dietary fiber. U.S. RDA: 40% niacin.*

## SCALLOP AND ARTICHOKE STIR-FRY

*To cook couscous, pour boiling water over the uncooked grain. Let mixture stand, uncovered, for 5 minutes—*

- 1 **pound fresh sea scallops**
- ¾ **cup water**
- 2 **tablespoons lime juice**
- 1 **tablespoon cornstarch**
- 1 **teaspoon sugar**
- 1 **teaspoon instant chicken bouillon granules**
- ⅛ **teaspoon pepper**
- 1 **9-ounce package frozen artichoke hearts**
- **Nonstick spray coating**
- ½ **of a green pepper, cut into thin strips**
- ½ **of a red sweet pepper, cut into thin strips**
- 1 **tablespoon cooking oil**
- 2 **cups hot cooked couscous (optional)**

Cut any large scallops in half and set aside. For sauce, combine water, lime juice, cornstarch, sugar, bouillon granules, and pepper.

Place artichoke hearts in a colander; run cold water over them till partially thawed.

Spray a cold wok or large skillet with nonstick spray coating. Cook over high heat. Stir-fry artichokes and peppers for 2 to 4 minutes or till peppers are crisp-tender. Remove vegetables from wok or skillet.

Add oil to wok or skillet; add *half* of the scallops. Stir-fry for 2 to 3 minutes or till scallops are opaque. Remove scallops. Stir-fry remaining scallops and remove from wok or skillet.

Stir sauce. Add to the wok or skillet. Cook and stir till thickened and bubbly. Return vegetables and scallops to wok. Cook and stir about 2 minutes or till mixture is heated through. Serve over hot cooked couscous, if desired. Makes 4 servings.

***Nutrition information per serving:*** *269 cal., 23 g pro., 36 g carbo., 4 g fat, 40 mg chol., 413 mg sodium, 518 mg potassium, and 6 g dietary fiber. U.S. RDA: 38% vit. A, 74% vit. C, 14% thiamine, 11% riboflavin, 14% niacin, 15% iron.*

## BEEF SALAD WITH FRESH BASIL DRESSING

*Chill the dressing in the freezer to get it cold FAST!*

- ½ cup buttermilk
- 3 tablespoons reduced-calorie mayonnaise *or* salad dressing
- 1 tablespoon snipped fresh basil *or* 1 teaspoon dried basil, crushed
- 1 tablespoon lemon juice
- 1 teaspoon sugar

Dash pepper
- 6 cups torn mixed greens
- 8 ounces lean cooked beef, cut into thin strips
- 1 small parsnip, thinly sliced
- 1 medium carrot, thinly sliced
- ½ of a small zucchini, sliced
- ½ cup broccoli flowerets
- ½ of a 16-ounce can julienne beets, well drained

For the dressing, in a small bowl stir together buttermilk, mayonnaise or salad dressing, basil, lemon juice, sugar, and pepper. Cover and chill in the freezer while preparing the salad.

To assemble the salad, toss together the greens, beef, parsnip, carrot, zucchini, and broccoli. Toss with the chilled dressing. Spoon onto serving plates. Top with the drained julienne beets. Makes 4 servings.

***Nutrition information per serving:*** *212 cal., 20 g pro., 13 g carbo., 9 g fat, 53 mg chol., 254 mg sodium, 684 mg potassium, and 7 g dietary fiber. U.S. RDA: 124% vit. A, 29% vit. C, 15% riboflavin, 18% niacin, 10% iron.*

## POACHED FISH IN ORANGE SAUCE

*Choose sole, flounder, or orange roughy fish fillets—*

- 1 medium cucumber
- 1 teaspoon finely shredded orange peel
- 1 cup orange juice
- 1 medium carrot, shredded
- ¼ teaspoon salt
- 1 pound fresh fish fillets
- 1 tablespoon cornstarch
- 1 tablespoon water

Orange wedges (optional)

Chop enough of the cucumber to equal ½ *cup*. Thinly slice the remaining cucumber.

In an ungreased 10-inch skillet stir together the orange peel, orange juice, carrot, and salt. Bring the mixture to boiling. Measure thickness of fish, then carefully add fish to skillet. Return the mixture just to boiling; reduce heat. Cover and simmer for 4 to 6 minutes per ½-inch thickness of fish or just till the fish flakes when tested with a fork.

Place cucumber slices on a platter. Use a slotted spatula to transfer fish to platter atop cucumber. Cover with foil to keep warm. For sauce, in a small bowl stir together the cornstarch and water. Stir into the mixture in the skillet. Cook and stir till mixture is thickened and bubbly. Cook and stir for 2 minutes more. Stir in the chopped cucumber. Spoon the sauce over all. Serve with orange wedges. Makes 4 servings.

**Microwave directions:** Chop and slice cucumber as directed. Set aside. Arrange fish fillets in a microwave-safe 8x8x2-inch baking dish. Turn under any thin portions to obtain an even thickness. Cover with microwave-safe clear plastic wrap; vent by leaving a small area unsealed at the edge of the dish. Micro-cook on 100% power (high) for 4 to 7 minutes or just till fish flakes with a fork, giving the dish a half-turn after 4 minutes. Cover to keep warm.

For sauce, in a 2-cup microwave-safe measure stir together orange peel, orange juice, carrot, salt, and cornstarch. *Omit* water. Cook, uncovered, on 100% power (high) for 3 to 5 minutes or till thickened and bubbly, stirring every minute. Cook on high for 30 seconds more. Stir in chopped cucumber. Place cucumber slices on a serving platter. Top with fish. Spoon sauce over all.

***Nutrition information per serving:*** *151 cal., 21 g pro., 12 g carbo., 2 g fat, 49 mg chol., 233 mg sodium, 770 mg potassium, 1 g dietary fiber. U.S. RDA: 104% vit. A, 34% vit. C, 10% thiamine, 12% niacin.*

## BROILED PARMESAN POTATOES

*Thinly slice the potatoes so they cook tender without burning—*

- 2 tablespoons margarine *or* butter, melted
- 1 teaspoon dried basil, crushed
- ½ teaspoon paprika
- ¼ teaspoon garlic powder
- ⅛ teaspoon pepper
- 2 medium potatoes, bias-sliced about ¼ inch thick
- ¼ cup grated Parmesan *or* Romano cheese

Stir together margarine or butter, basil, paprika, garlic powder, and pepper. Place potato slices in a single layer on the unheated rack of a broiler pan. Brush margarine mixture over both sides of potato slices. Broil about 5 inches from the heat for 8 to 9 minutes or till potatoes begin to brown.

Using a wide spatula, turn potatoes. Sprinkle with cheese. Broil for 4 to 6 minutes more or till potatoes are tender. Makes 4 servings.

***Nutrition information per serving:*** *142 cal., 4 g pro., 14 g carbo., 8 g fat, 5 mg chol., 188 mg sodium, 442 mg potassium, and 2 g dietary fiber. U.S. RDA: 10% vit. A, 18% vit. C, 10% calcium.*

## PEAS AND ONIONS AU GRATIN

*Here's a tasty vegetable side-dish recipe that goes together just as fast as plain peas, but tastes even better! The creamy shortcut sauce blends soft-style cream cheese with pepper and garlic. Herb-seasoned croutons give this side dish a crunchy finish.*

- 1 16-ounce package loose-pack frozen peas and pearl onions
- 2 tablespoons water
- 2 ounces reduced-calorie soft-style cream cheese (¼ cup)
- 2 tablespoons milk
- ¼ to ½ teaspoon cracked black pepper
- 1 clove garlic, minced, *or* ⅛ teaspoon bottled minced garlic
- ½ cup herb-seasoned croutons

In a microwave-safe 1-quart casserole micro-cook the frozen peas and pearl onions and water, covered, on 100% power (high) for 3 to 5 minutes or just till the vegetables are tender. Drain off the water.

Stir in the soft-style cream cheese, milk, pepper, and fresh or bottled garlic. Cook, covered, on high for 2 to 4 minutes or till heated through, stirring twice. Sprinkle the herb-seasoned croutons atop the vegetable mixture. Makes 4 servings.

*Nutrition information per serving: 124 cal., 5 g pro., 13 g carbo., 6 g fat, 1 mg chol., 169 mg sodium, 140 mg potassium, and 3 g dietary fiber. U.S. RDA: 14% vit. A, 13% vit. C, 10% thiamine.*

## ITALIAN TOMATO AND RICE SOUP

*A warming soup for a blustery day—*

- 2 cups water
- 1 12-ounce jar mild chunky salsa
- 1 cup sodium-reduced tomato juice
- ⅓ cup quick-cooking brown rice
- 1 tablespoon dried minced onion
- 1 teaspoon dried Italian seasoning
- ½ teaspoon instant chicken bouillon granules
- ⅛ teaspoon dried minced garlic
- ⅛ teaspoon pepper
- 1 16-ounce package loose-pack frozen zucchini, carrots, cauliflower, lima beans, and Italian beans
- ⅓ cup finely shredded *or* grated Parmesan cheese (optional)

In a large saucepan combine the water, salsa, tomato juice, rice, onion, Italian seasoning, bouillon granules, garlic, and pepper. Bring mixture to boiling; reduce heat. Cover and simmer for 10 minutes.

Meanwhile, place vegetables in a colander. Run cold water over vegetables till thawed. Stir into the rice mixture. Return to boiling; reduce heat. Cover and simmer for 5 to 10 minutes or till rice and vegetables are tender. Top each serving with cheese. Makes 6 side-dish servings.

*Nutrition information per serving: 86 cal., 3 g pro., 15 g carbo., 1 g fat, 0 mg chol., 628 mg sodium, 324 mg potassium, and 4 g dietary fiber. U.S. RDA: 30% vit. A, 34% vit. C.*

## CREAMY PASTA AND CABBAGE SALAD

*Keep your meal on the lean side; serve this vegetable side dish with grilled chicken or turkey—*

- 4 ounces corkscrew macaroni (1½ cups uncooked)
- ½ cup plain low-fat yogurt
- ⅓ cup reduced-calorie creamy Italian salad dressing
- 1 tablespoon grated Parmesan cheese
- 1 small clove garlic, minced
- 2 cups mixed shredded cabbage and carrots
- 1 medium cucumber, chopped
- 1 medium tomato, seeded and chopped

Lettuce leaves (optional)
Cucumber rings (optional)
Purple basil (optional)

Cook pasta in boiling water according to package directions. Immediately drain. Rinse under cold running water. Drain pasta well.

Meanwhile, in a small bowl stir together the low-fat plain yogurt, creamy Italian salad dressing, Parmesan cheese, and garlic.

In a large bowl toss together the pasta, salad dressing mixture, shredded cabbage and carrots, cucumber, and tomato. Cover and quick-chill the salad in the freezer for 10 minutes. Serve chilled mixture atop lettuce leaves. Garnish with cucumber and purple basil, if desired. Makes 6 servings.

*Nutrition information per serving: 131 cal., 5 g pro., 21 g carbo., 3 g fat, 2 mg chol., 155 mg sodium, 269 mg potassium, and 2 g dietary fiber. U.S. RDA: 108% vit. A, 14% vit. C, 15% thiamine.*

## CHILI PEPPER POTATO SALAD

*Canned potatoes and bottled salad dressing keep it simple—*

- 2 **16-ounce cans sliced potatoes, drained**
- 1 **yellow *or* red sweet pepper, coarsely chopped**
- 1 **cup loose-pack frozen peas**
- ¼ **cup reduced-calorie creamy bacon salad dressing**
- 1 **4-ounce can diced green chili peppers, drained**
- ½ **teaspoon salt**
- ⅛ **teaspoon pepper**
- ⅛ **teaspoon bottled minced garlic**

**Lettuce leaves (optional)**

In a large mixing bowl toss together potatoes, sweet pepper, and peas. In a blender container combine salad dressing, chili peppers, salt, pepper, and garlic. Cover and blend till smooth. Toss with the potato mixture. If desired, cover and quick-chill in the freezer for 10 to 15 minutes or till cold. Serve on lettuce leaves. Makes 6 servings.

***Nutrition information per serving:*** *103 cal., 3 g pro., 19 g carbo., 2 g fat, 0 mg chol., 532 mg sodium, 291 mg potassium, 3 g dietary fiber. U.S. RDA: 28% vit. A, 94% vit. C, 10% thiamine, and 11% iron.*

## HONEY-LIME FRUIT WITH FROZEN YOGURT

*Here's a fruit and dessert combined in one. The colorful fruit quartet includes bananas, peaches, kiwi fruit, and fresh strawberries—*

- 3 **tablespoons margarine *or* butter**
- 1 **tablespoon lime juice**
- 1 **tablespoon honey**
- 2 **medium bananas, bias-sliced ¼ inch thick**
- ½ **cup frozen unsweetened peaches, chopped**
- 2 **kiwi fruit, peeled and sliced**
- 1½ **cups halved strawberries**
- 2 **cups frozen yogurt**

In a 10-inch skillet melt the margarine or butter. Stir in the lime juice and honey. Add the bananas and peaches. Heat and gently stir for 1 to 2 minutes or till the fruit is heated through. In dessert bowls arrange kiwi fruit and strawberries. Top with frozen yogurt. Spoon the warm fruit-honey mixture over all. Makes 4 servings.

**Microwave directions:** In a microwave-safe 1½-quart casserole, microcook margarine or butter, uncovered, on 100% power (high) for 45 to 60 seconds or till melted. Stir in the lime juice and honey. Add the bananas and the peaches, stirring to coat. Cook, uncovered, on high for 2 to 2½ minutes or till fruit is heated through, stirring once. Continue as directed.

***Nutrition information per serving:*** *334 cal., 5 g pro., 51 g carbo., 14 g fat, 8 mg chol., 173 mg sodium, 712 mg potassium, and 5 g dietary fiber. U.S. RDA: 17% vit. A, 151% vit. C, 17% riboflavin, 13% calcium.*

## FRUITED FLOATING ISLANDS

- 3 **cups water**
- 2 **egg whites**
- 1 **teaspoon vanilla**
- ¼ **cup sugar**
- 1 **10-ounce package frozen mixed fruit (in quick-thaw pouch), thawed**
- 2 **teaspoons cornstarch**

**Crème de strawberry, crème de almond, *or* grenadine syrup**
**Toasted sliced almonds**

In a 10-inch skillet heat water to simmering. Meanwhile, for meringues, in a small mixer bowl beat egg whites and vanilla with an electric mixer on medium speed till soft peaks form (tips curl). Gradually add sugar, beating on high speed till stiff peaks form (tips stand straight).

Drop egg white mixture in 8 portions into simmering water. Simmer, uncovered, about 5 minutes or till meringues are firm. (Knife comes out clean.) Using a slotted spoon, gently lift from water. Drain on paper towels, and place on waxed paper. Chill meringues while preparing the fruit.

Drain fruit, reserving syrup. Add enough water to syrup to make ⅔ cup liquid. In a small saucepan stir together syrup mixture and cornstarch. Cook and stir till thickened and bubbly. Cook and stir for 2 minutes more. Stir in fruit. Spoon into 4 dessert dishes. Top each serving with 2 meringues. Drizzle liqueur or grenadine over meringues. Sprinkle with toasted almonds. Makes 4 servings.

***Nutrition information per serving:*** *161 cal., 3 g pro., 36 g carbo., 1 g fat, 0 mg chol., 28 mg sodium, 135 mg potassium, and 1 g dietary fiber. U.S. RDA: 62% vit. C.*

# APRIL

# CHICKEN

SCOTT LITTLE

By
Barbara Johnson

## MEXICAN CHICKEN SKILLET

*There's plenty of time to toss together a green salad, cut up fresh fruit, slice a loaf of bakery-fresh bread, and pour glasses of milk while the chicken simmers for 35 minutes—*

- **8** chicken drumsticks (about 1½ pounds total) *or* 4 chicken thighs (about 1 pound total)
- **2** tablespoons cooking oil
- • • •
- **1** 12-ounce jar chunky red salsa
- • • •
- **½** cup shredded Monterey Jack cheese (2 ounces)
- **½** cup broken tortilla chips

● **Rinse** the chicken drumsticks or thighs. Pat dry with paper towels.

● **In a 10-inch skillet cook** the chicken in hot cooking oil, uncovered, over medium-high heat for 10 to 15 minutes or till chicken is light brown, turning occasionally so chicken browns evenly. Drain off the fat.

● **Pour the salsa over the chicken** in the skillet. Reduce the heat; cover and simmer for 35 to 40 minutes or till chicken is tender enough to be easily pierced with a fork. Transfer the chicken and salsa sauce to a serving platter. Sprinkle with the cheese. Serve with the tortilla chips. Makes 4 servings.

**Kids will love the taste of this fun-to-eat meal.**

*Nutrition information per serving:* *342 cal., 29 g pro., 12 g carbo., 18 g fat, 94 mg chol., 814 mg sodium, 426 mg potassium, 2 g dietary fiber. U.S. RDA: 10% vit. A, 18% riboflavin, 27% niacin, 15% calcium, 10% iron.*

PHOTOGRAPH: SUSAN SCHELLING. FOOD STYLIST: STEVIE BASS

● **Use tongs to turn the chicken pieces occasionally so the chicken browns evenly.**

44

# DINNERS

## CHICKEN IN MUSHROOM CREAM SAUCE

*Look for marinated fresh chicken in your grocer's refrigerated meat case. Any of the several flavors available will work in this 15-minute recipe—*

- 2 **8-** *or* **12-ounce packages lemon- and pepper-marinated chicken breasts (4 breast halves total)**
- ¼ **cup margarine** *or* **butter**

• • •

- 2 **cups packaged sliced fresh mushrooms**
- 2 **teaspoons fresh** *or* **frozen snipped chives**
- ½ **cup whipping cream**

● **In a large skillet cook** the chicken breasts in hot margarine or butter over medium heat for 8 to 10 minutes or till chicken is tender enough to be easily pierced with a fork and no pink remains, turning occasionally so chicken browns evenly.

● **Transfer chicken** to a serving platter, reserving the drippings in the skillet. Cover the chicken and keep warm.

● **Add the mushrooms and chives** to the reserved drippings in the skillet. Cook and stir for 1 to 2 minutes or till the mushrooms are tender. Stir in the whipping cream; boil gently for 3 minutes or till the sauce is slightly thickened, scraping up the browned bits on the bottom of the skillet. To serve, spoon the sauce over the chicken. Makes 4 servings.

Cook this dish for your special someone.

*Nutrition information per serving:* *401 cal., 37 g pro., 3 g carbo., 27 g fat, 137 mg chol., 231 mg sodium, 450 mg potassium, and 1 g dietary fiber. U.S. RDA: 19% vit. A, 19% riboflavin, and 85% niacin.*

● **Add the cream to the skillet drippings, then cook and stir at a gentle boil till the sauce thickens.**

# FABULOUS FOODS

SPECIAL RECIPES FOR THOSE SPECIAL OCCASIONS

By Joy Taylor

Looking for a knock-'em-dead recipe? For your next all-out cooking and dining extravaganza, concentrate your time and efforts on one spectacular recipe. Then, complete the menu with no-fuss accompaniments. One glorious recipe makes for one grand dinner.

## ROAST PORK WITH MUSHROOM-BUTTER SAUCE

- ● **Preparation time:** 1 hour
- ● **Roasting time:** 2 hours

### MENU
Chilled Avocado Soup
•
Roast Pork with Mushroom-Butter Sauce
•
Turmeric Rice
•
Steamed Seasonal Vegetables
•
Apricot Custard

**Make dinner easy on yourself: Fix and chill the soup and dessert ahead.**

### FOR ROAST PORK ...
- 2 **cups finely chopped fresh shiitake, oyster, *or* morel mushrooms**
- 2 **cups finely chopped leeks**
- ¼ **cup butter**
- ¼ **cup dry white wine**
- ¾ **cup soft bread crumbs**
- ½ **cup chopped water chestnuts**
- ½ **cup shredded carrot**
- ¼ **teaspoon salt**
- 1 **4-to-5-pound pork loin center rib roast, backbone loosened (8 ribs)**
- 1 **recipe Mushroom-Butter Sauce (see recipe, page 53)**

For stuffing, in a saucepan cook mushrooms and leeks in butter till tender. Add wine; simmer, uncovered, 5 minutes or till liquid evapo-

rates. Remove from heat. Stir in bread crumbs, water chestnuts, carrot, salt, and ⅛ teaspoon *pepper*.

Place roast, rib side down. On the meaty side, cut a pocket above each rib, making 8 pockets total. Spoon stuffing into pockets. Place roast, rib side down, in a shallow roasting pan. Insert meat thermometer. Roast in a 325° oven 1¾ to 2¼ hours or till thermometer registers 160°. Cover loosely with foil after 1 hour to prevent overbrowning. About 30 minutes before serving, prepare sauce. Keep sauce warm. Remove roast from oven; let stand 10 minutes before carving. To serve, slice meat between ribs. Serve with sauce. Makes 8 servings.

*Nutrition information per serving:* 529 cal., 31 g pro., 16 g carbo., 37 g fat, 146 mg chol., 261 mg sodium, 713 mg potassium, and 2 g dietary fiber. U.S. RDA: 58% vit. A, 13% vit. C, 49% thiamine, 29% riboflavin, 35% niacin, and 17% iron.

**Cut pockets on meaty side above ribs. Spoon about ⅓ cup stuffing into each pocket.**

# SMOKED SALMON SALAD WITH LEMON VINAIGRETTE

**S**et the stage for an elegant evening. Succulent salmon, tender greens, and a silky dressing create this first-course masterpiece.

- ● *Preparation time:* 55 minutes
- ● *Final assembly:* 35 minutes

## MENU

Smoked Salmon Salad
With Lemon Vinaigrette
•
Assorted Breads
•
Cornish Game Hens with
Wild Rice Dressing
•
Steamed Broccoli Spears
•
Almond-Raspberry Torte

After the seafood first course, follow with a simple poultry dish. Because the rest of the meal is light, go ahead and serve a decadant dessert.

### FOR SALAD...

- 1 **large cucumber**
- 2 **ounces rice sticks, broken**
- **Cooking oil for deep frying**
- 1 **head red tip lettuce**
- 1 **head Bibb lettuce**
- 4 **cups thinly shredded mixed greens**
- 6 **ounces thinly sliced smoked salmon (lox)**
- **Edible flowers (such as nasturtium, borage, *or* pansy)\***
- 1 **recipe Lemon Vinaigrette (see recipe, page 54)**

Using a very sharp knife, thinly slice the cucumber. Soak slices in iced salt water for 5 minutes. Remove slices. To make cucumber flowers, tightly roll up a small cucumber slice. Wrap the next largest slice around the first slice. Continue wrapping more slices around center slice till flower is of desired

size. Secure with a toothpick at one end. Fold out ends of cucumber to resemble a flower. Place in iced salt water for 5 minutes. Drain. Cover and chill till needed.

One hour before serving time, fry unsoaked rice sticks, a few at a time, in deep hot oil (375°) about 5 seconds or till sticks puff and rise to the top. Remove; drain on paper towels. (If rice sticks are fried too early, they may become soggy.)

At serving time, remove large outer leaves from red tip and Bibb lettuce; line 4 plates with leaves. Top with rice sticks. Fill center of each plate with shredded greens. Cut salmon into strips and roll up. Remove toothpicks from cucumber flowers. Arrange salmon, cucumber flowers, and edible flowers on each plate. Serve immediately; pass Lemon

Vinaigrette to drizzle over each serving. Makes 4 first-course salads.

*Nutrition information per serving:* 296 cal., 12 g pro., 9 g carbo., 24 g fat, 84 mg chol., 2,793 mg sodium, and 3 g dietary fiber. U.S. RDA: 20% vit. A, 30% vit. C, 12% riboflavin, and 10% iron.

**\*Note:** Use only flowers that are grown specifically for eating.

**Tightly roll up cucumber slices into a flower shape. Secure; soak in salted ice water. Drain.**

# CHOCOLATE TERRINE WITH SPRING FRUITS

**Y**our guests will "ooh" and "aah," when you serve this outrageous dessert. Enjoy the praise!

- *Preparation time:* 30 minutes plus cooling
- *Chilling time:* 6 hours
- *Final touches:* 5 minutes

## MENU
Hearts of Palm Salad
•
Sweet Mustard Lamb
•
Lemon Snap Peas
•
Dinner Rolls
•
Chocolate Terrine with Spring Fruits
•
Café au Lait

**A lightly dressed salad and simple entrée balance the creamy, rich dessert.**

### FOR TERRINE...

- 1 **envelope unflavored gelatin**
- ¾ **cup sugar**
- ¾ **cup water**
- 4 **slightly beaten egg yolks**
- 4 **egg whites**
- ¾ **cup whipping cream**
- 6 **ounces semisweet chocolate, melted and cooled**
- 2 **tablespoons orange liqueur**
- 1 **recipe Rhubarb-Strawberry Sauce (see recipe, page 55)**
**Whole and sliced strawberries**
**Fresh mint, orange sections, and chocolate curls (optional)**

In a 1½-quart saucepan combine unflavored gelatin and sugar; stir in water, then egg yolks. Cook and stir over medium heat till gelatin is dissolved and mixture comes to a gentle boil; cook and stir 2 minutes more. Cover surface with clear plastic wrap. Cool to room temperature (about 1 hour).

In a large mixer bowl beat egg whites with an electric mixer on high speed till stiff peaks form (tips stand straight); fold in gelatin mixture. Beat the whipping cream just till soft peaks form; fold into gelatin mixture. Divide into two equal portions (about 2 cups each).

Lightly fold melted chocolate into one portion and fold orange liqueur into remaining portion. Pour the liqueur portion into an 8x4x2-inch loaf pan, spreading evenly in pan. Cover and chill liqueur layer till partially set (20 to 30 minutes). (Meanwhile, keep chocolate mixture, covered, at room temperature.) Carefully spoon on the chocolate portion when the liqueur layer is almost set but still slightly sticky to the touch. Cover and chill the terrine for 6 hours or till it is firm.

To serve, unmold the terrine onto a serving platter. Decorate terrine and serve slices with Rhubarb-Strawberry Sauce, fresh berries, mint, orange sections, and chocolate curls. Serves 6 to 8.

***Nutrition information per serving:*** *390 cal., 6 g pro., 54 g carbo., 19 g fat, 167 mg chol., 41 mg sodium, and 2 g dietary fiber. U.S. RDA: 11% vit. A and 45% vit. C.*

**Add the chocolate layer when the white layer is almost set and sticky to the touch.**

51

# CAMEMBERT SPREAD WITH WALNUT FLAT BREAD

Send out the word, "Come for hors d'oeuvres." Then plan to make an impression with this beautiful food.

- **Preparation time:** 1½ hours
- **Chilling time:** 2 hours
- **Final touches:** 10 minutes

## MENU

Camembert Spread with Walnut Flat Bread
•
Appetizer Frittata
•
Chilled Shrimp with Spinach Sauce
•
Mixed Nuts
•
Sparkling Apple Cider

**Contrast this cheesy center-piece with crisp and zesty finger foods.**

**FOR SPREAD...**

2 4½-ounce containers Camembert cheese
4 ounces fresh pea pods
1 large artichoke, cooked and chilled
1 8-ounce carton dairy sour cream
¼ to ½ teaspoon garlic powder
2 tablespoons crumbled blue cheese
2 teaspoons snipped chives
Red leaf lettuce
2 tablespoons snipped sun-dried tomatoes
Garlic chive blossom (optional)
1 recipe Walnut Flat bread (see recipe, page 56)

Bring Camembert to room temperature. Meanwhile, cook pea pods in a small amount of boiling water 30 seconds. Immediately immerse in ice water. Drain; chill.

Discard small outer leaves on artichoke. Pull off large leaves; cover and chill leaves till serving time. Discard choke. Finely chop heart.

Cut up Camembert (do not remove white outer coating); place in a food processor bowl or blender container. Add sour cream and garlic powder. Cover; blend till smooth, stopping occasionally to scrape down sides. Stir in artichoke heart, blue cheese, and chives. Spread mixture in a large lettuce-lined platter. Cover; chill till serving time.

To serve, arrange artichoke leaves and pea pods around edge of platter. Sprinkle with sun-dried tomatoes. Garnish with a garlic chive blossom. Serve with Walnut Flat Bread. Makes 12 appetizer servings.

***Nutrition information per serving with ½ of a flat bread:*** *211 cal., 9 g pro., 15 g carbo., 13 g fat, 47 mg chol., 370 mg sodium, and 1 g dietary fiber. U.S. RDA: 11% vit. A, 37% thiamine, 14% riboflavin, 14% calcium.*

## MUSHROOM-BUTTER SAUCE (FOR ROAST PORK)

*Roast pork recipe appears on page 46—*

- 1 cup sliced leeks
- 1 cup sliced shiitake, oyster, *or* morel mushrooms
- ¼ cup dry white wine
- 1 teaspoon fines herbes, crushed
- ½ cup whipping cream
- ½ cup butter
- 2 teaspoons lemon juice
- 1 teaspoon instant chicken bouillon granules
- ⅛ teaspoon pepper

Combine leeks, mushrooms, wine, and fines herbes. Bring to boiling; reduce heat. Simmer, uncovered, for 5 minutes or till most of the liquid is evaporated. Stir in whipping cream.

Add butter, a little at a time, stirring till melted. *Do not boil.* Stir in lemon juice, bouillon granules, and pepper. Keep sauce warm for up to 30 minutes. Serve with roast pork. Makes 2 cups.

## TURMERIC RICE

- 1½ cups long grain rice
- ½ teaspoon ground turmeric

Prepare rice according to package directions, adding turmeric to the water before cooking. Makes 8 servings.

***Nutrition information per serving:***
*127 cal., 2 g pro., 28 g carbo., 0 g fat, 0 mg chol., 2 mg sodium, 35 mg potassium, and 0 g dietary fiber. U.S. RDA: 10% thiamine.*

## CHILLED AVOCADO SOUP

- ¼ cup chopped onion
- 1 tablespoon margarine *or* butter
- 1 tablespoon all-purpose flour
- ¼ teaspoon dried dillweed
- 2 cups chicken broth
- 2 medium avocados, seeded, peeled, and cut into chunks
- 1 cup milk
- ½ cup dairy sour cream
- 1 small tomato, seeded and coarsely chopped
  Fresh dill sprigs

Cook onion in margarine or butter till tender. Stir in flour and ¼ teaspoon dillweed. Stir in broth. Cook and stir till slightly thickened and bubbly. Cook and stir 1 minute more. Cool slightly.

In a blender container or food processor bowl combine *half* of the broth mixture and *half* of the avocados. Cover and blend or process till smooth. Pour into a mixing bowl. Repeat, blending or processing remaining broth mixture and avocado; transfer to the bowl. Stir milk into avocado mixture. Place clear plastic wrap on the surface; chill in the refrigerator for 3 to 4 hours or till cold. (*Do not* store longer; the avocado may darken the soup.)

To serve, ladle chilled avocado mixture into 8 soup bowls. Garnish *each* serving with *1 tablespoon* of the sour cream, chopped tomato, and a sprig of fresh dill. Makes 8 servings.

***Nutrition information per serving:***
*168 cal., 4 g pro., 8 g carbo., 14 g fat, 9 mg chol., 235 mg sodium, 490 mg potassium, and 1 g dietary fiber. U.S. RDA: 14% vit. A, 10% riboflavin, and 10% niacin.*

## APRICOT CUSTARD

- ½ cup apricot preserves
- 2 tablespoons apricot nectar *or* orange juice
- 4 eggs
- 2 cups milk
- ⅓ cup sugar
- ¼ teaspoon vanilla
  Boiling water
- ¼ cup slivered almonds, toasted
- ¼ cup chopped macadamia nuts
  Fresh mint leaves (optional)

In a saucepan combine preserves and nectar. Cook and stir till preserves are melted. Spread in bottom of an 8-inch round baking dish. Set aside.

For custard, in a large mixing bowl lightly beat eggs. Stir in milk, sugar, and vanilla. Place baking dish with preserves mixture in a larger baking pan; set in the center of an oven rack. To prevent spattering, hold a large spoon upside down just above the preserves mixture. Pour egg mixture over spoon into the baking dish. Carefully pour boiling water into larger pan around baking dish to a depth of 1 inch.

Bake in a 325° oven about 35 minutes or till a knife inserted near the center comes out clean. Cool. Chill for several hours. About 1 hour before serving, loosen sides of custard with a knife. Invert onto a serving plate. Chill till serving time. Arrange the almonds and macadamia nuts atop. Garnish with fresh mint leaves, if desired. Cut into wedges to serve. Makes 8 servings.

***Nutrition information per serving:***
*202 cal., 6 g pro., 26 g carbo., 9 g fat, 141 mg chol., 68 mg sodium, 188 mg potassium, and 1 g dietary fiber. U.S. RDA: 12% riboflavin and 10% calcium.*

## ALMOND RASPBERRY TORTE

*Make cake and filling a day in advance. Frost with whipped cream and garnish with jam and almonds before serving—*

1½ cups all-purpose flour
2¼ teaspoons baking powder
¼ teaspoon salt
¾ cup margarine *or* butter
1 cup sugar
1½ teaspoons vanilla
3 eggs
¾ cup milk
½ cup seedless red raspberry jam
1 recipe Almond Filling
1¼ cups whipping cream
¼ cup seedless red raspberry jam
Sliced almonds, toasted

Grease and lightly flour two 9-inch round cake pans; set aside. For cake, in a bowl stir together flour, baking powder, and salt. Beat margarine on medium speed about 30 seconds. Add sugar and vanilla; beat till well combined.

Add eggs, one at a time, beating after each addition. Add dry ingredients and milk alternately to beaten mixture, beating after each addition. (Batter may appear curdled.) Spread batter in prepared pans.

Bake in a 375° oven for 20 to 25 minutes or till a wooden toothpick inserted in the center comes out clean. Cool for 10 minutes in pans on wire racks. Remove from pans. Cool.

Cut cake layers in half horizontally. Stir the ½ cup raspberry jam. To assemble, spread *one* cake layer with *one-third* of the Almond Filling, then with *2 rounded tablespoons* of jam. Repeat, layering with 2 more of the cake

layers, Almond Filling, and jam 2 more times. Top with the final cake layer. Cover cake tightly and refrigerate for at least 6 hours or overnight.

No more than 1 hour before serving, beat cream to stiff peaks; spread over cake. Press almonds around the base of the cake.

Just before serving, stir the remaining ¼ cup raspberry jam. Drizzle jam atop cake. Serve immediately. Makes 10 servings.

**Almond Filling:** In a small mixer bowl crumble one 8-ounce can *almond paste*. With an electric mixer beat in ⅓ cup softened *margarine* or *butter*. Add 2 tablespoons *milk;* beat till smooth.

*Nutrition information per serving: 637 cal., 9 g pro., 63 g carbo., 41 g fat, 125 mg chol., 398 mg sodium, 290 mg potassium, and 2 g dietary fiber. U.S. RDA: 28% vit. A, 14% thiamine, 23% riboflavin, 17% calcium, 12% iron.*

## LEMON VINAIGRETTE (FOR SMOKED SALMON SALAD)

*The recipe for Smoked Salmon Salad appears on page 48—*

1 egg yolk
½ teaspoon finely shredded lemon peel
3 tablespoons lemon juice
½ teaspoon sugar
¼ teaspoon salt
¼ teaspoon dry mustard
⅛ teaspoon pepper
⅓ cup hazelnut oil, almond oil, *or* olive oil

In a blender container combine egg yolk, finely shredded lemon peel, lemon juice, sugar, salt, mustard, and pepper. Cover and blend till smooth.

With blender on low speed, add oil in a slow, steady stream. Blend till mixture is slightly thickened and creamy. Transfer to a covered container. Chill for several hours in the refrigerator. Stir mixture before serving with salad. Makes about ½ cup salad dressing.

## CORNISH GAME HENS WITH WILD RICE DRESSING

2 1- to 1½-pound Cornish game hens, halved lengthwise
½ cup chopped onion
1 tablespoon margarine *or* butter
1¾ cups chicken broth
½ cup wild rice
¼ cup regular brown rice
¼ teaspoon ground sage
¼ teaspoon dried oregano, crushed
⅛ teaspoon pepper
1 cup shredded carrot
Melted margarine *or* butter

Rinse hen halves. Twist wing tips under backs. Cover and chill. For stuffing, cook onion in margarine or butter till tender. Stir in broth, wild rice, brown rice, ground sage, oregano, and pepper. Bring to boiling; reduce heat. Simmer, covered, for 40 to 50 minutes or till liquid is absorbed. Stir in carrot. Cool; cover and chill for up to 24 hours.

To bake, spoon rice stuffing into 4 mounds on bottom of a 13x9x2-inch baking dish. Place Cornish hens, cut side down, over rice mounds. Brush with melted margarine. Bake, covered, in a 375° oven for 45 minutes. Uncover. Brush hens with melted margarine. Bake, uncovered, for 30 to 35 minutes more or till tender. Arrange hens atop rice stuffing on 4 plates. Garnish with a sprig of fresh sage, if desired. Makes 4 servings.

*Nutrition information per serving: 440 cal., 39 g pro., 29 g carbo., 18 g fat, 101 mg chol., 540 mg sodium, 563 mg potassium, and 3 g dietary fiber. U.S. RDA: 163% vit. A, 17% thiamine, 23% riboflavin, 70% niacin, 16% iron.*

## RHUBARB-STRAWBERRY SAUCE (FOR CHOCOLATE TERRINE)

*The recipe for Chocolate Terrine appears on page 50—*

- 2 cups fresh rhubarb cut into ½-inch pieces *or* half of a 16-ounce package frozen rhubarb, thawed
- 1 cup sliced strawberries
- ½ cup sugar
- 4 teaspoons cornstarch

In a saucepan combine rhubarb, strawberries, and ¼ cup *water.* Bring to boiling; reduce heat. Cover; simmer for 5 to 8 minutes or till tender. Drain, reserving liquid. Add enough *water* to liquid to equal 1¼ cups. Discard pulp.

Return liquid to saucepan. Stir together sugar and cornstarch. Stir into liquid in saucepan. Cook and stir till thickened and bubbly. Cook and stir for 2 minutes more. Cool. Cover and chill. Makes about 1 cup sauce.

## LEMON SNAP PEAS

- 1½ pounds fresh *or* frozen snap peas
- 1 tablespoon margarine *or* butter
- 2 teaspoons cornstarch
- ⅛ teaspoon white pepper
- ⅛ teaspoon salt
- 1 cup light cream
- ½ teaspoon finely shredded lemon peel
- 1 teaspoon lemon juice

If using fresh peas, in a medium saucepan cook peas, covered, in a small amount of boiling water for 5 to 6 minutes or till tender. (If using frozen peas, cook in a small amount of boiling water about 2 minutes or till heated through.) Drain peas. Cover to keep warm.

Meanwhile, melt margarine or butter. Stir in cornstarch, pepper, and salt. Add cream all at once. Cook and stir till thickened and bubbly. Cook and stir for 2 minutes more. Stir in lemon peel and lemon juice. Serve over snap peas. Makes 6 servings.

***Nutrition information per serving:***
*186 cal., 7 g pro., 18 g carbo., 10 g fat, 26 mg chol., 210 mg sodium, 220 mg potassium, and 5 g dietary fiber. U.S. RDA: 24% vit. A, 25% vit. C, 20% thiamine, 10% riboflavin, 10% niacin.*

## HEARTS OF PALM SALAD

- 6 cups torn fresh spinach
- 1 small carrot, shredded
- ½ cup oil and vinegar salad dressing
- ¼ teaspoon dried oregano, crushed
- 1 14-ounce can hearts of palm, drained, sliced, and chilled

Fresh summer savory sprigs (optional)
Fresh oregano sprigs (optional)

Toss together spinach and carrot. Cover; chill. In a screw-top jar combine salad dressing and oregano. Cover and shake to combine. Chill.

Before serving, mound spinach onto 6 salad plates. Top with hearts of palm. Drizzle dressing over spinach. Garnish with savory and oregano, if desired. Serve immediately. Serves 6.

***Nutrition information per serving of Hearts of Palm Salad:*** *109 cal., 2 g pro., 5 g carbo., 10 g fat, 0 mg chol., 204 mg sodium, 337 mg potassium, and 1 g dietary fiber. U.S. RDA: 121% vit. A, 27% vit. C.*

## SWEET MUSTARD LAMB

*Serve with Lemon Snap Peas. And for a festive touch, garnish each lamb chop with fresh chives that are in blossom —*

- 2 tablespoons margarine *or* butter, melted
- 2 tablespoons honey
- 1 tablespoon Dijon-style mustard
- ¼ teaspoon dried rosemary, crushed
- ⅛ teaspoon pepper
- 6 lamb leg sirloin chops, cut 1 inch thick

Fresh chives

In a bowl combine the margarine or butter, honey, mustard, rosemary, and pepper. Trim excess fat from the lamb chops. Place the lamb chops on a rack in a shallow baking pan. Brush with some of the honey mixture. Roast in a 325° oven till of desired doneness (allow 35 to 40 minutes for medium doneness).

Before serving, brush each chop with a little of the honey mixture again. Top each lamb chop with chives, if desired. Makes 6 servings.

***Nutrition information per serving:***
*180 cal., 18 g pro., 6 g carbo., 9 g fat, 65 mg chol., 163 mg sodium, 215 mg potassium, and 0 g dietary fiber. U.S. RDA: 11% riboflavin, 20% niacin.*

## WALNUT FLAT BREAD
## (FOR CAMEMBERT SPREAD)

*It takes a little extra time to roll the dough into thin circles, but the crispy-baked results you get are worth it. The recipe for Camembert Spread appears on page 52—*

 1 10-ounce package
      refrigerated white bread
      dough
 1 beaten egg
 1 tablespoon water
 ¼ cup ground walnuts

Divide the refrigerated white bread dough into 6 equal pieces. Use your hands to roll each piece into a ball.

On a lightly greased baking sheet roll a ball of the white bread dough into a 10-inch paper-thin circle. Repeat with the remaining balls of white bread dough. (If the bread dough is difficult to roll, cover the bread dough and let it rest for 5 minutes. Then, you can resume rolling the dough and it should be easier for you to work with.)

In a custard cup stir together the beaten egg and the water. Brush over the bread dough circles. Sprinkle *each* circle with *1 rounded teaspoon* of the ground walnuts.

Bake the bread dough circles in a 350° oven for 8 to 10 minutes or till the bread dough circles are golden brown and crisp. Transfer to wire racks. Cool completely. To store, stack carefully in a tightly covered container.

To serve, stack bread on a serving plate. Break off portions of the bread to dip into the Camembert Spread. Makes 6 flat breads.

## CHILLED SHRIMP
## WITH SPINACH SAUCE

*Making the sauce ahead leaves just 5 minutes prep time on serving day—*

 1 pound fresh *or* frozen shelled
      shrimp
 1 recipe Spinach Sauce
Lemon wedges
Cherry tomatoes (optional)
Lettuce leaves

Cook fresh or frozen shrimp in boiling salted water for 1 to 3 minutes or till pink. Drain; chill for at least 2 hours.

Prepare Spinach Sauce. Cover and chill in the refrigerator.

At serving time, arrange chilled shrimp, lemon wedges, and cherry tomatoes on a lettuce-lined serving platter. Serve with Spinach Sauce. Makes 8 servings.

*Spinach Sauce:* In a blender container combine ⅓ cup *mayonnaise or salad dressing;* ⅓ cup dairy *sour cream;* ¼ cup snipped *parsley;* ¼ cup frozen chopped *spinach,* thawed and well drained; 1 tablespoon *lemon juice;* 1 tablespoon *water;* ¼ teaspoon dried *tarragon,* crushed; and ⅛ teaspoon *garlic salt.* Cover and blend till smooth. Cover; chill till serving time. Makes 1 cup.

*Nutrition information per serving:* *140 cal., 11 g pro., 2 g carbo., 10 g fat, 95 mg chol., 168 mg sodium, 162 mg potassium, and 0 g dietary fiber.*

## APPETIZER FRITTATA

 ¼ cup chopped celery
 ¼ cup chopped onion
 2 tablespoons margarine *or* butter
 8 beaten eggs
 ½ cup dairy sour cream
 ½ cup grated Parmesan cheese
 1 3½-ounce package sliced
      pepperoni
Sliced green onion (optional)

In an ovenproof 10-inch skillet or omelet pan cook celery and chopped onion in hot margarine till tender but not brown. Combine eggs, sour cream, and Parmesan cheese. Chop *half* of the pepperoni and stir into egg mixture.

Pour egg mixture into skillet and cook over medium heat, lifting edges occasionally to allow uncooked portion to flow underneath. Cook for 8 to 10 minutes or till eggs are almost set.

Arrange the remaining pepperoni around edge of egg mixture. Broil 5 inches from heat for 1 to 2 minutes or till eggs are set. Sprinkle green onion atop. Cut into wedges. Serves 12.

*Nutrition information per serving:* *153 cal., 8 g pro., 2 g carbo., 13 g fat, 198 mg chol., 322 mg sodium, 105 mg potassium, and 0 g dietary fiber.*

# 12 TWENTY-MINUTE DINNERS

## SO QUICK TO FIX; THEN RELAX AND ENJOY

By Lisa Mack

Despite busy lives, families today are rediscovering the pleasure and importance of sharing a home-cooked meal at day's end. Our streamlined recipes can help because they're:

●**RIGHT FOR YOU!**
*They fit your busy lifestyle.*

●**EASY!**
*Kids can make these meals, too.*

●**FAST!**
*We mean it—20 minutes.*

●**GREAT TASTING!**
*Super-quick doesn't mean so-so.*

### CANADIAN BACON PIZZAS ▲

When a pizza craving hits, satisfy it in 10 minutes flat. For this healthful, hand-size dinner, layer spinach, bacon, tomatoes, and cheese on chewy French bread slices. Pop the pizzas under the broiler, then enjoy.

### HONEY CHICKEN STIR-FRY ▶

In the time it usually takes just to chop the vegetables, you can have a delicious stir-fry dinner on the table. Simply rely on frozen Chinese vegetables, boneless chicken breasts, and a four-ingredient sweet-sour sauce.

# TWENTY-MINUTE DINNERS

## SPICED-UP TURKEY SAUTÉ ▲

If you like spicy food, this cumin-seasoned dish is bound to be a hit. It's nutritious, and sure to satisfy even hearty appetites.

## GLAZED LAMB WITH PEPPERS ▶

Stir together orange marmalade and hoisin sauce to glaze tender lamb chops with ease. Simmer peppers with the chops; they pick up a mellow, roasted taste.

## PORK CHOPS WITH PEANUT GINGER SAUCE ▶

Peanut butter makes more than just sandwiches and this savory dinner proves it! Soak up the 30-second sauce with quick-cooking oriental rice noodles.

## HAM WITH CHUNKY CRANBERRY SAUCE ◀

One of the butcher's best time-savers: Heat-and-eat sliced ham. The sauce: A medley of cranberry-orange sauce, apples, celery, and allspice. The payoff: A great dinner in 15 minutes!

# TWENTY-MINUTE DINNERS

### BEEF AND APPLE SALAD ▲

Treat yourself to a one-of-a-kind salad when you're on your own for dinner. Sliced roast beef, jicama, apple wedges, and carrot slices make a stellar combination. Fix it ahead, then sprinkle with raisins and dressing just before eating.

### POACHED SALMON WITH ZUCCHINI MAYONNAISE ▶

Good taste needn't take a lot of time. Creamy tarragon- and zucchini-topped poached salmon answers your quest for terrific flavor in a mere 17 minutes.

### EASY ASPARAGUS LOBSTER NEWBURG ▶

Frozen Newburg, rice pilaf, and asparagus make a stylish dinner combination.

### PICADILLO FRITTATA ◀

Olives, raisins, and almonds—from the Spanish dish, picadillo—flavor this robust open-faced omelet.

# NUTRITION INFORMATION
## HOW TO MAKE IT WORK

Our seal assures you that every recipe has been tested in the *Better Homes and Gardens*® Test Kitchen. This means that each recipe is practical and reliable, and meets our high standards of taste appeal.

### EVERY RECIPE ANALYZED

● With each recipe we give important nutrition information. This information, which includes the calorie count of individual servings and the amount, in grams, of protein, fat, carbohydrate, cholesterol, sodium, potassium, and dietary fiber, helps you keep tabs on what you eat.

● Also, you can check the vitamin and mineral levels contained in each individual serving of each recipe. These vitamins and minerals are noted in percentages of the United States Recommended Daily Allowance (U.S. RDA) whenever the value exceeds 10 percent of the recommended amounts. (The U.S. RDAs are dietary standards developed by the U.S. Food and Drug Administration.)

### HOW WE ANALYZE

● When ingredient options appear in a recipe's ingredient list, we use the first ingredient choice for calculating the nutrition analysis.
● We use the first serving size listed.
● We omit optional ingredients from the nutrition analysis.
● When milk is an ingredient, we figure the nutrition information using *low-fat* milk.

### WHAT YOU NEED

● Use our analyses to chart the nutritional value of the foods you eat. These guidelines are based on daily needs of moderately active females, 23 to 50 years old (in general, males and teens need more calories):

**calories—2,000
protein—45 to 65 grams
fat—67 grams
cholesterol—300 milligrams
sodium—1,100 to 3,300 milligrams
fiber—25 to 30 grams**

There's no real harm in going over or under these figures in any single day, but aim for a balanced diet overall.

**Four ingredients and voilà—a refreshing alfresco dinner for two. If you use hot salsa in your gazpacho, serve breadsticks and iced tea to cool your taste buds.**

# CHILLED COD WITH EASY GAZPACHO SAUCE ▲

*In case you don't have time to stop at the deli for the salad, make your own. Stir ¼ cup chopped cucumber and 1 tablespoon vinegar with 1 tablespoon sugar—*

½ **pound fresh *or* frozen thawed cod, cusk, flounder *or* orange roughy fillets, cut ½ inch thick**
½ **of a lemon, sliced**
¼ **cup deli marinated cucumber salad *or* mixed vegetable salad, drained**
¼ **cup mild or hot chunky salsa**

● ● ●

**Chopped greens (optional)
Breadsticks (optional)**

In a large skillet or Dutch oven place a large open steamer basket over ½ inch of *water*. Bring water to boiling; reduce heat. Carefully place the fish fillets in the steamer basket. (Cut the fish into 2 pieces, if necessary, to fit.) Top with lemon slices. Cover skillet or Dutch oven and steam fish about 6 min-

utes or till fish flakes easily when tested with a fork. Discard lemon.

Remove fish from steamer basket. Carefully immerse the fish in a bowl of ice water. Let the fish stand in the ice water for 1 to 2 minutes or till fish is thoroughly chilled. Using a slotted spoon, carefully remove fish from water and drain on paper towels.

Meanwhile for sauce, cut up any large pieces of deli salad or prepare the cucumber salad as directed. Stir together the cucumber salad and the mild or hot salsa.

Arrange salad greens on two dinner plates; place half of the chilled fish atop each plate of greens. Spoon the salsa mixture over fish. Serve with breadsticks. Makes 2 servings.

***Nutrition information per serving:*** *128 cal., 20 g pro., 9 g carbo., 1 g fat, 0 mg chol., 281 mg sodium, 528 mg potassium, 1 g dietary fiber. U.S. RDA: 12% niacin.*

## CANADIAN BACON PIZZAS

*These nouvelle pizzas feature fresh spinach and Swiss cheese layered on top of crusty bread slices—*

- ¼ **cup mayonnaise** *or* **salad dressing**
- ½ **teaspoon dried thyme, crushed; dried basil, crushed;** *or* **dried oregano, crushed**
- ⅛ **teaspoon garlic powder**
- 2 **cups torn fresh spinach**
- 6 **slices French bread, bias-sliced ½ inch thick**
- 6 **slices Canadian-style bacon, cut ⅛ inch thick**
- 6 **cherry tomatoes, quartered**
- 6 **slices Swiss cheese**

Preheat the broiler. Stir together the mayonnaise or salad dressing; thyme, basil, or oregano; and garlic powder. Toss with the spinach. Spread spinach mixture on 1 side of each bread slice.

Place bread slices, spinach side up, on the unheated rack of a broiler pan. Place bacon slices and cherry tomato quarters atop spinach mixture.

Broil bread slices about 3 inches from heat for 2 to 3 minutes or till heated through. Top with Swiss cheese slices; broil about 1 minute more or till cheese just starts to melt. Serves 3.

***Nutrition information per serving:*** *636 cal., 34 g pro., 44 g carbo., 36 g fat, 89 mg chol., 1,336 mg sodium, 555 mg potassium, 3 g dietary fiber. U.S. RDA: 66% vit. A, 10% vit. C, 15% thiamine, 32% riboflavin, 29% niacin, 62% calcium, 22% iron.*

## BEEF TENDERLOIN WITH PEPPERCORNS

*To sauté mushrooms, cook halved mushrooms in a little margarine and red wine over medium heat till tender and the liquid evaporates—*

- 2 **tablespoons margarine** *or* **butter**
- **Multicolored peppercorns, cracked,** *or* **black peppercorns, cracked**
- 2 **beef tenderloin steaks, cut 1¼ inches thick (about 10 ounces total)**
- 2 **teaspoons margarine** *or* **butter**
- 1 **teaspoon all-purpose flour**
- **Dash salt**
- **Dash pepper**
- ⅓ **cup light cream** *or* **milk**
- 1 **tablespoon horseradish mustard**
- **Cooked green beans (optional)**
- **Sautéed mushrooms (optional)**

In a heavy 8-inch skillet melt 2 tablespoons margarine or butter. Meanwhile, generously sprinkle the cracked peppercorns over both sides of steaks. (Use about *1 teaspoon* pepper for each steak.) With your fingers, press pepper into steaks.

Add steaks to skillet and cook, uncovered, over medium-high heat for 4 minutes. If steaks brown too quickly, reduce heat to medium. Turn the steaks over. Cook for 3 to 4 minutes more for medium-rare to medium doneness. Transfer steaks to 2 dinner plates. Keep warm while preparing sauce.

Meanwhile, for sauce, in a small saucepan melt the 2 teaspoons margarine or butter. Stir in flour, salt, and dash pepper. Add the cream or milk all at once. Cook and stir over medium heat till thickened and bubbly. Cook and stir for 2 minutes more. Stir in the horseradish mustard.

To serve, pour the sauce over the steaks. If desired, serve steaks with cooked green beans and sautéed mushrooms. Makes 2 servings.

***Nutrition information per serving:*** *410 cal., 25 g pro., 3 g carbo., 33 g fat, 100 mg chol., 361 mg sodium, 411 mg potassium. U.S. RDA: 18% vit. A, 20% riboflavin, 15% niacin, 19% iron.*

## HONEY CHICKEN STIR-FRY

*The seasoning packet from the frozen vegetables flavors this stir-fried dish—*

- 1 **pound skinned and boned chicken breasts**
- ½ **cup apple juice**
- 1 **tablespoon honey**
- 1 **tablespoon Dijon-style mustard**
- 2 **teaspoons cornstarch**
- 1 **10-ounce package frozen Chinese-style stir-fry vegetables with seasonings**
- 1 **tablespoon cooking oil**
- 3 **green onions, bias-sliced into 1-inch pieces**
- **Chow mein noodles**

Rinse chicken; pat dry. Cut chicken into 1-inch pieces. For sauce, stir together the apple juice, honey, mustard, cornstarch, and seasonings from the frozen stir-fry vegetables. Set sauce mixture aside.

Preheat a wok or large skillet over high heat; add oil. (Add more oil as necessary during cooking.) Stir-fry vegetables and onions in oil for 3 to 4 minutes or till crisp-tender. Remove vegetables from wok.

Add *half* of the chicken to the hot wok. Stir-fry about 3 minutes or till no longer pink. Remove chicken. Repeat with remaining chicken. Return all of the chicken to the wok. Push from center of wok.

Stir sauce; add to the center of the wok. Cook and stir till thickened and bubbly. Cook and stir for 2 minutes more. Return vegetables to wok; toss to coat with sauce. Cook and stir for 1 minute or till heated through. Serve chicken mixture over chow mein noodles. Makes 4 servings.

***Nutrition information per serving:*** *351 cal., 31 g pro., 29 g carbo., 12 g fat, 75 mg chol., 802 mg sodium, 468 mg potassium, 2 g dietary fiber. U.S. RDA: 32% vit. A, 15% vit. C, 10% thiamine, 12% riboflavin, 62% niacin, 11% iron.*

## SPICED-UP TURKEY SAUTÉ

*Traditional seasonings—coriander, turmeric, and cumin—season this Middle Eastern dish—*

 2 tablespoons all-purpose flour
 ¾ teaspoon instant chicken bouillon granules
 ¼ teaspoon ground coriander
 ¼ teaspoon ground turmeric
 ⅛ teaspoon garlic powder
 1 8-ounce carton plain yogurt
 2 medium carrots, thinly bias sliced
 3 green onions, bias-sliced into 1-inch pieces
 ½ teaspoon ground cumin
 1 tablespoon margarine *or* butter
 ½ cup water
 8 ounces fully cooked smoked turkey breast portion, cut into strips
 ½ of a 15-ounce can garbanzo beans, drained
 ¼ cup mixed dried fruit bits
Hot cooked couscous

In a small bowl stir flour, chicken granules, coriander, turmeric, and garlic powder into yogurt. Set aside.

In a large skillet cook and stir carrots, green onions, and cumin in margarine or butter over medium-high heat about 5 minutes or till carrots are tender. Reduce heat. Add yogurt mixture to skillet. Add water all at once. Cook and stir till thickened and bubbly.

Stir in turkey, beans, and fruit bits. Cover and cook for 1 to 2 minutes more or till heated through. Serve over hot cooked couscous. Makes 4 servings.

***Nutrition information per serving:***
*339 cal., 27 g pro., 46 g carbo., 5 g fat, 51 mg chol., 188 mg sodium, 673 mg potassium, 6 g dietary fiber. U.S. RDA: 208% vit. A, 10% vit. C, 14% thiamine, 16% riboflavin, 27% niacin, 15% calcium, 16% iron.*

## PORK CHOPS WITH PEANUT GINGER SAUCE

*Look for rice noodles in the Oriental food section of your supermarket—*

 2 tablespoons cooking oil
 2 pork loin chops, cut ¾ inch thick (about 12 ounces total)
 ¼ cup chicken broth
 1 tablespoon peanut butter
 1 green onion, thinly sliced
 1 teaspoon lemon juice
 ¼ teaspoon garlic powder
 ¼ teaspoon ground ginger
Hot cooked rice noodles
 2 tablespoons chopped peanuts

Preheat a large skillet over medium-high heat; add oil. Add chops to skillet, then reduce heat to medium. Cook for 7 minutes. Turn chops over. Continue cooking for 5 to 8 minutes more or till chops are no longer pink.

Remove chops from skillet. Cover to keep warm. Drain off fat in skillet.

For sauce, in the same skillet stir together broth, peanut butter, green onion, lemon juice, garlic powder, and ground ginger. Cook and stir over medium heat about 30 seconds or till slightly thickened. (Sauce should be smooth.) Serve chops atop noodles. Spoon sauce over all. Top with peanuts. Makes 2 servings.

***Nutrition information per serving:***
*658 cal., 45 g pro., 23 g carbo., 43 g fat, 145 mg chol., 259 mg sodium, 760 mg potassium, 3 g dietary fiber. U.S. RDA: 87% thiamine, 30% riboflavin, 52% niacin, 12% iron.*

## GLAZED LAMB WITH PEPPERS

*Because there's plenty of sauce, this dish goes well with hot cooked pasta or rice—*

 1 tablespoon cooking oil
 4 lamb leg sirloin chops, cut ¾ inch thick (about 1 pound total)
 ¼ cup orange marmalade
 3 tablespoons hoisin sauce
 2 tablespoons water
 1 sweet red pepper, cut into strips
 1 green pepper, cut into strips

Preheat a large skillet over medium-high heat. Add oil. Add chops to skillet, then reduce heat to medium. Cook the chops without turning for 7 minutes.

Meanwhile, stir together the marmalade, hoisin sauce, and water.

Turn chops over. Top with red and green pepper strips. Pour marmalade mixture evenly over all. Cover and simmer for 5 to 8 minutes or till chops are desired doneness. Serves 4.

***Nutrition information per serving:***
*227 cal., 19 g pro., 19 g carbo., 9 g fat, 65 mg chol., 145 mg sodium, 348 mg potassium, 1 g dietary fiber. U.S. RDA: 39% vit. A, 113% vit. C, 10% thiamine, 13% riboflavin, 22% niacin, 13% iron.*

## HAM WITH CHUNKY CRANBERRY SAUCE

*To save time, have your butcher slice the ham, or purchase ham steaks—*

 ½ pound fully cooked ham, sliced ⅛ inch thick
 1 small green apple, cored and chopped (½ cup)
 1 stalk celery, sliced (½ cup)
 1 tablespoon margarine *or* butter
 ½ cup cranberry-orange sauce
 2 tablespoons vinegar
Several dashes ground allspice
Hot cooked sweet potatoes, sliced (optional)

In a large skillet cook ham over medium heat about 5 minutes or till heated through, turning once. (Overlap the slices in the skillet, if necessary.) Remove ham slices from skillet. Cover ham to keep warm.

For sauce, in the same skillet cook apple and celery in margarine or butter till tender. Stir in cranberry-orange sauce, vinegar, and allspice. Cook and stir till heated through.

On 2 dinner plates, arrange ham slices. Spoon sauce atop. If desired, serve with hot cooked sliced sweet potatoes. Makes 2 servings.

***Nutrition information per serving:***
*365 cal., 24 g pro., 41 g carbo., 12 g fat, 60 mg chol., 1,481 mg sodium, 493 mg potassium. U.S. RDA: 47% vit. C, 59% thiamine, 15% riboflavin, 24% niacin, 12% iron.*

## BEEF AND APPLE SALAD

*A great way to enjoy last night's roast beef, or use sliced beef from the deli—*

- **3 ounces thinly sliced cooked beef**
- **½ of a medium apple, cored and cut into thin wedges**
- **3 ounces jicama, peeled and cut into thin sticks, *or* ½ of an 8-ounce can sliced water chestnuts, drained**
- **½ of a medium carrot, cut into thin strips**
- **Lettuce leaves**
- **1 tablespoon raisins**
- **¼ cup apple juice**
- **¼ cup salad oil**
- **2 tablespoons red wine vinegar**

Arrange beef, apple, jicama or water chestnuts, and carrot on a lettuce-lined dinner plate. Sprinkle with raisins. Cover with clear plastic wrap and chill till serving time or serve immediately. (If chilling the salad, first dip apple in a mixture of lemon juice and water.)

For dressing, in a screw-top jar combine apple juice, oil, and wine vinegar. Cover and shake well. Pour desired amount of dressing over salad. Store remaining dressing, covered, in the refrigerator. Makes 1 serving.

***Nutrition information per serving:*** *429 cal., 27 g pro., 33 g carbo., 22 g fat, 77 mg chol., 77 mg sodium, 597 mg potassium, 6 g dietary fiber. U.S. RDA: 204% vit. A, 44% vit. C, 11% thiamine, 15% riboflavin, 25% niacin, 25% iron.*

## POACHED SALMON WITH ZUCCHINI MAYONNAISE

- **4 fresh *or* frozen salmon, cod, halibut, *or* shark steaks, cut 1 to 1¼ inches thick**
- **½ cup dry white wine**
- **½ teaspoon dried tarragon, crushed**
- **½ of a small zucchini, finely chopped (about ½ cup)**
- **¼ cup mayonnaise *or* salad dressing**
- **¼ cup plain yogurt**
- **2 tablespoons frozen snipped chives**
- **Fresh radishes (optional)**
- **Steamed pea pods (optional)**

Thaw fish, if frozen.

In a large skillet combine wine, tarragon, and 1½ cups *water*. Bring just to boiling. Carefully add fish. Return to boiling; reduce heat. Cover and simmer just till fish flakes with a fork. (Allow 8 to 12 minutes for 1-inch-thick fish steaks and 10 to 15 minutes for 1¼-inch-thick fish steaks.) Remove the fish steaks from the wine mixture and drain thoroughly on paper towels.

Meanwhile, for sauce, in a small bowl stir together the zucchini, mayonnaise or salad dressing, yogurt, and snipped chives.

To serve, arrange the fish steaks on 4 dinner plates. Spoon some of the sauce over each fish steak. Serve with fresh radishes and steamed pea pods. Makes 4 servings.

***Nutrition information per serving:*** *348 cal., 25 g pro., 3 g carbo., 24 g fat, 49 mg chol., 145 mg sodium, 562 mg potassium. U.S. RDA: 12% thiamine, 42% niacin, 18% calcium, 10% iron.*

## EASY ASPARAGUS LOBSTER NEWBURG

- **1 10-ounce package frozen long grain and wild rice**
- **1 6½-ounce package frozen lobster Newburg**
- **3 cups water**
- **½ pound asparagus spears**
- **¼ cup slivered almonds (optional)**
- **Lemon wedges**

Place the pouches of frozen rice and frozen lobster Newburg in a large saucepan with the water. Cook according to the Newburg package directions.

In a medium saucepan cook the asparagus, covered, in a small amount of boiling water for 3 to 4 minutes or till asparagus is crisp-tender. If desired, stir almonds into the rice mixture.

To serve, place *half* of the rice mixture on *each* of 2 dinner plates. Top *each* serving with *half* of the asparagus spears and *half* of the lobster Newburg. Squeeze the juice from the lemon wedges over each serving. Serves 2.

***Nutrition information per serving:*** *361 cal., 14 g pro., 37 g carbo., 18 g fat, 31 mg chol., 110 mg sodium, 469 mg potassium, and 5 g dietary fiber. U.S. RDA: 24% vit. A, 48% vit. C, 28% thiamine, 15% riboflavin, 16% niacin, 16% iron.*

## PICADILLO FRITTATA

*A one-skillet dinner that's easy to make and serve—*

- **4 ounces bulk Italian sausage**
- **½ cup tomato sauce**
- **¼ cup raisins**
- **Dash ground cloves**
- **Dash ground cinnamon**
- **5 eggs**
- **¼ cup milk**
- **¼ cup slivered almonds**
- **6 pimiento-stuffed olives, drained and halved**
- **2 tablespoons grated Parmesan cheese**

Preheat the broiler. In an 8-inch oven-proof omelet pan or skillet cook the Italian sausage over medium heat till done. Drain the fat from the skillet.

Meanwhile, for sauce, in a small saucepan combine tomato sauce, raisins, cloves, and cinnamon. Cook and stir over low heat till mixture is heated through. Remove from heat. Cover to keep warm.

In a mixing bowl use a fork or rotary beater to beat together the eggs and the milk till well combined. Pour the egg mixture over the cooked Italian sausage in the skillet.

Cook over medium heat, lifting the edges occasionally to allow uncooked egg portions to flow underneath. Cook about 4 minutes or till the top of the egg mixture is almost set.

Sprinkle almonds, olives, and cheese over egg mixture. Broil 5 inches from the heat about 2 minutes or till top is light brown.

To serve, cut into wedges and spoon sauce atop. Makes 3 servings.

***Nutrition information per serving:*** *333 cal., 19 g pro., 17 g carbo., 22 g fat, 477 mg chol., 803 mg sodium, 513 mg potassium, 2 g dietary fiber. U.S. RDA: 18% vit. A, 17% thiamine, 27% riboflavin, 18% calcium, 17% iron.*

# A MEXICAN DINNER FOR KIDS TO MICRO-COOK

## A 25-MINUTE MICROWAVE DINNER

By Joy Taylor

SCOTT LITTLE

Chili-Muffin Dinner—A simple recipe to teach your children the basics of microwave cooking. Second time around, let them try it on their own.

## UTENSILS YOU'LL NEED

- fork
- colander
- can opener
- wooden spoon
- table knife
- small spoon
- 3-quart microwave-safe casserole with lid

## CHILI-MUFFIN DINNER

*Cleanup is a breeze, too!*

- 1 12½-ounce package (6) frozen corn muffins
- 1 pound lean ground beef
- 1 15½-ounce can chili beans
- 1 12-ounce can whole kernel corn
- 1 14½-ounce can Mexican-style stewed tomatoes
- 1 8-ounce jar taco sauce
- 6 slices American cheese, cut into triangles

18-ounce container sour cream dip with toasted onion

- **Gather utensils** (see list) and ingredients, and read through the recipe.
- **Thaw muffins** in the microwave oven following package directions. Remove from oven; set aside.
- **Use your hands to crumble meat** into a 3-quart microwave-safe casserole. Cover and place in the microwave oven; set on full or 100% power (high). Set the microwave timer for 3 minutes. Start oven.
- **After 3 minutes of cooking,** stir meat with a fork to break up large pieces. Cover and micro-cook meat on high for 2 minutes more. Drain meat in a colander to get rid of fat. Return cooked meat to the casserole.

- **Use a can opener to open beans,** corn, and tomatoes. Drain the beans and corn in the colander.
- **Using a wooden spoon, stir beans,** corn, *undrained* tomatoes, and taco sauce into meat in casserole. Micro-cook, uncovered, on high for 3 minutes then stir mixture. Cook 4 to 6 minutes more or till bubbly and hot; stir again.
- **Cut muffins** in half. Place 2 muffin halves on each plate. Spoon chili mixture over each. Top each serving with cheese and sour cream dip. Serves 6.

*Nutrition information per serving:* 538 cal., 30 g pro., 47 g carbo., 26 g fat, 129 mg chol., 1,308 mg sodium, 840 mg potassium, 12 g fiber. U.S. RDA: 25% vit. A, 23% vit. C, 27% riboflavin, 27% niacin, 28% calcium, 29% iron.

# JUNE

THE MAGAZINE FOR AMERICAN FAMILIES
• 36 MILLION READERS •

Better Homes and Gardens

$1.50
JUNE 1988

Page 57
SUMMER
HEALTH
AT HOME ON VACATION

**GARDENING WITH KIDS**
SHARING THE WONDER

**SUMMER FOOD**
• CARE-FREE ENTERTAINING
• 15 FESTIVE RECIPES
• EASY COOKING
• STYLISH DINING

SUMMERTIME
**LIVING IN STYLE**
FABULOUS NEW IDEAS FOR YARDS, DECKS, PORCHES, AND PATIOS

**KITTY CRAFTS**
12 PURR-FECT HOLIDAY MAKE-AHEADS

**GLORIOUS SALADS**

**PRETTY PORCHES**
Romance Is Back

**FOR FUN**
Build Your Kids A Treehouse!

# CELEBRATING SUMMER

## EASY COOKING, STYLISH DINING

### By Barbara Johnson

PHOTOGRAPH: SUSAN SCHELLING. FOOD STYLIST: STEVIE BASS

PHOTOGRAPHS: JOAN HIX VANDERSCHUIT. FOOD STYLING: MABLE HOFFMAN

**A**h, summer! Time to get together with friends—talk, laugh, play, and, of course, dine in lighthearted style. That means you want festive, tasty, luscious-looking recipes. What's more, they should be easy to fix so everyone can join in the fun. That's just the kind of recipes and menus we give you here—grilled meats, fresh salads, frosty desserts, and more. All to help you, your family, and your friends enjoy summer to the hilt.

## M E N U

**Boursin-Pesto Pâté**
*Layer aromatic pesto and spiced cheese.*

•

**Shrimp-Salmon Kabobs**
*Thread your favorite vegetables on, too.*

•

**Wheat-Berry-Melon Toss**
*A classy alternative to traditional potato salad.*

•

**Cranberry-Lemon Sipper**
*Choose to spike it or not.*

# CELEBRATING SUMMER

Play all day, yet dine fancy tonight. These start-ahead or fix-on-the-spot recipes let you!

### 3-INGREDIENT TOFFEE FREEZE ◄

You won't need an ice-cream freezer to make this rich and creamy ice cream. Combine sweetened condensed milk, whipping cream, and almond brickle pieces. Pour into a pan; freeze. It takes less time to make than a quick jaunt to the store!

### PEACH-GLAZED BABY BACK RIBS ▶

Stir together 4 ingredients (preserves, lemon juice, mustard, and cardamom) to turn baby backs, the king of ribs, into a glistening showstopper. Slather the easy glaze on the ribs and slow-grill 1¼ hours. Meantime, you can hang out in a hammock.

### SUMMER VEGETABLE POTPOURRI ◄

Ten minutes—that's all you need to cut up fresh summer squash, mushrooms, onions, and celery and drench them in a tarragon and white Worcestershire vinaigrette. Grill alongside meat, fish, or poultry 30 minutes till perfectly crisp-tender.

### ORIENTAL STEAK PINWHEELS ◄

Distinctive but simple kabobs! Just roll up a round steak, slice into pinwheels, and thread onto skewers. Marinate in a five-spice and teriyaki sauce, then grill. For an interesting presentation, serve them on crisp-fried Oriental rice sticks.

No debate here: Ribs are just plain fun to eat!

# CELEBRATING SUMMER

Honey Limeade: a sweet and sassy sipper.

### BERRY BLENDER MOUSSE◄

Here's a dessert that's extraordinary and easy: Puree fresh berries with cream cheese and a touch of sugar. Fold in whipped topping, and chill. That's it!

### JICAMA-CILANTRO SLAW◄

Absolutely refreshing! Add jicama to preshredded coleslaw vegetables, then pour on anything but the typical coleslaw dressing. Here it's a peppered lime vinaigrette.

### CHOCOLATE-BERRY WEDGES; HONEY LIMEADE►

Raspberry preserves are the secret ingredient in these moist, decadent brownies. Top off the refreshing limeade with kiwi fruit slices.

### SMOKED JALAPEÑO TURKEY◄

Wondering what to do with a jar of jalapeño jelly? Combine it with cumin; spread under turkey breast skin. Use a little more jelly to fire up the fresh-fruit salsa.

## MICROWAVE NEW POTATO SALAD ◄

Potato salad is a favorite at any summer outdoor food gathering. This recipe is particularly good because you can micro-cook, chill, and serve this salad all in the same dish! For a twist, start with tiny whole new potatoes and snapping-fresh green beans. After cooking them in your microwave oven (no heating up the kitchen), add an Italian herb buttermilk dressing plus ripe olives. Potato salad has never been so easy!

## PICKLED BABY CORN ON THE COB ◄

Whether you grow them fresh in your own garden plot or harvest them off the shelf at a local produce market, these tiny sweet cobs are so good, we bet they won't last long around your house! In this recipe there's no fussing around with canning, either. Simply add the baby corn to a seasoned vinegar brine; let them pickle right in your own refrigerator.

## BOURSIN-PESTO PÂTÉ

- 1½ cups firmly packed snipped parsley
- ¾ cup grated Parmesan cheese
- ¼ cup shelled hazelnuts *or* walnuts
- ¼ cup olive *or* cooking oil
- ¼ teaspoon *each of* dried basil, oregano, marjoram, thyme, dillweed, *and* rosemary, crushed
- 1 8-ounce package cream cheese, softened
- 1 4-ounce container semisoft cheese spiced with French onion *or* ½ of an 8-ounce container cream cheese with chives and onion
- ½ cup whipping cream
Lemon peel strips (optional)
Fresh savory *or* thyme sprigs (optional)
Pita wedges and carrot sticks (optional)

Line six 6-ounce custard cups with clear plastic wrap. Set aside.

In a blender container or food processor bowl combine parsley, Parmesan cheese, and nuts. Cover and blend or process with several on/off turns till mixture is crumbly, stopping frequently to scrape down sides of container. With machine running slowly, add oil and blend or process till mixture is the consistency of soft butter.

Divide mixture evenly among prepared custard cups. Stir a *different* herb into the mixture in *each* cup. Press mixture down evenly.

In a small mixer bowl beat cream cheese and semisoft cheese with an electric mixer on low speed till nearly smooth. In another bowl beat cream till soft peaks form. Fold into cheese mixture. Spread *one-sixth* (about ⅓ *cup*) of the cheese mixture evenly over herb mixture in *each* custard cup. Cover and chill for several hours or overnight.

To serve, invert cups onto a serving platter. Remove cups and plastic wrap. Top with lemon peel strips tied into knots. Arrange fresh herb sprigs on platter. Serve with pita wedges and carrot sticks. Makes about 14 servings.

*Nutrition information per serving:* *191 cal., 5 g pro., 2 g carbo., 19 g fat, 43 mg chol., 177 mg sodium, 89 mg potassium, 0 g dietary fiber. U.S. RDA: 17% vit. A, 10% vit. C, 11% calcium.*

## SHRIMP-SALMON KABOBS

*A seaside treat—shrimp and salmon with fresh vegetables—*

- 2 cups long-cooking vegetables (whole tiny new potatoes, halved; zucchini, cut into ½-inch slices; *or* baby corn on the cob)
- ¾ pound fresh *or* frozen large shrimp in shells (about 16)
- ½ pound fresh *or* frozen salmon fillet, 1 inch thick
- ¼ cup wine vinegar
- ¼ cup catsup
- 2 tablespoons cooking oil
- 2 tablespoons soy sauce
- 1 teaspoon prepared mustard
- ½ teaspoon bottled minced garlic
- ¼ teaspoon pepper
- 2 cups quick-cooking vegetables (fresh pea pods; red sweet pepper, cut into 1-inch pieces; *or* small whole fresh mushrooms)

Cooking oil

In a medium saucepan cook long-cooking vegetables in a small amount of boiling water till nearly tender. (Allow 12 to 15 minutes for new potatoes, 3 to 4 minutes for baby corn, and 1 to 2 minutes for zucchini.) Drain and cool.

Meanwhile, thaw shrimp and salmon, if frozen. Peel and devein shrimp, keeping tails intact. Cut salmon into 1-inch pieces.

For marinade, in a small mixing bowl stir together wine vinegar, catsup, the 2 tablespoons oil, soy sauce, mustard, garlic, and pepper.

Place long-cooking vegetables, shrimp, salmon, and quick-cooking vegetables in a plastic bag in a shallow dish. Pour marinade over all; close the bag. Marinate in the refrigerator for 2 to 4 hours, turning once.

Drain vegetables, shrimp, and salmon, reserving marinade. Thread vegetables, shrimp, and salmon alternately on eight 8- to 10-inch skewers.

Brush grill rack with oil. Grill kabobs on an uncovered grill over *hot* coals (see tip, page 78) for 10 to 12 minutes or till shrimp turn pink and salmon just flakes with a fork. Turn and brush with the reserved marinade frequently. Makes 4 servings.

***Nutrition information per serving:*** *239 cal., 26 g pro., 14 g carbo., 9 g fat, 115 mg chol., 300 mg sodium, 782 mg potassium, 3 g dietary fiber. U.S. RDA: 49% vit. A, 106% vit. C, 15% thiamine, 37% niacin, 14% calcium, 17% iron.*

## WHEAT-BERRY-MELON TOSS

*Orzo, also called rosamarina, is a tiny ricelike pasta—*

- 2½ cups water
- ⅓ cup wheat berries
- ¼ cup orzo *or* tiny star macaroni
- ⅓ cup plain yogurt
- ⅓ cup frozen whipped dessert topping, thawed
- 1 tablespoon honey
- 1 teaspoon finely shredded lemon peel
- ⅛ teaspoon salt
- ½ cup sliced celery
- 1½ cups cubed melon *or* melon balls (watermelon, honeydew melon, *or* cantaloupe)

Lettuce leaf cups (optional)

In a large saucepan bring the water to boiling. Stir in the wheat berries. Return to boiling; reduce heat. Cover and simmer for 45 minutes. Stir in the orzo. Return to boiling. Boil, uncovered, for 5 to 8 minutes or till both the berries and the orzo are tender, stirring occasionally. Drain in a colander. Rinse with cold water. Drain well.

In a mixing bowl stir together the plain yogurt, whipped dessert topping, honey, finely shredded lemon peel, and salt. Add the wheat-berry-orzo mixture and the sliced celery; toss to mix well. Cover and chill thoroughly in the refrigerator. At serving time, stir in the cubed melon or melon balls. Spoon the mixture into lettuce leaf cups. Cover and chill any leftover salad in the refrigerator. Makes 6 servings.

***Nutrition information per serving:*** *99 cal., 3 g pro., 19 g carbo., 2 g fat, 1 mg chol., 68 mg sodium, 227 mg potassium, 2 g dietary fiber. U.S. RDA: 27% vit. A, 30% vit. C.*

## CRANBERRY-LEMON SIPPER

*Make half with a carbonated beverage for kids, half with wine for adults—*

- 1 12-ounce can frozen pink lemonade concentrate
- 1 6-ounce can frozen cranberry juice cocktail concentrate
- 1 67.6-ounce bottle lemon-lime carbonated beverage *or* two 750-milliliter bottles dry white wine, chilled

Cracked ice
Lemon twists (optional)

In a 3-quart pitcher combine frozen pink lemonade and cranberry juice cocktail concentrates. Stir in lemon-lime carbonated beverage or wine. Serve over ice with lemon twists. Makes about 10 (8-ounce) servings.

***Nutrition information per serving:*** *225 cal., 0 g pro., 59 g carbo., 0 g fat, 0 mg chol., 4 mg sodium, 49 mg potassium, 0 g dietary fiber. U.S. RDA: 75% vit. C.*

## 3-INGREDIENT TOFFEE FREEZE

- 1 14-ounce can (1¼ cups) *sweetened condensed* milk
- 1 6-ounce package (1 cup) almond brickle pieces *or* miniature semisweet chocolate pieces
- 2 cups whipping cream

Combine sweetened condensed milk and almond brickle pieces or semisweet chocolate pieces. In a small bowl beat whipping cream with an electric mixer on low speed till soft peaks form; fold into condensed milk mixture.

Transfer mixture to a 9x9x2-inch baking pan. Cover tightly with moisture- and vaporproof wrap. Freeze for 6 hours or till firm. To serve, scoop into individual dessert dishes. Makes about 1½ quarts (10 to 12 servings).

***Nutrition information per serving:*** *394 cal., 5 g pro., 34 g carbo., 28 g fat, 79 mg chol., 71 mg sodium, 192 mg potassium, 0 g dietary fiber. U.S. RDA: 17% vit. A, 13% riboflavin, 15% calcium.*

## PEACH-GLAZED BABY BACK RIBS

- 1 10-ounce jar peach preserves
- 2 tablespoons lemon juice
- 1 teaspoon Dijon-style mustard
- ¼ teaspoon ground cardamom *or* ground cinnamon
- 4 to 5 pounds pork loin back ribs *or* spareribs

Salt *or* onion salt
Pepper
Fresh peach slices (optional)

For glaze, in a small saucepan cook and stir peach preserves, lemon juice, Dijon-style mustard, and cardamom or cinnamon over low heat till preserves melt. Set aside.

In a covered grill arrange preheated coals around a drip pan; test for *medium* heat above pan (see tip, below).

Sprinkle loin back ribs or spareribs with salt or onion salt and pepper. Place the ribs on a rib rack, if desired. Place ribs, meaty side up, on grill rack over drip pan, but not over the coals. Lower grill hood.

Grill ribs for 1 hour, brushing with glaze after the first 30 minutes. Uncover; grill for 15 to 30 minutes more or till ribs are tender, brushing occasionally with glaze. Serve with fresh peach slices and any additional glaze. Makes 5 or 6 servings.

*Nutrition information per serving:*
*719 cal., 42 g pro., 40 g carbo., 43 g fat, 171 mg chol., 194 mg sodium, 513 mg potassium, 0 g dietary fiber. U.S. RDA: 39% thiamine, 33% riboflavin, 39% niacin, 18% iron.*

### TESTING COAL TEMPERATURE

To determine the temperature of the lighted coals in your grill box, hold your hand, palm down, above the coals at the height your food will be cooked. Then count the seconds, "one thousand one, one thousand two . . . ." If you need to remove your hand after two seconds, the coals are *hot;* after three seconds, they're *medium-hot;* after four seconds, they're *medium;* after five seconds, they're *medium-slow;* and after six seconds, they're *slow.*

## SUMMER VEGETABLE POTPOURRI

*This is great totable food for an away-from-home picnic: Just bundle up everything in foil and take along—*

- 1 tablespoon cooking oil
- 1 tablespoon white wine vinegar
- 1 tablespoon white wine

Worcestershire sauce
- 1 teaspoon snipped fresh tarragon *or* ¼ teaspoon dried tarragon, crushed
- ½ teaspoon finely shredded lemon peel
- ⅛ teaspoon salt
- 8 ounces large whole fresh mushrooms, halved (about 12)
- 2 small yellow summer squash, halved lengthwise and cut into ½-inch-thick slices
- 1 cup pearl onions *or* 1 large onion, cut into chunks
- 1 large stalk celery, bias-sliced into 1-inch pieces
- 2 tablespoons sliced pimiento

Tear off a 36x18-inch piece of heavy foil. Fold in half to make an 18-inch square. Fold up sides, using your fist to form a pouch.

In a small mixing bowl stir together the cooking oil, white wine vinegar, white wine, Worcestershire sauce, tarragon, lemon peel, and salt.

In the foil pouch combine the mushrooms, summer squash, onions, celery, and pimiento. Pour oil mixture over the vegetables. Fold edges of foil to seal pouch securely, leaving space for expansion of steam.

Grill on an uncovered grill directly over *medium-hot* coals (see tip, left) about 30 minutes or till the vegetables are crisp-tender, turning the pouch occasionally. Makes 4 to 6 servings.

*Nutrition information per serving:*
*76 cal., 2 g pro., 9 g carbo., 4 g fat, 0 mg chol., 92 mg sodium, 449 mg potassium, 3 g dietary fiber. U.S. RDA: 19% vit. C, 17% riboflavin, 14% niacin.*

## ORIENTAL STEAK PINWHEELS

*Can't find five-spice powder? Substitute ¼ teaspoon ground cinnamon and ¼ teaspoon crushed aniseed—*

- ¼ cup packed brown sugar
- ¼ cup teriyaki sauce
- 1 tablespoon rice wine vinegar *or* white wine vinegar
- ½ teaspoon five-spice powder
- ½ teaspoon bottled minced garlic
- ¼ teaspoon ground ginger
- 1 1- to 1¼-pound boneless beef top round steak, cut about ¾ inch thick
- 2 yellow *and/or* green sweet peppers, cut into 1½-inch squares

Fried rice sticks (optional)*

For marinade, in a small bowl combine brown sugar, teriyaki sauce, rice wine or white wine vinegar, five-spice powder, garlic, and ginger. Set mixture aside.

Use a meat mallet to pound beef to ¼- to ½-inch thickness. Brush about *2 tablespoons* of the marinade over beef. Roll up from long side. Cut into 1-inch slices. Thread beef pinwheels and peppers alternately onto 4 or 5 skewers. Place in a shallow baking dish. Pour remaining marinade over kabobs. Cover; marinate in the refrigerator for 6 hours or overnight, turning the skewers occasionally.

Remove skewers from marinade, reserving marinade. Grill, on an uncovered grill, directly over *medium-hot* coals (see tip, left) till beef reaches desired doneness (allow 14 to 16 minutes for medium), turning and brushing with reserved marinade often. If desired, serve kabobs over fried rice sticks. Makes 4 or 5 servings.

*\*Note:* Fry unsoaked rice sticks, a few at a time, in deep hot cooking oil (375°) about 5 seconds or just till sticks puff and rise to the top. Remove rice sticks; drain on paper towels. Keep warm in the oven.

*Nutrition information per serving:*
*187 cal., 26 g pro., 7 g carbo., 5 g fat, 67 mg chol., 224 mg sodium, 493 mg potassium, 1 g dietary fiber. U.S. RDA: 88% vit. C, 10% thiamine, 15% riboflavin, 26% niacin, 18% iron.*

## BERRY BLENDER MOUSSE

*Strawberries peak May through June—*

1½ cups fresh strawberries *or* ½ of a
   16-ounce package frozen
   unsweetened whole strawberries, thawed
1 8-ounce package cream cheese,
   cut into small cubes
½ cup sifted powdered sugar
1 4-ounce container frozen
   whipped dessert topping,
   thawed
Sliced almonds

In a blender container or food processor bowl combine strawberries,
cream cheese, and powdered sugar.
Cover and blend or process till mixture
is smooth, stopping and scraping sides
as necessary. Pour into a mixing bowl.
Fold in dessert topping.

Spoon mousse mixture into 6 dessert dishes. Chill for 3 to 4 hours or
overnight. To serve, sprinkle with almonds. Makes 6 servings.

*Nutrition information per serving:*
*241 cal., 4 g pro., 16 g carbo., 19 g fat, 42*
*mg chol., 117 mg sodium, 118 mg potas-*
*sium, 1 g dietary fiber. U.S. RDA: 14%*
*vit. A, 35% vit. C.*

## HONEY LIMEADE

*For added pizzazz, freeze wedges of kiwi*
*fruit in ice cubes to use in each drink—*

5 cups water
1 cup lime juice (juice from 4 to 5
   limes)
⅔ cup sugar
2 tablespoons honey
Kiwi fruit ice cubes *or* ice cubes
2 kiwi fruit, sliced (optional)

In a 2-quart pitcher combine water, lime juice, sugar, and honey. Stir to
dissolve sugar. Serve over ice cubes.
Garnish each glass with a slice of kiwi
fruit. Makes about 6 (8-ounce) servings.

*Nutrition information per serving:*
*117 cal., 0 g pro., 31 g carbo., 0 g fat, 0 mg*
*chol., 1 mg sodium, 48 mg potassium, 0 g*
*dietary fiber. U.S. RDA: 20% vit. C.*

## JICAMA-CILANTRO SLAW

*Look for bags of shredded coleslaw vege-*
*tables (a mix of cabbage and carrots) in*
*your supermarket's produce aisle—*

¼ cup salad oil
¼ cup lime juice
2 tablespoons snipped cilantro *or*
   parsley
1 tablespoon sugar
¼ teaspoon salt
⅛ teaspoon ground red pepper
3 cups shredded coleslaw
   vegetables
1 pound jicama, peeled and cut
   into thin strips (about
   2 cups)
1 to 2 medium green onions,
   thinly sliced
Crinkle-cut carrots (optional)
Cilantro sprigs (optional)

In a medium bowl stir together salad oil, lime juice, snipped cilantro or
parsley, sugar, salt, and red pepper till
sugar is dissolved.

Add the shredded coleslaw vegetables, jicama strips, and sliced green onions; toss to coat. Cover and chill
mixture in the refrigerator about 3
hours or overnight.

Before serving, toss slaw; if desired, top with crinkle-cut carrots and
cilantro sprigs. Makes 6 servings.

*Nutrition information per serving:*
*132 cal., 1 g pro., 12 g carbo., 9 g fat, 0 mg*
*chol., 100 mg sodium, 139 mg potassi-*
*um, 3 g dietary fiber. U.S. RDA: 105%*
*vit. A, 48% vit. C.*

## CHOCOLATE-BERRY WEDGES

1 cup all-purpose flour
½ cup cornstarch
⅛ teaspoon salt
½ cup margarine *or* butter,
   softened
½ cup sugar
½ cup packed brown sugar
3 eggs
4 squares (4 ounces) semisweet
   chocolate, melted and cooled
½ teaspoon vanilla
½ cup raspberry *or* apricot
   preserves
⅓ cup raspberry *or* apricot
   preserves
1 recipe Chocolate Glaze
Fresh raspberries (optional)

Grease an 11x7x1½-inch baking
pan. Set aside.

In a small mixing bowl stir together flour, cornstarch, and salt. Set aside.

Combine margarine or butter, sugar, and brown sugar. Stir in eggs, one at
a time. Stir in chocolate and vanilla.
Stir in flour mixture. Stir in the ½ cup
preserves. Pour into prepared pan.

Bake in a 350° oven for 35 to 40
minutes or till brownies spring back
when lightly touched in center. Cool on
a wire rack for 10 minutes. Spread with
the ⅓ cup preserves. Pour Chocolate
Glaze over brownies. Cool completely.
To serve, cut into triangular wedges. If
desired, top each wedge with a raspberry. Makes about 32 wedges.

*Chocolate Glaze:* In a medium
saucepan cook and stir 3 tablespoons
*margarine or butter,* 2 tablespoons *un-*
*sweetened cocoa powder,* and 2 tablespoons *milk* till mixture comes to a boil.
Remove from heat. Stir in 1½ cups sifted *powdered sugar* and ½ teaspoon *va-*
*nilla* till smooth. Makes ⅔ cup.

*Nutrition information per serving:*
*147 cal., 1 g pro., 24 g carbo., 6 g fat, 26*
*mg chol., 66 mg sodium, 46 mg potassi-*
*um, 0 g dietary fiber.*

## MICROWAVE NEW POTATO SALAD

*Don't have a microwave? Cook the vegetables on your range top—*

- ¾ **pound whole tiny new potatoes**
- ¼ **cup water**
- ¾ **pound fresh whole green beans *or* one 9-ounce package frozen cut green beans**
- ¼ **cup mayonnaise *or* salad dressing**
- ¼ **cup dairy sour cream**
- ¼ **cup buttermilk *or* milk**
- ¼ **teaspoon salt**
- ¼ **teaspoon onion salt**
- ¼ **teaspoon Italian seasoning, crushed**
- ¼ **cup sliced pitted ripe olives**

**Tomato wedges**
**Whole pitted ripe olives**
**Salad savoy leaves (optional)**

Scrub potatoes; quarter lengthwise. In a 1½-quart microwave-safe casserole combine potatoes and water. Micro-cook, covered, on 100% power (high) for 8 to 10 minutes or till potatoes are tender, stirring once. Drain in a colander; set aside.

If using fresh beans, remove ends and strings. Break into 1-inch pieces. In same casserole, cook fresh beans and ¼ cup *water*, covered, on high for 13 to 15 minutes or till tender. (If using frozen beans, cook beans, covered, on high for 5 to 7 minutes or till tender, stirring once.) Drain in a colander; set aside.

In same casserole stir together mayonnaise or salad dressing, sour cream, buttermilk or milk, salt, onion salt, and Italian seasoning. Stir in potatoes, beans, and olives. Cover; chill for 4 hours or till completely chilled.

To serve the salad, gently stir the mixture. Place tomato wedges and whole pitted ripe olives on top and to 1 side of the salad. If desired, tuck the salad savoy leaves in 1 side of the casserole dish, just behind the tomatoes and olives. Makes 6 servings.

***Nutrition information per serving:***
*164 cal., 3 g pro., 16 g carbo., 10 g fat, 10 mg chol., 278 mg sodium, 495 mg potassium, 3 g dietary fiber. U.S. RDA: 13% vit. A, 27% vit. C.*

## SMOKED JALAPEÑO TURKEY

*Young children might prefer apple jelly instead of spicy jalapeño jelly—*

- 4 **cups mesquite wood chips**
- 2 **tablespoons jalapeño *or* apple jelly**
- ½ **teaspoon salt**
- ¼ **teaspoon ground cumin**
- ¼ **teaspoon pepper**
- 1 **3- to 3½-pound fresh breast half of turkey with bone**

**Cooking oil**
- 1 **pineapple**
- 2 **fresh apricots, pitted and chopped**
- 1 **red sweet pepper, seeded and chopped**
- ¼ **cup jalapeño *or* apple jelly**

At least 1 hour before cooking, soak the wood chips in enough water to cover. In a bowl stir together the 2 tablespoons jelly, salt, cumin, and pepper.

Use a sharp knife to remove bone from turkey breast; discard bone. Rinse turkey; pat dry. To loosen turkey skin, slip your fingers under skin of turkey breast, pulling it away from meat, but leaving skin attached at 1 long edge. Spread jelly mixture over the meat under the skin. Replace skin over jelly mixture, securing with wooden toothpicks, if necessary. Insert a meat thermometer into the center of the thickest portion of turkey breast.

Drain wood chips. In a covered grill arrange preheated coals around a drip pan; test for *medium* heat above pan (see tip, page 78). Pour water into pan to a depth of 1 inch. Sprinkle *half* of the drained wood chips over coals.

Brush grill rack with cooking oil. Place turkey breast, skin side up, on the rack over drip pan, but not over coals. Brush turkey skin with a little oil. Lower the grill hood.

Grill turkey breast for 2¼ to 3 hours or till thermometer registers 170°. Sprinkle remaining wood chips over the coals after 45 minutes of cooking. Add more water to the drip pan, as necessary. Add 6 to 8 new coals to the firebox every 20 to 30 minutes during cooking to maintain the coal's heat.

Meanwhile, cut six ½-inch-thick slices off bottom of unpeeled pineapple. Halve slices; set aside. For the salsa, peel, core, and chop the remaining pineapple (should have 1½ to 2 cups). In a small mixing bowl combine the chopped pineapple, fresh apricots, red sweet pepper, and ¼ cup jelly. Cover and chill salsa in the refrigerator till serving time.

During the last 10 minutes of grilling, add halved pineapple slices on the side of the grill to heat through. Slice turkey; serve with salsa and grilled pineapple. Makes 6 to 8 servings.

***Nutrition information per serving:***
*307 cal., 43 g pro., 30 g carbo., 2 g fat, 117 mg chol., 259 mg sodium, 629 mg potassium, 2 g dietary fiber. U.S. RDA: 29% vit. A, 95% vit. C, 13% thiamine, 14% riboflavin, 56% niacin, 18% iron.*

## PICKLED BABY CORN ON THE COB

*For crisp pickles, eat within a week—*

- 1½ **cups sugar**
- 1 **cup vinegar**
- ½ **teaspoon ground turmeric**
- ½ **teaspoon celery seed**
- ¼ **teaspoon dry mustard**
- ¼ **teaspoon bottled minced garlic**
- 1½ **pounds fresh baby corn on the cob, husked, *or* two 8-ounce packages frozen baby corn on the cob**

In a large saucepan stir together sugar, vinegar, turmeric, celery seed, mustard, and garlic. Add fresh or frozen corn. Bring to a full boil. For fresh corn, boil gently for 2 minutes. (For frozen corn, omit boiling for 2 minutes.) Remove from heat. Cool slightly.

Transfer corn to a moisture- and vaporproof container. Add enough of the cooking liquid to cover. Cover; chill in the refrigerator for up to 1 week. Makes 8 to 10 servings.

***Nutrition information per serving:***
*64 cal., 1 g pro., 16 g carbo., 0 g fat, 0 mg chol., 5 mg sodium, 94 mg potassium, 2 g dietary fiber.*

# GLORIOUS SALADS

**Garden-fresh, crisp, and luscious—summer's vegetables are perfect
for the light salads we like for lunch, for supper.
The new exotic veggies make those salads even better!**

By Joy Taylor

## SAVOY AND RADICCHIO CHICKEN SALAD ▲

Savoy cabbage leaves encase a splendid concoction of chicken, radicchio, peanuts, and pineapple. Serve the bundles, drizzled with a sumptuous peanut dressing, on radicchio and white salad savoy leaves.

Gather your favorite standby salad ingredients
then mix them with fruits and vegetables you haven't
tried before. You'll love the results!

## ROASTED-PEPPER PEPPERONI SALAD ▶

Pick your favorite colored peppers to roast for this savory salad.

Team roasted pepper strips with pepperoni, cheese, garbanzo beans, Italian plum tomatoes, Greek olives, and a heavenly garlic dressing. Serve on a bed of curly endive and arugula.

Cap off this Mediterranean supper with a sprinkling of arugula flowers.

## CARIBBEAN SHRIMP AND PAPAYA SALAD ◀

Spoon chili-spiced shrimp into succulent papaya halves for a resplendent tropical dinner. Nestle each papaya half into Oak Leaf lettuce, sweet coconut, and peppery nasturtium leaves.

Tangy carambola (star fruit) and nasturtium blossoms complete this stylish summer salad plate.

## ROAST BEEF SALAD WITH HORSERADISH DRESSING ▶

A scattering of fresh thyme leaves along with piquant horseradish dressing defines this salad of sliced roast beef and crisp, fresh vegetables. Create your own unique arrangement on a bed of red leaf lettuce and spinach leaves.

Freshly grated horseradish in the dressing provides pungent results.

83

# THE NEW FIXIN'S

**Look for exotic fruits, vegetables, and greens in the produce section of your supermarket.**

### 1. Edible Flowers
Choose only pesticide-free flowers that have been grown especially for eating. Flowers pictured from left to right are rosemary, chamomile, arugula, orchid, and red and gold nasturtiums.

### 2. Varietal Peppers
Red, yellow, and orange peppers taste similar to green peppers, but they have a subtle sweetness. Look for purple peppers, too.

### 3. Italian Plum Tomatoes
Yellow and red plum tomatoes are sweeter than traditional tomatoes and about the size of an oval cherry tomato.

### 4. Salad Savoy
Known also as flowering kale, this green has a cabbagelike flavor and comes in purple, pink, green, and creamy white varieties.

### 5. Oak Leaf Lettuce
Named for its oak-leaf shape, this loose-leaf lettuce is available in red or green.

### 6. Enoki Mushrooms
These unique mushrooms have a crisp texture and mild flavor.

### 7. Radicchio
A member of the chicory family, radicchio adds a mild bitterness to salads.

### 8. Arugula
Also known as rocket salad, arugula has a refreshing mustardlike flavor.

### 9. Savoy Cabbage
Crinkly leaves and a loose head distinguish this mild flavored cabbage.

## SAVOY AND RADICCHIO CHICKEN SALAD

*Serve the filled bundles either whole or sliced. When they're sliced, you can see the splendid chicken filling inside!*

- 1 head Savoy cabbage *or* Napa cabbage
- 1 head radicchio
- 2 whole medium chicken breasts, skinned, boned, cooked, and cubed (about 2 cups)
- 1 cup finely chopped fresh pineapple *or* one 8¼-ounce can crushed pineapple, drained
- 2 medium green onions, thinly sliced
- ¼ cup raisins
- ¼ cup unsalted cocktail peanuts, chopped
- ¾ cup mayonnaise *or* salad dressing
- ¼ cup milk
- ¼ cup peanut butter
- 1 teaspoon curry powder
- ½ teaspoon paprika
- ¼ teaspoon lemon juice *or* lime juice
- 1 to 2 tablespoons milk
- Green onion tops, steamed (optional)
- Salad savoy leaves
- Fresh pineapple wedges (optional)
- Lemon twists (optional)
- Fresh rosemary sprigs, savory sprigs, and chamomile (optional)

Remove 8 of the large outer leaves from cabbage. Place the leaves in a microwave-safe casserole. Set remaining cabbage aside.

Cover the casserole with vented microwave-safe plastic wrap. Microcook on 100% power (high) for 2 to 3 minutes or till the cabbage leaves are limp. Drain. Cover and chill in the refrigerator. Remove 16 of the larger leaves from the radicchio. *Do not* cook. Cover leaves and chill.

Meanwhile, coarsely shred the remaining cabbage and radicchio. Measure 1½ cups of the shredded mixture. Set the remaining shredded cabbage aside. In a large bowl combine the 1½ cups shredded mixture, chicken, chopped pineapple, sliced green onions, raisins, and peanuts.

For dressing, in a small bowl combine mayonnaise or salad dressing, the ¼ cup milk, peanut butter, curry powder, paprika, and lemon or lime juice.

Pour ½ cup of the dressing over the chicken mixture; stir to coat. Stir 1 to 2 tablespoons milk into the remaining dressing till of drizzling consistency. Set dressing aside.

For each cabbage roll, place about ½ cup of the chicken mixture at 1 end of *each* cabbage leaf. Fold in sides of leaf. Roll leaf around the chicken mixture. If desired, tie the roll with the steamed green onion tops.

Line 4 dinner plates with the remaining shredded mixture, radicchio leaves, and salad savoy leaves. Top each plate with 2 cabbage rolls. Drizzle dressing over the cabbage rolls. If desired, serve with pineapple wedges and garnish with a lemon twist, rosemary sprigs, savory sprigs, and chamomile. Makes 4 servings.

***Nutrition information per serving:*** *651 cal., 33 g pro., 26 g carbo., 49 g fat, 85 mg chol., 401 mg sodium, 880 mg potassium, 6 g dietary fiber. U.S. RDA: 47% vit. A, 70% vit. C, 17% thiamine, 14% riboflavin, 70% niacin, 14% calcium, 18% iron.*

## ROASTED-PEPPER PEPPERONI SALAD

*Roasting the peppers mellows their flavor. If you can't find an assortment of colored sweet peppers, you can use all green peppers.*

- 2 large green peppers
- 2 red *or* purple sweet peppers
- 2 yellow *or* orange sweet peppers
- ½ of a 15-ounce can garbanzo beans, drained
- 4 ounces Monterey Jack cheese, cut into strips
- ¼ cup olive oil *or* salad oil
- ¼ cup red wine vinegar
- 2 cloves garlic, minced, *or* 1 teaspoon bottled minced garlic
- ½ teaspoon dry mustard
- ¼ teaspoon salt
- ⅛ teaspoon pepper
- 6 cups torn mixed greens (arugula leaves, curly endive, oak leaf lettuce)
- 1 3½- to 4-ounce package sliced pepperoni
- Black Greek olives (optional)
- Yellow Italian plum tomatoes, halved (optional)
- Arugula flowers (optional)

Quarter peppers lengthwise. Remove the stems and seeds. Cut small slits on the ends of the pepper pieces to make them lie flat. Place, peel side up, on the unheated rack of a broiler pan. Broil 2 inches from the heat about 15 minutes or till completely charred. Immediately place in a paper bag; close bag tightly and allow peppers to cool.

Peel the peppers with a sharp paring knife. Cut lengthwise into ½-inch-wide strips. In a large bowl combine pepper strips, garbanzo beans, and cheese strips. In a screw-top jar combine oil, vinegar, garlic, dry mustard, salt, and pepper. Cover; shake well. Toss with roasted pepper mixture.

Arrange torn greens on 4 salad plates. Mound the pepper mixture in the center. Arrange pepperoni around edge of plate. If desired, garnish with olives, yellow plum tomatoes, and arugula flowers. Makes 4 servings.

***Nutrition information per serving:*** *491 cal., 18 g pro., 26 g carbo., 37 g fat, 45 mg chol., 1,048 mg sodium, 1,006 mg potassium, 8 g dietary fiber. U.S. RDA: 150% vit. A, 433% vit. C, 27% thiamine, 23% riboflavin, 16% niacin, 30% calcium, 31% iron.*

## CARIBBEAN SHRIMP AND PAPAYA SALAD

*Line the salad plates with any delicate lettuce leaves. We used red oak and green oak leaf lettuce in the photo on page 82. If you can't find nasturtiums, use more lettuce and decorate the plate with any edible flower—*

6 to 8 ounces fresh *or* frozen cooked medium shrimp
¼ cup chili sauce
2 medium green onions, sliced
¼ teaspoon ground cinnamon
2 to 3 drops bottled hot pepper sauce
1 large ripe papaya
1 ripe carambola (star fruit)
2 nasturtiums (including leaves and stems)
Lettuce leaves
½ cup coconut
Fresh oregano sprigs
Green onions

Thaw shrimp, if frozen. Drain. In a medium bowl combine chili sauce, sliced green onions, cinnamon, and hot pepper sauce; stir in shrimp. Let stand, covered, while preparing papaya.

Halve the papaya lengthwise. Scoop out the seeds and the stringy pulp; discard. Lightly score the top edges of the papaya halves with a sharp knife to make an X. Slice carambola crosswise into ¼-inch-thick slices. Remove the flower portions of the nasturtiums from the stems and set aside.

Remove the leaves from the stems. Discard the stems.

Line 2 salad plates with the lettuce leaves and the nasturtium leaves. Sprinkle the coconut over the leaves. Place a papaya half on each plate. Spoon the shrimp mixture inside the papaya halves. Arrange carambola slices, nasturtium flowers, oregano sprigs, and green onions on plates. Makes 2 servings.

*Nutrition information per serving:* 296 cal., 21 g pro., 38 g carbo., 8 g fat, 166 mg chol., 658 mg sodium, 880 mg potassium, 6 g dietary fiber. U.S. RDA: 78% vit. A, 191% vit. C, 18% niacin, and 21% iron.

## ROAST BEEF SALAD WITH HORSERADISH DRESSING

*It takes just a few extra minutes to arrange the simple salad ingredients into a beautiful meal—*

⅔ cup mayonnaise *or* salad dressing
2 to 3 tablespoons freshly grated horseradish *or* 2 to 3 teaspoons prepared horseradish
½ teaspoon paprika
⅓ cup plain yogurt
1 pound whole tiny new potatoes
¾ pound baby carrots, halved lengthwise, *or* regular carrots, cut into julienne strips
1 cup fresh pea pods, stems and strings removed
Spinach leaves
Red leaf lettuce
½ of a medium red onion, sliced and separated into rings
3 ounces enoki mushrooms
8 ounces thinly sliced, cooked beef
Fresh thyme, snipped (optional)

For horseradish dressing, in a small bowl stir together the mayonnaise or salad dressing, the freshly grated or prepared horseradish, and the paprika. Stir in the plain yogurt. Cover and chill.

Scrub the new potatoes. Cut potatoes into wedges. In a large saucepan cook potato wedges, covered, in a small amount of lightly salted boiling water for 5 minutes.

Add the baby carrots; cook for 10 minutes more or till vegetables are nearly tender. Drain. Rinse with cold water. Drain; cover. Chill.

Blanch pea pods by pouring boiling water over them in a colander. Drain; cover and chill.

Line 4 dinner plates with spinach and lettuce leaves. Arrange portions of the potato wedges, carrots, pea pods, onion rings, enoki mushrooms, and sliced cooked beef on each plate. Spoon some horseradish dressing on each plate. If desired, sprinkle each serving with snipped fresh thyme. Serves 4.

*Nutrition information per serving:* 544 cal., 23 g pro., 37 g carbo., 35 g fat, 74 mg chol., 310 mg sodium, 1,373 mg potassium, 8 g dietary fiber. U.S. RDA: 502% vit. A, 56% vit. C, 21% thiamine, 24% riboflavin, 34% niacin, 12% calcium, 26% iron.

# JULY

# SALSAS/SAUCES

## SUMMER-FRESH FROM YOUR MICROWAVE, GREAT WITH GRILLED MEATS

We all love grilled steaks, chops, and chicken, but plain grilled foods just don't cut it. So, fix a simple sauce or salsa (the Italian and Spanish word for sauce) in micro-minutes. Special taste, little work.

### CORN-CUCUMBER SALSA

  1  to 2 fresh ears of corn
  ¼  cup water
  ¼  cup vinegar
  4  teaspoons sugar
  1  red chili pepper, seeded and chopped (about 1 tablespoon)
  1  teaspoon cornstarch
  ⅛  teaspoon salt
  1  cup finely chopped cucumber

Cut corn from cob; measure *1 cup.* In a microwave-safe 4-cup measure micro-cook corn and water, covered, on 100% power (high) for 3 to 5 minutes (low-wattage ovens: 5 to 6 minutes) or till tender, stirring after 2 minutes. *Do not drain.* Combine vinegar, sugar, chili pepper, cornstarch, and salt. Stir into corn. Micro-cook, uncovered, on high for 2 to 3 minutes (low-wattage ovens: 3 to 4 minutes) or till thickened and bubbly, stirring every minute. Cook for 30 seconds more. Cool. Stir in cucumber. Cover; chill. Serve with grilled pork or beef. Makes 2 cups.
    *Nutrition information per tablespoon:* 8 cal., 2 g carbo., 0 g fat, 0 mg chol., 14 mg sodium, 22 mg potassium.

### APRICOT-GRAPE SALSA

  1  tablespoon honey
  1  teaspoon cornstarch
  ⅛  teaspoon ground nutmeg
Dash salt
Dash ground ginger
  ½  cup quartered seedless red grapes

*These fix-quick microwave sauces add taste to grilled meat, poultry, and fish.*

  ½  cup chopped pitted apricots
  ¼  cup finely chopped celery
  3  tablespoons orange juice
  1  teaspoon lemon juice

In a microwave-safe 2-cup measure combine honey, cornstarch, nutmeg, salt, and ginger. Stir in grapes, apricots, celery, orange juice, and lemon juice. Micro-cook, uncovered, on 100% power (high) for 3 to 4 minutes (low-wattage ovens: 4 to 6 minutes) or till thickened and bubbly, stirring twice. Cover; chill. Serve with grilled chicken or turkey. Makes 1 cup.
    *Nutrition information per tablespoon:* 12 cal., 3 g carbo., 0 g fat, 0 mg chol., 10 mg sodium, 36 mg potassium.

---

### SAUCES MADE EASY

    Measure, mix, and cook a sauce in one container. Choose a microwave-safe glass measure that's twice the volume of your sauce.
    Our recipes make less than 3 cups. We found that larger amounts take as long to micro-cook as to cook on the stove top.

---

### SHIITAKE MUSHROOM AND SHALLOT SAUCE

  ¾  cup sliced shiitake mushrooms
  2  tablespoons finely chopped shallot *or* onion
  1  tablespoon margarine *or* butter
  4  teaspoons all-purpose flour
  ⅛  teaspoon salt
Dash pepper
  ⅔  cup milk
  ½  cup dairy sour cream

In a microwave-safe 2-cup measure combine mushrooms, shallot, and margarine. Cover with waxed paper. Micro-cook on 100% power (high) for 1½ to 2 minutes or till mushrooms are just tender. Stir in flour, salt, and pepper. Stir in milk. Micro-cook, uncovered, for 1½ to 2 minutes or till thickened and bubbly, stirring every minute. Cook for 30 seconds more. Stir in sour cream. Serve immediately with beef or pork. Makes 1⅓ cups sauce.
    *Nutrition information per tablespoon:* 24 cal., 1 g pro., 1 g carbo., 2 g fat, 3 mg chol., 26 mg sodium, 33 mg potassium, and 0 g dietary fiber.

---

### CHERRY-LIME SALSA

  1½  cups fresh *or* frozen pitted tart red cherries, quartered
  3  tablespoons sugar
  1½  teaspoons cornstarch
Dash ground cloves
  1  teaspoon grated lime peel
  4  teaspoons lime juice

Partially thaw cherries, if frozen. In a microwave-safe 2-cup measure combine sugar, cornstarch, and cloves. Stir in remaining ingredients. Micro-cook, uncovered, on 100% power (high) for 2½ to 3½ minutes (low-wattage ovens: 3½ to 4½ minutes) or till thickened and bubbly, stirring twice. Cook for 30 seconds more. Cover; chill. Serve with grilled beef or chicken. Makes 1 cup.
    *Nutrition information per tablespoon:* 16 cal., 4 g carbo., 0 g fat, 0 mg chol., 0 mg sodium, 21 mg potassium.

# OLD-FASHIONED SUMMER DESSERTS

## • Fresh Fruit  • Sweet Cream  • Flaky Pastry

By Joy Taylor

### FRUIT MEDLEY SLUMP

Plentiful fruits—berries, plums, and peaches—made their way into a simmered pudding that early Americans called, oddly enough, slump. (Some cooks even referred to it as grunt!) No matter what you call the warm fruit dessert, tender dumplings and "pour" cream make it even more sumptuous.

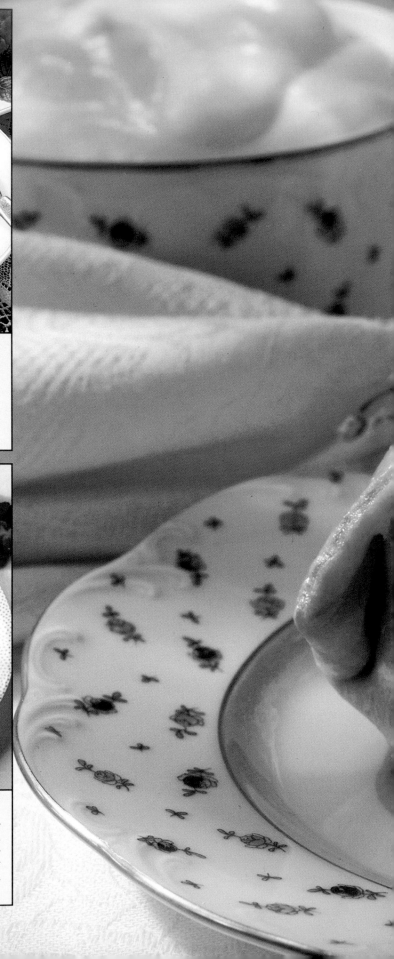

## RASPBERRY CHARLOTTE

Queen Charlotte of Great Britain, wife of George III, is often credited with this regal dessert. Fortunately, the recipe made its way across the Atlantic. In early versions, strips of dry bread lined a special charlotte mold. Today, ladyfingers are a sweet substitute; raspberries the fitting filling.

## CHERRY SWIRL SHERBET

Until 1896 when Fannie Farmer published her cookbook, ingredients were measured by handfuls, pinches, and a shot glass. Miss Farmer's collection of exact recipes includes a basic sherbet calling for 4 cups milk; our tangy cherry sherbet uses 2 cups buttermilk (about a quarter pailful). It's divine!

# OLD-FASHIONED SUMMER DESSERTS

### NECTARINE DUMPLINGS

Ah, sweet dumpling! Ingenious colonial cooks wrapped bits of pastry around fresh fruit after pie making. Though apples were the fruit of choice decades ago, nowadays anything goes, nectarines included. A spoonful of foamy sauce enriches each flaky, fork-tender dumpling.

# OLD-FASHIONED SUMMER DESSERTS

### WATERMELON ICE
Fourth of July and icy-cold watermelon—they've been an all-American duo for generations. When the fireworks explode this Fourth, serve generous scoops of the pink ice alongside the requisite slices of fresh melon. A sparkling, chilling way to celebrate our independence!

## APRICOT FLUMMERY

What a funny name for such an easy idea! Flummery, originally an English dessert, means "thickened fruit." The warm sauce (made with almost any abundant fruit) is sometimes mixed right into custard or spooned over individual servings of chilled custard. Either way, it's simply delicious.

## LEMON MINT ICE CREAM

Thanks to the father of our country, Americans have cranked, scooped, and licked ice cream since the 1700s. And no summer (winter, fall, and spring for many of us!) would be complete without a cone (or two or . . .). On sun-streaked summer days, the blend of lemon and mint tastes oh-so-right.

## FRUIT MEDLEY SLUMP

*Serve warm for the ultimate treat—*

  2 **cups sliced, peeled peaches**
    **(4 medium)**
1½ **cups sliced, pitted red plums**
  ½ **cup blueberries** *or* **raspberries**
  ¾ **cup sugar**
  2 **tablespoons water**
  1 **cup all-purpose flour**
1½ **teaspoons baking powder**
  1 **teaspoon sugar**
  ¼ **teaspoon cream of tartar**
  ⅛ **teaspoon salt**
  ⅛ **teaspoon baking soda**
  ¼ **cup shortening**
  ¼ **cup milk**
  1 **tablespoon sugar**
  ¼ **teaspoon ground cinnamon**
**Light cream (optional)**

In a 10-inch skillet mix peaches, plums, and berries. Stir in the ¾ cup sugar and water. Bring to boiling; reduce heat. Cover; simmer for 5 minutes.

Meanwhile, in a mixing bowl combine flour, baking powder, 1 teaspoon sugar, cream of tartar, salt, and baking soda. Cut in shortening till mixture resembles coarse crumbs. Make a well in the center; add milk all at once. Stir just till dough clings together.

On a lightly floured surface knead dough for 10 to 12 strokes. Roll or pat dough ¼ inch thick. Using cookie cutters, cut into desired shapes, dipping cutter in flour between cuts. *Or,* cut dough into 2x1-inch rectangles. Drop cutouts onto hot fruit. Combine the 1 tablespoon sugar and the cinnamon. Sprinkle over cutouts.

Cook, covered, for 10 to 15 minutes or till dumplings are golden brown. To serve, spoon fruit and dumplings into serving bowls. If desired, serve with light cream. Makes 8 servings.

***Nutrition information per serving:***
*237 cal., 3 g pro., 43 g carbo., 7 g fat, 112 mg sodium, 174 mg potassium, and 2 g dietary fiber. U.S. RDA: 12% vit. C.*

## RASPBERRY CHARLOTTE

*Depending on the size of the ladyfingers, you may use a few more or less than the 20 specified below—*

  4 **cups fresh** *or* **frozen raspberries**
  ¾ **cup peach** *or* **apricot nectar**
  ⅓ **cup sugar**
  1 **envelope unflavored gelatin**
  1 **tablespoon lemon juice**
  ⅛ **teaspoon almond extract**
  2 **egg whites**
  ⅓ **cup raspberry jam**
 20 **ladyfingers, split lengthwise**
  ¾ **cup whipping cream**
  ⅓ **cup raspberry jam, melted**
**Fresh raspberries (optional)**
**Fresh mint sprigs (optional)**

Thaw berries, if frozen; do not drain. In a blender container or a food processor bowl combine raspberries and nectar. Cover and blend or process till smooth. Strain mixture to remove seeds. (You should have 2 cups raspberry puree.)

In a small saucepan combine sugar and gelatin; stir in ¾ *cup* of the puree. Cook and stir over low heat till gelatin dissolves. Remove from heat. Add remaining raspberry puree, lemon juice, and almond extract; gradually stir into unbeaten egg whites. Cool about 30 minutes or till gelatin mixture reaches room temperature.

Meanwhile, spread the first ⅓ cup jam over the cut side of 11 ladyfinger halves; top with 11 more ladyfinger halves. Arrange 7 of these ladyfinger sandwiches crosswise on bottom of a 9x5x3-inch loaf pan lined with waxed paper. Set aside the remaining 4 sandwiches with jam. Arrange the 18 remaining ladyfinger halves around sides of pan, cut side toward center of pan.

Beat cooled gelatin mixture with electric mixer for 4 to 5 minutes or till light. Beat cream till soft peaks form; fold into gelatin mixture. Chill about 2 hours or till mixture mounds when spooned, stirring occasionally.

Carefully turn half of the gelatin mixture into the ladyfinger-lined pan. Place remaining 4 ladyfinger sandwiches lengthwise atop; top with remaining gelatin mixture. Cover and chill for 6 to 8 hours or till firm.

To serve, invert the pan over a serving platter; remove pan and waxed paper. Spread the melted jam on the top and garnish with raspberries and mint, if desired. Makes 16 servings.

***Nutrition information per serving:***
*163 cal., 2 g pro., 27 g carbo., 5 g fat, 64 mg chol., 23 mg sodium, 88 mg potassium, and 3 g dietary fiber. U.S. RDA: 10% vit. C.*

## CHERRY SWIRL SHERBET

*The buttermilk gives this icy dessert a tangy taste. And it makes each serving low in fat!—*

  1 **envelope unflavored gelatin**
  ¼ **cup cold water**
  2 **cups buttermilk**
  ¾ **cup sugar**
  1 **teaspoon vanilla**
  2 **cups pitted dark sweet cherries**
  ¼ **cup orange** *or* **pineapple juice**
  1 **egg white**
  2 **tablespoons sugar**

In a small saucepan combine gelatin and cold water; let stand for 5 minutes. Cook and stir over medium heat till gelatin is dissolved.

In a medium mixing bowl combine the gelatin mixture, buttermilk, the ¾ cup sugar, and vanilla. Turn into an 8x8x2-inch pan. Cover; freeze till firm.

In a blender container or a food processor bowl combine cherries and orange juice. Cover and blend or process till finely chopped.

In a small mixer bowl beat egg white till soft peaks form (tips curl); gradually add 2 tablespoons sugar, beating till stiff peaks form (tips stand straight).

Break frozen mixture into chunks with a wooden spoon; turn into a chilled mixer bowl. Beat with an electric mixer till fluffy. Fold in beaten egg white. Return mixture to cold pan. Spoon cherry mixture over buttermilk layer; use a fork to marble.

Cover; freeze till firm. Let stand for 20 minutes before serving. Makes 1½ quarts (10 to 12 servings).

***Nutrition information per serving:***
*113 cal., 3 g pro., 25 g carbo., 1 g fat, 2 mg chol., 57 mg sodium, 149 mg potassium.*

## NECTARINE DUMPLINGS

*To decorate each dumpling with pastry cutouts, roll out the pastry into a slightly larger rectangle than called for. Trim rough edges and cut these scraps into desired shapes. Brush top of dumpling with egg white and water mixture and press cutouts into place before baking—*

2¼  cups all-purpose flour
½  teaspoon salt
⅔  cup shortening
6  to 8 tablespoons cold water
6  medium nectarines *or* peaches
    (about 1¾ pounds total)
¼  cup finely chopped pecans
¼  cup sugar
1  egg white
1  tablespoon water
1  recipe Foamy Sauce *or* light
    cream

In a large bowl combine flour and salt. Cut in shortening till mixture resembles coarse crumbs. Sprinkle water atop, a little at a time, mixing till moistened. Form into a ball. On a floured surface roll out into a 21x14-inch rectangle. Cut into six 7-inch squares.

If using peaches, remove peel. With a small-bladed knife or a grapefruit knife, working from blossom end of nectarine or peach, cut a small hole (about ¾ inch) to expose pit. Carefully slide the blade of the knife around the pit to loosen. Remove pit by pushing the pit through blossom end from stem end, keeping nectarine intact. Repeat with remaining fruit.

In a small bowl combine pecans and sugar. Place a nectarine or peach in the center of each pastry square. Spoon pecan mixture evenly in holes in fruit. Moisten edges of pastry. Fold corners to center atop fruit, tucking in corners. Pinch the edges together. Place in a buttered 13x9x2-inch baking dish, making sure dumplings do not touch. Combine egg white and water. Brush on dumplings.

Bake in a 400° oven about 35 minutes or till golden brown. Serve warm with Foamy Sauce or light cream. Makes 6 servings.

*Foamy Sauce:* Beat ½ cup *whipping cream* till soft peaks form; cover and chill. In a small mixer bowl immediately beat 2 *egg yolks,* ⅓ cup *sifted powdered sugar,* and ¼ teaspoon *vanilla* about 5 minutes or till thick and lemon colored. Wash beaters thoroughly. In a large mixer bowl beat 2 *egg whites* till stiff peaks form, gradually adding ⅔ cup *sifted powdered sugar.* Fold beaten yolks into whites. Fold whipped cream into egg mixture. Chill for up to 1 hour. Makes about 3 cups sauce.

***Nutrition information per serving:*** *657 cal., 10 g pro., 78 g carbo., 36 g fat, 118 mg chol., 217 mg sodium, 396 mg potassium, and 5 g dietary fiber. U.S. RDA: 28% vit. A, 13% vit. C, 26% thiamine, 20% riboflavin, 19% niacin, 15% iron.*

## WATERMELON ICE

*Light, low calorie, and economical!—*

1  5-pound piece of watermelon
½  cup sugar
1  teaspoon finely shredded orange
    peel
3  tablespoons orange juice
    Watermelon wedges (optional)

Seed and cut up watermelon piece, removing rind (should have about 5 cups). In a blender container or a food processor bowl puree watermelon. (You should have about 3 cups puree.)

In a mixing bowl stir together watermelon puree, sugar, orange peel, and orange juice. Stir till sugar is dissolved. Pour mixture into a 9x9x2-inch pan. Cover and freeze for 3 to 4 hours or till almost firm.

Break frozen mixture into chunks. Transfer frozen mixture to a chilled large mixer bowl. Beat with an electric mixer till smooth but not melted. Return quickly to the cold pan. Cover and freeze for 6 to 8 hours or till firm.

To serve, let ice stand about 5 minutes at room temperature. Scoop or scrape across the frozen mixture with a spoon and mound in individual dessert dishes. Serve with watermelon wedges, if desired. Makes 6 to 8 servings.

***Nutrition information per serving:*** *110 cal., 1 g pro., 27 g carbo., 1 g fat, 3 mg sodium, 170 mg potassium. U.S. RDA: 10% vit. A, 27% vit. C.*

*Blackberry Fool: an English dessert traditionally made with gooseberries.*

## BLACKBERRY FOOL

2  cups fresh *or* frozen blackberries
    *or* huckleberries
¼  cup water
⅓  cup powdered sugar
½  teaspoon finely shredded orange
    peel
¾  cup whipping cream
¼  cup crumbled macaroons
    (optional)

In a medium saucepan bring berries and water to boiling. Simmer, uncovered, about 15 minutes or till berries are very tender. Remove from heat. Use a wooden spoon to press berries through a sieve. Discard seeds. Stir sugar and orange peel into berry puree. Cover and chill.

Beat whipping cream to soft peaks. Fold in cooled berry mixture. Spoon into dessert cups. Sprinkle crumbled macaroons on top, if desired. Serve immediately. Makes 4 servings.

***Nutrition information per serving:*** *250 cal., 2 g pro., 25 g carbo., 17 g fat, 61 mg chol., 17 mg sodium, 274 mg potassium, and 8 g dietary fiber. U.S. RDA: 17% vit. A, 44% vit. C.*

## APRICOT FLUMMERY

*Look for rosewater, a fragrant flavoring, in a pharmacy or specialty food shop. Always use it in small amounts—*

- 4 eggs
- 2 cups milk
- ½ cup sugar
- 1 teaspoon rosewater *or* 2 teaspoons vanilla
- ⅓ cup sugar
- 2 tablespoons cornstarch
- Dash salt
- ½ cup apricot nectar
- 1½ pounds apricots (12 to 16), peeled, pitted, and chopped (2 cups)

In a medium bowl lightly beat eggs. Stir in milk, ½ cup sugar, and rosewater or vanilla. Oil six ½-cup molds or one 1-quart casserole. Place molds or casserole in a 13x9x2-inch baking pan on oven rack. Pour egg mixture into molds or casserole. Pour boiling water into pan around molds or casserole to a depth of 1 inch.

Bake in a 325° oven until a knife inserted near the center comes out clean. Allow 25 to 30 minutes for the molds, 50 to 60 minutes for the casserole. Chill.

Just before serving, in a saucepan combine the ⅓ cup sugar, cornstarch, and salt. Stir in apricot nectar. Cook and stir till thickened and bubbly. Stir in apricots. Cook and stir for 2 minutes more. Set aside to cool slightly.

To serve, unmold custards by first loosening edges with a spatula; slip point of spatula down sides to let in air. Invert onto a serving plate. Spoon warm apricot sauce over the chilled custard. Cover and chill any remaining sauce. Makes 6 servings.

***Nutrition information per serving:*** *246 cal., 7 g pro., 43 g carbo., 5 g fat, 189 mg chol., 110 mg sodium, 347 mg potassium, and 1 g dietary fiber. U.S. RDA: 39% vit. A, 29% vit. C, 15% riboflavin, 13% calcium.*

*Honey-Pear Sherbet: a fresh-tasting and creamy blend of fruit and buttermilk.*

## HONEY-PEAR SHERBET

- 1 envelope unflavored gelatin
- ¼ cup cold water
- 1 cup chopped, peeled pear
- ⅓ cup pear, apricot, *or* peach nectar
- 2 cups buttermilk
- ¾ cup honey
- 1 teaspoon vanilla
- 1 egg white
- 2 tablespoons sugar

In a small saucepan combine gelatin and cold water; let stand for 5 minutes. Cook and stir over medium heat till gelatin is dissolved.

In a blender container combine chopped pear and nectar. Cover and blend till smooth. In a large mixing bowl combine gelatin mixture, pear mixture, buttermilk, honey, and vanilla. Turn into an 8x8x2-inch pan. Cover and freeze about 4 hours or till firm.

In a small mixer bowl beat egg white till soft peaks form (tips curl); gradually add sugar, beating till stiff peaks form (tips stand straight). Break frozen mixture into chunks with a wooden spoon; turn into a chilled mixer bowl. Beat with an electric mixer till fluffy. Fold in egg white. Return mixture to cold pan. Cover; freeze till firm. Makes 1½ quarts (about 12 servings).

***Nutrition information per serving:*** *102 cal., 1 g pro., 25 g carbo., 0 g fat, 1 mg chol., 48 mg sodium, 95 mg potassium.*

## LEMON MINT ICE CREAM

*You can serve scoops of the ice cream in lemon cups. Just halve the lemons and spoon out the flesh; save the juice for another use—*

- 2 eggs
- 4 cups whipping cream
- 3 cups light cream
- 2 cups sugar
- ¼ cup finely snipped fresh mint
- 1 tablespoon finely shredded lemon peel
- ¼ cup lemon juice
- Crushed ice
- Rock salt
- Lemon peel curls (optional)
- Fresh mint sprigs (optional)

In a large mixing bowl beat eggs. Stir in whipping cream, light cream, sugar, mint, lemon peel, and lemon juice. Stir till sugar is dissolved. Pour mixture into the freezer can of a 4- or 5-quart ice-cream freezer. Fit can into the outer freezer bucket. Add the dasher, then cover with the freezer can lid. Alternate layers of ice and rock salt in the outer freezer bucket.

Fit the motor or crank into place. Turn the motor on or start cranking. Freeze till done according to manufacturer's directions, adding ice and salt occasionally as ice melts. Unplug freezer. Carefully drain off the water through drain hole in the side of the bucket. Remove the motor or crank and the dasher.

Cover the can with lid and repack with ice and salt. Ripen ice cream for 4 hours. Garnish servings with lemon peel curls and mint sprigs, if desired. Makes 3 quarts (24 servings).

***Nutrition information per serving:*** *267 cal., 2 g pro., 19 g carbo., 21 g fat, 97 mg chol., 33 mg sodium, 79 mg potassium. U.S. RDA: 17% vit. A.*

# TREASURED FAMILY RECIPES

## From Family Reunion Cookbooks

By Barbara Johnson

"Can I please have your recipe?" It's a familiar request at family reunions. And, when three families heard it, they decided to create cookbooks full of cherished recipes and nostalgia. Try their best-loved dishes. Then, turn to *page 104* for how to make your own family cookbook.

PERRY STRUSE

# THE THOMASES' DOWN-HOME BUFFET

*"When our Thomas clan convenes every 4th of July weekend in Alabama, there's plenty of reminiscing, cooling swims in the nearby pond, and tables full of great food."*
—*Marly Thomas*

A hundred-plus relatives attend the annual Thomas family gala, now approximately in its 75th year. No Thomas reunion would be complete without *Brunswick Stew, Reunion Apples,* or *Lemon Jelly Cake.* And, everyone pitches in to do the big-batch cooking and cleanup. No one minds, though, because the work takes place in the family's homeplace—a stately 91-year-old home that their ancestors built. Proceeds from the family's anecdote-packed cookbook go toward helping preserve this restored home and its bountiful land.

Uncle Russell is chief stew maker.

● **MEET THE THOMASES**
The Alabama-based folks (above) live nearest the homeplace, so they do most of the reunion planning and grocery shopping. Other Thomases who travel farther pitch in when they arrive.

●**CROWD-SIZE RECIPES**
The Thomases' recipe treasury brims with crowd-size recipes. Uncle Russell's stew and Aunt Edith's apples both feed 100 relatives.

▶ **DINNER IS SERVED!**
Cousin Catherine beams over her *Lemon Jelly Cake.* Other foods on the menu (clockwise from front): *Marinated Eye of Round, Reunion Apples, Tossed Artichoke and Orange Salad, Sheepherder's Bread, Curried Seafood-Pasta Salad,* and *Brunswick Stew.*

Granmomma holds bread-baking "class."

Aunt Edith serves her Reunion Apples.

Grandpa snitches a zucchini bar.

Two Maxey cousins get to lickin'!

Ben polishes off a drumstick.

# THE MAXEYS' SUMMERTIME FAVORITES

*"Eating home-cooked food, hugging relatives, exchanging recipes, and meeting new cousins are some of the most popular pastimes at our family reunions."*

—*Coyal Gorman*

Coyal and her sister, Frances Garrett, (both Maxeys before marriage) put together their family cookbook five years ago as a way to get to know their widely scattered family a little better.

"When the mail carrier delivered letters from relatives across the country, we both laughed and cried as we read the recipes plus the timeless stories behind them," recalls Coyal. She still has the collection of letters and recipes tucked away in a box, saved for posterity.

With the Maxey roots in Texas, the obvious emphasis in their cookbook is on barbecued foods and the dishes that are natural barbecue accompaniments. We think you'll find their recipes to be the perfect type of dishes for any summertime family gathering.

● **MEET THE MAXEYS**
Though many of these Maxeys live in Louisiana, their roots and their reunions remain in Texas. Because most of the family lives only a few hours from the reunion site, everyone cooks ahead and totes food to the gathering.

● **GREAT EATING**
The all-weekend event begins Friday night with a salad supper. Saturday and Sunday the Maxeys enjoy chicken and barbecue favorites plus lots of ice cream.

▶ **COME TO A TEXAS FEAST!**
Coyal pours *Black Jack Barbecue Sauce* onto barbecued venison and pork, while Aunt Martha reaches for a taste. The whole gang will dig into (clockwise from center): *Cinnamon-Frosted Zucchini Bars, Parmesan Chicken, Cucumber Salad with Spicy Dressing,* and *Fat Man's Ice Cream.*

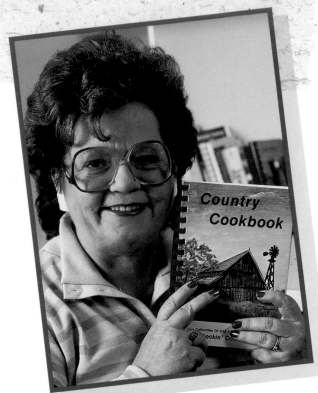

Country Cookbook

# THE FEATHERINGILLS' SCRUMPTIOUS DESSERTS

*"The Featheringills' love of family and family reunions runs deep. And, our family cookbook,* Country Cookbook, *is just one proof of that feeling."*
—*Marge Featheringill Waterfield*

The Featheringills' love of family also shows up in their history of reunions. Marge is curator of antique announcement flyers and printed programs from reunions that date back to the early 1900s. Family reunions still take place every summer in Attica, Ohio.

Just as strong as the family's commitment to reunions is their intense love of desserts. Almost half of the 100-page family cookbook is devoted to recipes for decadent cakes, luscious pies, incredible cookies, and other irresistible desserts. In fact, we're sure that any of the three delightful desserts shown here will be a hit with your own family this summer.

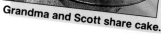
Mike treats his wife to pie.

● **MEET THE FEATHERINGILLS**
These folks live close to the fairgrounds where the family gathers for reunions. They accept most of the legwork for the event. Other relatives come from as far away as Florida and Mississippi.

Grandma and Scott share cake.

● **NOSTALGIC RECIPES**
Much of the food that family members bring to the annual reunion has touching stories behind it. *Burnt Sugar Cake,* for instance, was Grandpa Dwight's favorite cake as a boy. But, the recipe was lost when his mother died in 1920. The 1986 recipe search for the family cookbook finally unearthed her old cookbook and the cake recipe. It's still Grandpa's favorite!

▶ **TIME FOR DESSERT!**
Jim Waterfield and granddaughter Abby with (clockwise from center): rich, chewy *Mississippi Mud Cake;* classic *Burnt Sugar Cake;* and, tart, creamy *Lemon Sponge Pie.*

Grandson Joshua digs in!

103

# HOW TO CREATE YOUR OWN FAMILY REUNION COOKBOOK

**MARINATED EYE OF ROUND**

*Grill or roast these tender, flavor-packed roasts. You can easily halve the recipe—*

     2  2- to 2½-pound boneless beef
         eye of round roasts
**Seasoned salt *or* salt**
**Lemon-pepper seasoning**
**Meat tenderizer (optional)**
   ½  cup soy sauce
   ¼  cup Italian salad dressing
   ¼  cup bourbon *or* whiskey
   ¼  cup Worcestershire sauce
**Carrot sticks (optional)**
**Parsley sprigs (optional)**

Pierce roasts in several places with a sharp knife. Season lightly with seasoned salt, the lemon-pepper seasoning, and meat tenderizer, if desired. Place roasts in a large plastic bag; set in a deep bowl.

For marinade, in a small bowl stir together the soy sauce, salad dressing, bourbon or whiskey, and Worcestershire sauce; pour over roasts. Seal bag and marinate in the refrigerator overnight, turning occasionally.

Remove eye of round roasts from marinade; discard marinade. Insert a meat thermometer in thickest part of *one* of the roasts.

To grill, in a covered grill arrange preheated coals around a drip pan; test for *medium-slow* heat above drip pan. Place roasts on grill rack over drip pan, but not over the coals. Lower grill hood. Grill roasts 1 to 1¼ hours or till the thermometer registers 140°.

To roast, place meat on a rack in a large shallow roasting pan. Roast in a 325° oven for 1¼ to 1¾ hours or till thermometer registers 140°.

To serve, slice roasts. If desired, serve hot or cold with carrot sticks and garnish with parsley. Serves 16 to 20.

***Nutrition information per serving:***
*164 cal., 26 g pro., 0 g carbo., 6 g fat, 67 mg chol., 205 mg sodium, 361 mg potassium, and 0 g dietary fiber. U.S. RDA: 13% riboflavin, 24% niacin, and 13% iron.*

**W**hen did you last taste Grandma's stew or cake? If it's been too long, why not preserve those recipes in a cookbook? Here's how.

## ENLIST HELP

All the work of compiling a family cookbook needn't fall on one person. Put a different relative in charge of each section, as Marly Thomas did. Or, gather a team as Marge Waterfield did. She and a few cousins met regularly to organize recipes.

## COLLECT THE RECIPES

It's easiest to compile a cookbook immediately following your reunion. That way, you can ask everyone to bring a favorite recipe to the gathering.

You may, though, want your cookbook done in time for an upcoming reunion. If so, ask for recipes to be turned in as far ahead of the reunion as possible (six months lead time is ideal).

Here are ideas of what to ask for:
● The recipe for each dish that families plan to bring to the upcoming reunion
● The recipes for any dishes that have been a hit at past reunions
● Any tried-and-true family favorites
● Any family trivia about the recipes
● Easy-to-read recipes specifying cooking times, temperatures, and so forth
● Reminiscences about family members and any old family photos.

Persistence pays! Be prepared to send a couple of pleading letters or make phone calls to get recipe contributions. You may even enlist the help of a cooperative family member or two.

## ORGANIZE THE RECIPES

Decide on the major recipe categories such as main dish, side dish, appetizer, beverage, salad, and desserts. Sort recipes into the categories.

## WRITE THE RECIPES

The next step is to transfer the recipes to pages for copying. You may go first class and have recipes professionally typeset. But, there are other ways to make a good-looking cookbook.

Use a family member's home computer and printer. Or, type recipes onto pages. Even calligraphy or a neat handwriting works well.

## GET THE BOOK PRINTED

There are several ways to get your recipe collection into print. Collate photocopies of the pages and tie them together with a ribbon. Or, go to a professional printer. Three hundred copies of an approximately 100-page book with about 200 typeset recipes will cost from $600 on up.

## OFFSET THE COST

You'll need money up front to defray the cost of assembling your cookbook. If your family stands firmly behind your effort, consider asking each family for an interest-free loan. Once the book is off the press, you can sell it (at a fair markup, of course) to help recoup the costs and pay back your debt.

## LEMON JELLY CAKE

*Cousin Catherine has been bringing this cake to reunions for over 25 years—*

- 1 recipe Lemon Jelly Filling
- 3 cups all-purpose flour
- 1 tablespoon baking powder
- ¾ cup margarine *or* butter
- 2 cups sugar
- 3 eggs
- 1 cup milk
- 1 teaspoon lemon extract *or* 1 teaspoon finely shredded lemon peel
- 1 recipe Seven-Minute-Plus Icing

Lemon slices (optional)
Mint sprig (optional)

Prepare and chill Lemon Jelly Filling. Grease and flour four 9x1½-inch round baking pans.*

For cake, in a small mixing bowl stir together the flour and the baking powder; set aside.

In a large mixer bowl beat margarine or butter with an electric mixer on medium speed for 30 seconds. Add sugar; beat till combined. Add eggs, one at a time, beating well after each addition. Add flour mixture and milk alternately, starting and ending with flour mixture. Add lemon extract or lemon peel. Divide and spread batter evenly in the 4 prepared pans.

Bake in a 350° oven about 20 minutes or till a wooden toothpick inserted in the center comes out clean. Cool the cake layers completely on wire racks.

Remove cake layers from pans. Spread 1 of the cooled cake layers with *one-third* of the Lemon Jelly Filling.

Repeat with *2* more of the cake layers and remaining filling. Stack the 3 layers. Top with the remaining cake layer. If possible, let the cake stand, covered, in the refrigerator overnight.

Frost with Seven-Minute-Plus Icing. If desired, cut 1 or 2 lemon slices into small wedges and arrange on top of the cake. If desired, garnish with a twisted lemon slice and a mint sprig. Makes 16 servings.

**Lemon Jelly Filling:** In a 2-quart saucepan stir together 2 cups *sugar*, ¼ cup *all-purpose flour,* and 2 tablespoons *cornstarch*. Slowly stir in 2 beaten *eggs* and 1 cup *cold water,* making a paste at first so that all lumps are dissolved. Stir in 1 tablespoon finely shredded *lemon peel* and 1 cup *lemon juice.* Cook and stir mixture over medium heat till thickened and bubbly; cook and stir for 2 minutes more. Stir 2 tablespoons *margarine* or *butter* into the mixture; cool. Cover and chill.

**Seven-Minute-Plus Icing:** In the top of a double boiler stir together 2 *egg whites,* 1½ cups *sugar,* ⅓ cup *cold water,* 2 teaspoons *light corn syrup* or ¼ teaspoon *cream of tartar,* and dash *salt.* Beat with an electric mixer on low speed for 30 seconds. Place the top of the double boiler over boiling water (the upper pan should not touch the water in the bottom of the double boiler). Cook while beating constantly with a heavy-duty portable electric mixer on high speed about 7 minutes or till the icing forms stiff peaks. Remove from the heat; add 1 teaspoon *vanilla.* Beat with an electric mixer on high speed for 2 to 3 minutes more or till the icing reaches spreading consistency.

**\*Note:** If you don't have the four 9x1½-inch round baking pans as called for, you can bake the cake layers two at a time. Simply remove the cooled cake layers as directed; then wash, grease, and flour the pans as directed before using the pans a second time.

**Nutrition information per serving of Lemon Jelly Cake:** *500 cal., 6 g pro., 92 g carbo., 13 g fat, 87 mg chol., 219 mg sodium, 102 mg potassium, 1 g dietary fiber. U.S. RDA: 11% vit. A, 13% thiamine, 11% riboflavin.*

## REUNION APPLES

*Aunt Edith makes her 100-serving recipe from apples grown right on the family homestead—*

- 8 cups cored and sliced cooking apples (about 9 medium)
- 1 cup sugar
- ½ teaspoon ground cinnamon
- ¼ teaspoon ground nutmeg
- ¼ cup margarine *or* butter
- ¼ cup water

Place apples in a 13x9x2-inch baking pan. In a small mixing bowl stir together sugar, cinnamon, and nutmeg. Stir the sugar mixture into apples. Dot margarine over top; pour water over all.

Bake, covered, in a 350° oven for 30 to 40 minutes or till apples are tender. Makes 8 to 10 servings.

**Nutrition information per serving:** *213 cal., 0 g pro., 42 g carbo., 6 g fat, 0 mg chol., 68 mg sodium, 131 mg potassium, 3 g dietary fiber.*

## TOSSED ARTICHOKE AND ORANGE SALAD

- 8 cups torn lettuce
- 3 cups torn escarole
- 3 cups torn curly endive
- 1 13¾-ounce jar marinated artichoke hearts
- 1 11-ounce can mandarin orange sections, drained and chilled
- 1 avocado, halved, seeded, peeled, and chopped
- 1 or 2 stalks celery, sliced
- 2 green onions, sliced
- ¾ cup Italian salad dressing
- ¼ cup blue cheese salad dressing

In a salad bowl toss together lettuce, escarole, and endive.

Drain artichoke hearts, reserving marinade; halve artichoke hearts. Arrange artichoke hearts, orange sections, avocado, celery, and green onions on top of tossed greens.

In a screw-top jar combine reserved marinade and salad dressings. Cover and shake well. Pour over salad. Toss. Makes 16 to 18 servings.

**Nutrition information per serving:** *124 cal., 2 g pro., 7 g carbo., 11 g fat, 0 mg chol., 167 mg sodium, 270 mg potassium, 1 g dietary fiber. U.S. RDA: 16% vit. A, 19% vit. C.*

## BRUNSWICK STEW

|   |   |
|---|---|
| 1 | 2½- to 3-pound broiler-fryer chicken, cut up |
| 6 | cups water |
| 1 | 2- to 2¼-pound boneless pork shoulder roast |
| 1 | 3- to 3½-pound boneless beef chuck pot roast |
| 1 | tablespoon cooking oil |
| ½ | cup water |
| 4 | pounds potatoes, peeled and cut into ¾-inch cubes (10 cups) |
| 6 | medium onions, chopped (3 cups) |
| 2 | 17-ounce cans whole kernel corn, drained |
| 2 | 14½-ounce cans tomatoes, cut up |
| 1 | 14-ounce bottle catsup |
| 1 | 10¾-ounce can condensed tomato soup |
| ½ | cup vinegar |
| ¼ | cup Worcestershire sauce |
| 1 | teaspoon bottled hot pepper sauce |
| 1 | teaspoon Kitchen Bouquet (optional) |
| ¾ | teaspoon salt |

Rinse chicken; pat dry. In a large kettle or Dutch oven bring chicken, the 6 cups water, and 1 teaspoon *salt* to boiling; reduce heat. Cover and simmer about 2 hours or till tender.

Remove chicken, reserving broth. Line a sieve with several layers of cheesecloth, then set sieve over a large bowl. Ladle broth through, and discard cheesecloth. Use a metal spoon to skim fat that rises to the surface of the broth. Set broth aside. When the chicken is cool enough to handle, remove meat from bones; discard skin and bones. Cube or shred meat; cover and chill.

Meanwhile, roast pork in a 325° oven about 2 hours or till a thermometer inserted in the thickest part registers 170°. Cool. Cube or shred meat, discarding fat; cover and chill.

In a large skillet brown beef on all sides in hot oil. Add the ½ cup water. Bring to boiling; reduce heat. Cover and cook over low heat about 2 hours or till tender. Cool. Cube or shred beef; cover and chill. (You should have about 10 to 12 cups of chicken, pork, and beef.)

In a 10-quart kettle or Dutch oven mix the reserved broth, the potatoes, and the onions. Bring to boiling; reduce heat. Cover; cook for 10 minutes.

Stir in corn, *undrained* tomatoes, catsup, soup, vinegar, Worcestershire sauce, hot pepper sauce, Kitchen Bouquet, salt, and ¼ teaspoon *pepper*. Return to boiling; reduce heat. Simmer, uncovered, about 30 minutes or till potatoes are tender.

Stir in chicken, pork, and beef; cook about 10 minutes more or till hot. Makes 16 to 18 main-dish servings.

***Nutrition information per serving:*** *409 cal., 35 g pro., 37 g carbo., 14 g fat, 95 mg chol., 935 mg sodium, 1,174 mg potassium, 7 g dietary fiber. U.S. RDA: 17% vit. A, 53% vit. C, 38% thiamine, 20% riboflavin, 44% niacin, 24% iron.*

## SHEEPHERDER'S BREAD

|   |   |
|---|---|
| 2½ | cups water |
| ½ | cup sugar |
| ½ | cup margarine *or* butter, cut up |
| 2 | packages active dry yeast |
| 7½ | to 8 cups all-purpose flour |

In a small saucepan heat water, sugar, margarine or butter, and 1½ teaspoons *salt* just till warm (105° to 115°) and the margarine is almost melted, stirring constantly. Pour mixture into a large mixing bowl. Stir in the yeast. Cover and let stand in a warm place about 15 minutes or till mixture is bubbly.

Using a wooden spoon, stir in *4 cups* of the flour, beating to form a thick batter. Stir in *3 cups* more flour to make a moderately soft dough. (To maintain a smooth dough, add the flour in portions; stir after each addition.)

Turn the dough out onto a lightly floured surface. Knead in enough of the remaining flour to make a moderately stiff dough that is smooth and elastic (6 to 8 minutes total).

Shape the dough into a ball. Place in a greased bowl; turn dough over once to grease the top surface.

Cover and let rise in a warm place till double (about 1 hour). The dough is ready when you can lightly and quickly press 2 fingertips ½ inch into the dough and the indentation remains.

Punch dough down; form into a smooth ball. Cover and let rest about 10 minutes. Grease the bottom and sides of an ovenproof 4½- or 5-quart Dutch oven. Place dough in prepared Dutch oven. Cover and let rise till dough is

about ½ inch below top edge of pan (about 1 hour).

Bake bread on the lowest rack of a 325° oven for 55 to 60 minutes or till the bread sounds hollow when tapped with your finger. Cover bread with foil, if necessary, to prevent overbrowning. Remove from pan; cool. Serves 16.

***Whole Wheat Sheepherder's Bread:*** Prepare Sheepherder's Bread as directed, *except* reduce the all-purpose flour to *4 cups*. Add the all-purpose flour to the yeast mixture as directed. Then, stir in 3 cups *whole wheat flour*. Knead as directed, using an additional ½ to 1 cup *whole wheat flour*.

***Nutrition information per serving of bread:*** *291 cal., 7 g pro., 51 g carbo., 6 g fat, 0 mg chol., 270 mg sodium, 76 mg potassium, and 3 g dietary fiber. U.S. RDA: 26% thiamine, 17% riboflavin, 17% niacin, and 15% iron.*

## CURRIED SEAFOOD-PASTA SALAD

|   |   |
|---|---|
| ½ | cup mayonnaise *or* salad dressing |
| ¼ | cup peanut oil *or* olive oil |
| 3 | tablespoons lemon juice |
| 1 | to 2 teaspoons curry powder |
| 1 | large clove garlic, minced |
| 1 | 6-ounce package frozen, peeled, cooked shrimp, thawed |
| 4 | cups cooked corkscrew macaroni |
| 2 | 7-ounce cans tuna (water pack), drained and broken into chunks |
| ½ | cup chopped celery |
| ½ | cup snipped parsley |
| ½ | cup sliced pitted ripe olives |

Mix mayonnaise, oil, lemon juice, curry powder, garlic, and ½ teaspoon *salt*.

Remove and chill a few of the shrimp to use for garnish, if desired. Add the remaining shrimp, macaroni, tuna, celery, the snipped parsley, and the ½ cup olives to the mayonnaise mixture; toss gently to coat, being careful not to tear macaroni. Cover; chill.

If desired, spoon salad into a lettuce-lined bowl; add reserved shrimp, additional olives, and parsley, if desired. Makes 6 to 8 side-dish servings.

***Nutrition information per serving:*** *478 cal., 30 g pro., 30 g carbo., 27 g fat, 108 mg chol., 479 mg sodium, 399 mg potassium, 2 g dietary fiber. U.S. RDA: 15% vit. C, 14% thiamine, 10% riboflavin, 54% niacin, 20% iron.*

# THE MAXEYS' SUMMERTIME FAVORITES

## BLACK JACK BARBECUE SAUCE

*Strong coffee plus hot fresh jalapeño chili peppers and chili powder give this barbecue sauce its oomph.*

- 4 medium onions, chopped (2 cups)
- 1 cup strong coffee
- 1 cup catsup
- ⅔ cup Worcestershire sauce
- ½ cup packed brown sugar
- ½ cup vinegar
- 4 to 6 fresh jalapeño chili peppers, seeded and cut up (¼ cup) (see tip for handling these peppers at lower right)
- 3 tablespoons chili powder
- 6 cloves garlic, sliced
- 2 teaspoons salt

In a 2-quart saucepan combine the chopped onions, strong coffee, catsup, Worcestershire sauce, brown sugar, vinegar, chili peppers, chili powder, garlic slices, and salt. Bring the mixture to boiling. Reduce the heat. Simmer the mixture, uncovered, for 25 minutes. Cool slightly.

In a blender container or a food processor bowl blend or process *half* of the mixture, covered, till mixture is nearly smooth. Remove from blender container or food processor bowl. Repeat with remaining mixture.

Use Black Jack Barbecue Sauce on barbecued venison and pork, brushing meat with the sauce during the last 15 to 20 minutes of grilling time. Pass extra sauce with meat, if desired. If you have some left, you can store it, covered, in the refrigerator for up to 1 week. Makes about 4 cups sauce.

*Nutrition information per ¼ cup of sauce: 66 cal., 1 g pro., 16 g carbo., 0 g fat, 0 mg chol., 571 mg sodium, 172 mg potassium, 1 g dietary fiber. U.S. RDA: 20% vit. A, 13% vit. C.*

## PARMESAN CHICKEN

*An easy way to make crispy chicken: bake it in the oven.*

- 1 2½- to 3-pound broiler-fryer chicken, cut up
- ½ cup grated Parmesan cheese
- ¼ cup whole wheat flour
- 1 teaspoon paprika
- ½ teaspoon salt
- Dash pepper
- 1 slightly beaten egg
- 2 tablespoons milk

Rinse chicken; pat dry. In a plastic bag combine cheese, flour, paprika, salt, and pepper. In a shallow dish stir together egg and milk.

Dip chicken in egg mixture; place chicken, 2 or 3 pieces at a time, in the plastic bag. Close bag and shake to coat chicken with cheese mixture.

Place chicken, skin side up, in a 13x9x2-inch baking pan. Bake in a 375° oven for 45 to 55 minutes or till chicken is tender. Transfer to a serving platter; garnish with carrot tops and cherry tomatoes, if desired. Serves 4 to 6.

*Nutrition information per serving: 281 cal., 34 g pro., 7 g carbo., 12 g fat, 160 mg chol., 599 mg sodium, and 304 mg potassium. U.S. RDA: 11% vit. A, 16% riboflavin, 44% niacin, 21% calcium, and 10% iron.*

## CINNAMON-FROSTED ZUCCHINI BARS

*The difference in these bars is that the spice is in the frosting, not the cookies.*

- 1¾ cups all-purpose flour
- 1½ teaspoons baking powder
- ¾ cup margarine *or* butter
- ½ cup sugar
- ½ cup packed brown sugar
- 2 eggs
- 1 teaspoon vanilla
- 2 cups shredded zucchini
- 1 cup coconut
- ¾ cup chopped walnuts
- 1 recipe Cinnamon Frosting

Generously grease a 15x10x1-inch baking pan. Set aside.

In a small mixing bowl stir together flour and baking powder; set aside.

In a large mixer bowl beat margarine or butter with an electric mixer on medium speed for 30 seconds. Add sugars; beat till fluffy. Add eggs and vanilla; beat well. Stir in flour mixture. Stir in zucchini, coconut, and nuts. Spread evenly in prepared pan.

Bake in a 350° oven about 30 minutes or till a wooden toothpick inserted near the center comes out clean. Cool completely in pan on a wire rack. Drizzle with the Cinnamon Frosting. Cut into bars. Makes 36 bars.

*Cinnamon Frosting:* In a large mixer bowl beat 2 cups sifted *powdered sugar;* 2 tablespoons *milk;* 2 tablespoons *margarine* or *butter,* melted; 1 teaspoon *ground cinnamon;* and 1 teaspoon *vanilla* till smooth.

*Nutrition information per bar: 137 cal., 2 g pro., 18 g carbo., 7 g fat, 15 mg chol., 71 mg sodium, 57 mg potassium, and 1 g dietary fiber.*

## CUCUMBER SALAD WITH SPICY DRESSING

- 3 to 4 medium cucumbers
- 1 tablespoon sugar
- 1 tablespoon vinegar
- 1 teaspoon sesame oil *or* salad oil
- 1 teaspoon soy sauce
- ½ teaspoon salt
- ¼ teaspoon bottled hot pepper sauce

Halve cucumbers lengthwise. Cut into ¼-inch slices. (You should have 4 cups.)

In a small bowl stir together the sugar, vinegar, sesame or salad oil, soy sauce, salt, and hot pepper sauce. Add cucumbers; toss to coat. Cover and chill before serving. If desired, top with whole radishes. Makes 8 servings.

*Nutrition information per serving: 21 cal., 1 g pro., 4 g carbo., 1 g fat, 0 mg chol., 181 mg sodium, 113 mg potassium, 1 g dietary fiber.*

# Handling Chili Peppers

Because fresh chili peppers contain volatile oils that can burn skin and eyes, avoid direct contact with the peppers. Wear plastic or rubber gloves or work under cold running water. If your bare hands touch the peppers, wash your hands and nails thoroughly with soap and water.

## FAT MAN'S ICE CREAM

*A creamy, rich treat that tastes just like a fudgy ice-cream bar*

- 1 pound chocolate-coated, caramel-topped nougat bars, cut up
- ½ of a 14-ounce can (⅔ cup) *sweetened condensed* milk
- 1 5½-ounce can chocolate-flavored syrup (½ cup)
- 4 cups whipping cream
- 4 cups light cream

In a 4-quart Dutch oven cook candy bars, sweetened condensed milk, and chocolate-flavored syrup over low heat, stirring frequently, till candy bars melt and mixture is smooth. Remove from heat. Stir in whipping cream and light cream. Pour into a storage container. Cover; chill completely.

Pour the chilled mixture into the freezer can of a 4- or 5-quart ice-cream freezer. Freeze according to the manufacturer's directions.

After cranking, remove ice to below level of can lid so no melted ice seeps into can. Wipe can and lid with a damp cloth to remove salt and ice. Remove lid and dasher, scraping the ice cream from the dasher back into the can. Cover the can with several layers of waxed paper or foil. Plug the opening in the lid with a cork. Replace lid.

To ripen the ice cream, pack additional layers of ice and salt into the outer container, using 4 parts ice to 1 part salt. Cover with a heavy cloth or newspaper. Let stand about 4 hours, repacking once or twice. Makes about 12 cups, 24 servings.

*Nutrition information per serving: 384 cal., 3 g pro., 24 g carbo., 31 g fat, 105 mg chol., 87 mg sodium, 169 mg potassium. U.S. RDA: 21% vit. A, 10% riboflavin, 10% calcium.*

# THE FEATHERINGILLS' SCRUMPTIOUS DESSERTS

## MISSISSIPPI MUD CAKE

- 1½ cups all-purpose flour
- 2 tablespoons unsweetened cocoa powder
- 1 cup margarine *or* butter
- 2 cups sugar
- 1 teaspoon vanilla
- 4 eggs
- 1½ cups chopped pecans
- 1 3½-ounce can (1⅓ cups) flaked coconut
- 1 7-ounce jar marshmallow creme
- 1 recipe Mississippi Mud Frosting

Grease and flour a 13x9x2-inch baking pan; set aside.

In a small mixing bowl stir together the flour and the cocoa powder; set mixture aside.

In a large mixer bowl beat margarine or butter with an electric mixer on medium speed for 30 seconds to soften. Add sugar and vanilla; beat till fluffy. Add eggs, one at a time, beating well after each addition. Beat in flour mixture. Stir in pecans and coconut. Turn mixture into prepared pan.

Bake in a 350° oven for 35 minutes or till cake tests done. Transfer cake to a wire rack. While cake is still hot, carefully spread with the marshmallow creme. Cool cake completely. Frost the cake with Mississippi Mud Frosting. Cut into squares. If desired, garnish with strawberries. Makes 16 servings.

***Mississippi Mud Frosting:*** In a small mixer bowl beat ½ cup *margarine or butter* with electric mixer on medium speed for 30 seconds. Add 1 cup sifted *powdered sugar* and ½ cup *unsweetened cocoa powder;* beat mixture with an electric mixer on low speed till combined. Beat in ½ cup *evaporated milk* and 1 teaspoon *vanilla.* Gradually beat in 3 cups sifted *powdered sugar.*

*Nutrition information per serving: 578 cal., 5 g pro., 76 g carbo., 30 g fat, 71 mg chol., 260 mg sodium, 152 mg potassium, 2 g dietary fiber. U.S. RDA: 16% vit. A, 13% thiamine.*

## BURNT SUGAR CAKE

- 2½ cups all-purpose flour
- 2 teaspoons baking powder
- ½ teaspoon salt
- ¼ cup packed brown sugar
- 1¼ cups hot water
- ¼ cup shortening
- ¼ cup margarine *or* butter
- 1½ cups sugar
- 3 eggs
- 1 recipe Caramel Frosting
- Chopped pecans (optional)
- Pecan halves (optional)

Grease and lightly flour two 8x1½-inch or 9x1½-inch round baking pans.

In a mixing bowl combine flour, baking powder, and salt. Set aside.

In an 8-inch skillet heat brown sugar over medium heat about 5 minutes or till sugar melts and turns deep golden brown, stirring constantly. Remove from heat.

Stir in ¼ *cup* of the hot water. Return to heat and continue stirring for about 2 minutes or till mixture is free of lumps. Stir in remaining water.

In a large mixer bowl beat shortening and margarine or butter with an electric mixer on medium speed for 30 seconds or till softened. Add sugar and beat till well combined. Add eggs, one at a time, beating well after each addition. Add the flour mixture and brown sugar mixture alternately to beaten mixture, beating on low speed after each addition just till combined. Divide and spread evenly in prepared pans.

Bake in a 350° oven for 25 to 30 minutes or till a wooden toothpick inserted in the center comes out clean. Cool for 10 minutes on wire racks. Remove cake from pans. Cool completely. Frost with Caramel Frosting. If desired, sprinkle cake top with chopped pecans and decorate edge of cake sides with pecan halves. Makes 12 servings.

***Caramel Frosting:*** In a medium saucepan melt ½ cup *margarine* or *butter;* stir in 1 cup packed *brown sugar.* Cook and stir till bubbly. Remove from heat. Add ¼ cup *milk;* beat vigorously till smooth. By hand, beat in 3½ cups sifted *powdered sugar* till frosting is of spreading consistency. Use at once.

*Nutrition information per serving: 563 cal., 5 g pro., 97 g carbo., 18 g fat, 69 mg chol., 301 mg sodium, 137 mg potassium, 2 g dietary fiber. U.S. RDA: 11% vit. A, 13% thiamine, 10% riboflavin, 13% iron.*

## LEMON SPONGE PIE

*An ingenious version of lemon pudding cake, put in a pie shell.*

    1 recipe Pastry for Single-Crust Pie
    2 egg yolks
    1 cup sugar
    ¼ cup lemon juice
    2 tablespoons all-purpose flour
    1 tablespoon margarine *or* butter,
        melted
    ⅛ teaspoon salt
    1 cup milk
    2 egg whites
Whipped cream
Lemon slices, halved

Prepare the Pastry for Single-Crust Pie as directed. Bake in a 450° oven for 5 minutes. Remove the foil and bake for 5 minutes more. Remove the pastry from the oven. Lower the oven temperature to 350°.

Meanwhile, for the filling, in a large mixing bowl beat egg yolks slightly with a rotary beater or fork. Stir in the sugar, lemon juice, flour, margarine or butter, and salt. Gradually stir the milk into the yolk mixture till all of the ingredients are well mixed.

In a small mixer bowl beat egg whites with an electric mixer on high speed till stiff peaks form (tips stand straight). Fold beaten whites into the egg yolk mixture.

Place partially baked pastry on the oven rack; pour the filling into the pastry. Bake in the 350° oven about 30 minutes or till a knife inserted near the center comes out clean. Cool completely on a wire rack.

Before serving, dollop pie with the whipped cream. Top each dollop with half of a lemon slice. To store, cover and chill. Makes 8 servings.

***Pastry for Single-Crust Pie:*** In a medium mixing bowl stir together 1¼ cups *all-purpose flour* and ½ teaspoon *salt*. Cut in ⅓ cup *shortening* till pieces are the size of small peas. Sprinkle 1 tablespoon *cold water* over *part* of the mixture; gently toss with a fork. Push to side of bowl. Repeat till all of the flour mixture is moistened, using a total of 3 to 4 tablespoons cold water.

On a lightly floured surface roll dough into a circle about 12 inches in diameter. Ease pastry into a 9-inch pie plate, being careful not to stretch the pastry. Trim excess pastry and flute edge. Line pastry with a double thickness of heavy-duty foil.

***Nutrition information per serving:*** *310 cal., 5 g pro., 44 g carbo., 13 g fat, 75 mg chol., 215 mg sodium, 96 mg potassium, 1 g dietary fiber. U.S. RDA: 11% thiamine, 11% riboflavin.*

## MARINATED VEGETABLE AND SPAGHETTI SALAD

*You can use other types of pasta in place of the spaghetti.*

    2 cups halved cherry tomatoes *or*
        chopped tomatoes
        (2 to 3 medium)
    ¾ cup chopped cucumber
    ¾ cup zucchini, halved and sliced
    1 small green pepper, cut into
        bite-size strips
    2 tablespoons chopped onion
    ¼ cup red wine vinegar
    3 tablespoons salad oil
    2 tablespoons sugar
    1 tablespoon lemon juice
    1 teaspoon snipped fresh parsley
    ¾ teaspoon snipped fresh basil *or*
        ¼ teaspoon dried basil,
        crushed
    1 small clove garlic, minced
    8 ounces spaghetti, broken
    1 tablespoon salad oil
Leaf lettuce

In a large mixing bowl combine tomatoes, cucumber, zucchini, green pepper, and onion. In a screw-top jar combine vinegar, the 3 tablespoons oil, sugar, lemon juice, parsley, basil, garlic, ⅛ teaspoon *salt*, and ⅛ teaspoon *pepper.* Cover and shake well; pour over vegetables. Cover; chill for 2 to 24 hours.

Meanwhile, cook spaghetti according to package directions. Drain; rinse under cold water. Toss with the 1 tablespoon oil. Cover and chill.

To serve, spoon vegetables around spaghetti in a lettuce-lined bowl. Sprinkle with grated Parmesan cheese, if desired. Toss before serving. Makes 8 to 10 servings.

***Nutrition information per serving:*** *193 cal., 4 g pro., 28 g carbo., 7 g fat, 0 mg chol., 38 mg sodium, 221 mg potassium, 2 g dietary fiber. U.S. RDA: 11% vit. A, 36% vit. C, 20% thiamine, 10% niacin.*

## DUTCH APPLE BRANDY CHEESECAKE

*No peeling of apples! Chunky applesauce is a clever timesaver.*

    1 recipe Cinnamon Crust
    4 8-ounce packages cream
        cheese, softened
    1 cup sugar
    3 tablespoons apple brandy
    1 teaspoon ground cinnamon
    ½ teaspoon vanilla
    ⅛ teaspoon ground nutmeg
    4 eggs
    1 cup chunk-style applesauce
    ¼ cup whipping cream
    1 recipe Crumb Topping

Prepare Cinnamon Crust; cool. Beat cream cheese till smooth. Gradually add sugar, beating well. Add brandy, cinnamon, vanilla, and nutmeg; blend well. Add eggs, one at a time, beating just till combined. Stir in the applesauce and cream. Pour into crust. Bake at 350° for 50 minutes or till center appears nearly set.

Meanwhile, prepare Crumb Topping; sprinkle over cake. Bake for 10 minutes more or just till cake is set. Cool for 5 minutes on a wire rack. Loosen sides of cake. Cool for 30 minutes. Remove sides of pan. Cover; chill thoroughly. Makes 16 servings.

***Cinnamon Crust:*** In a bowl mix 1¼ cups *graham cracker crumbs;* ⅓ cup ground *walnuts* or *pecans;* ⅓ cup *margarine* or *butter*, melted; and ½ teaspoon *ground cinnamon.* Press on the bottom and 1½ inches up sides of a 10-inch springform pan. Bake in a 350° oven about 10 minutes or till golden. Cool completely before using.

***Crumb Topping:*** In a bowl combine ¾ cup packed *brown sugar;* ¾ cup *all-purpose flour;* ⅓ cup *margarine* or *butter*, melted; ½ teaspoon *ground cinnamon;* and ¼ teaspoon *ground nutmeg* till crumbly.

***Nutrition information per serving:*** *462 cal., 7 g pro., 37 g carbo., 32 g fat, 136 mg chol., 328 mg sodium, 176 mg potassium, 0 g dietary fiber.*

# SUMMER SALAD
## FRESH VEGETABLES AND SMOKED TURKEY MAKE A MEAL!

By Barbara Johnson

**M**icro-cook garden-fresh vegetables, strips of smoked turkey, and a jazzed-up salad dressing, and you have a summer supper salad ready fast. What's more, your kitchen stays cool.

**Enjoy fresh summer vegetables in this quick and healthful salad.**

When you'd rather spend your summer hours playing instead of cooking, toss together this simple and light dinner salad.

## TURKEY AND VEGETABLES WITH GARDEN GREENS

*Heat the turkey and vegetables in the salad dressing. Then, pour over the torn greens to wilt ever so slightly—*

- **6** cups torn mixed greens (such as green *or* red leaf lettuce, radicchio, romaine, sorrel, arugula, *or* butter head lettuce)
- **2** small yellow summer squash *or* zucchini, bias-sliced ¼ inch thick (1½ cups)
- **1** medium red, yellow, green *or* purple sweet pepper, cut into thin strips (¾ cup)
- **¾** pound fully cooked smoked turkey, cut into thin strips
- **¼** cup oil and vinegar salad dressing
- **2** tablespoons grated Parmesan cheese
- **1½** teaspoons snipped fresh thyme, oregano, *or* basil *or* ½ teaspoon dried thyme oregano, *or* basil, crushed
- **1** teaspoon sugar

● **Place the torn mixed greens** in a large salad bowl; set aside.

● **In a 1½-quart** microwave-safe casserole micro-cook the summer squash, sweet pepper, and 2 tablespoons *water* on 100% power (high), covered, for 2 minutes. Drain.

● **Stir in** the smoked turkey, salad dressing, Parmesan cheese, herb, and sugar. Cook, covered, on high for 2 to 4 minutes or till vegetables are tender and turkey is heated through; stir once.

● **Immediately pour the hot mixture** over the torn mixed greens; toss about 1 minute or till the greens are slightly wilted. Serve immediately. Makes 4 main-dish servings.

*Nutrition information per serving: 211 cal., 19 g pro., 7 g carbo., 12 g fat, 40 mg chol., 893 mg sodium, 597 mg potassium, and 2 g dietary fiber. U.S. RDA: 67% vit. A, 86% vit. C, 11% thiamine, 13% riboflavin, 32% niacin, and 10% iron.*

# SEPTEMBER

THE MAGAZINE FOR AMERICAN FAMILIES

## Better Homes and Gardens

SEPTEMBER 1988
●$1.50

**15 PROJECTS**
**MAKE-AHEAD GIFTS!**

BUILD
A PLAYHOUSE
BUNK BED
**FOR KIDS**

**PROBLEM-SOLVING**
**FURNITURE**
**ARRANGEMENTS**

STEP-BY-STEP
**MICROWAVE**
**MAIN DISHES**
QUICK—
EASY ENOUGH
FOR BEGINNERS

PERRY STRUSE

● Gerrianne Jordan did it! And she doesn't even own a microwave. "Now I see lots of possibilities!"

**Q.** How thin should I pound the chicken breasts?

**A.** To ¼-inch thickness, so that they'll roll easily and cook evenly.

**Q.** Is there an art to rolling the roll-ups?

**A.** Just spread the stuffing evenly over the flattened chicken breast, fold in the sides, and roll up the three layers together, starting from a narrow end. Secure with wooden toothpicks or skewers, if necessary.

**Q.** How will I know when the chicken is done?

**A.** At the end of the suggested minimum cooking time, check the center of the chicken with the tip of a sharp knife. If the chicken is done, juices will run clear and no pink will remain.

# MICROWAVE COOKING...
## You Can Do It!

### By Barbara Goldman

Are you a microwave novice? Turn pro with these easy recipes. Thirty beginners tested them in our kitchens. Their response? "A piece of cake!"

## 3 MICROWAVE CHICKEN ROLL-UPS

● The happy combination of chicken and the microwave oven produces three fabulous chicken dinners.

PHOTOGRAPHS: TIM SCHULTZ. FOOD STYLIST: JANET HERWIG

**REUBEN- ▶ STYLE CHICKEN**
Micro-cook this corned beef, coleslaw, and chicken winner in just 6 to 8 minutes.

**◀ APPLE-PROSCIUTTO CHICKEN**
An appealing flavor blend creates a homey yet sophisticated entrée.

**◀ BACON-MUSHROOM CHICKEN**
A savory 30-minute roll-up with an easy cheddar sauce—fantastic!

Recipes begin on *page 118;* timings for low-wattage microwave ovens and conventional directions included.

## MEAT SAUCES
### QUESTIONS AND ANSWERS

● **Steve Johnson did it!** "It's surprisingly easy," he told us, "and the sauce tastes great!"

**Q.** How small do I cut the vegetables?

**A.** Cut the onion and celery into ½-inch pieces. For even microwave cooking it's important for the pieces to be about the same size and thickness.

**Q.** Why do I *crumble* the ground turkey into the bowl?

**A.** You don't want the ground meat to clump. By crumbling the meat, it cooks more evenly.

**Q.** Why do I stir the meat mixture during cooking?

**A.** Moving foods during micro-cooking ensures that all portions cook evenly. Stirring from the outside in brings heat from the fast-cooking edges to the slow-heating center.

# 3 MICROWAVE MEAT SAUCES

● **After-work cooking is a snap with ready-in-minutes micro-cooked meals from ground meat.**

### TURKEY MOLE ▶
Ground turkey lends a contemporary touch to a south-of-the-border favorite.

### ▲ LAMB CURRY
This lively mix of ingredients will turn you into a curry lover fast. It micro-cooks in just 15 minutes.

### ▲ BEEF ITALIANO
Pasta sauce just like Mom used to make! But in a fraction of the time in your microwave oven.

Recipes begin on page 121; timings for low-wattage microwave ovens and conventional directions included.

## FISH DINNERS
### QUESTIONS AND ANSWERS

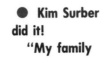

● **Kim Surber did it!**

"My family will love this dish," she said of her salmon and rice entrée.

**Q.** Why does this recipe suggest that I fold under the thin ends of the fish?

**A.** Fish fillets vary in thickness and shape and may need help to cook evenly. To obtain an even thickness of ½ inch, you may have to fold the edges under.

**Q.** Why is the dish covered with vented microwave-safe plastic wrap?

**A.** Covering food prevents splattering and keeps steam inside the dish so that food will be moist. "Venting" refers to turning back a corner of the plastic wrap.

**Q.** How will I know when the fish is done?

**A.** As when cooked in a conventional oven, perfectly micro-cooked fish should *just* flake with a fork.

# 3 MICROWAVE FISH DINNERS

● **Fast! Simple! And oh so healthful! These dinners take to the microwave oven like fish take to water.**

### RICE FLORENTINE SALMON ▶
Impress guests with this elegant entrée, and you'll be impressed, too. It cooks in less than 10 minutes.

### ▲ TOMATO COD FILLETS
The proverbial cod dinner takes on a new twist. Partner the microwave-moist fish with a tangy rice.

### ▲ HERBED PEPPER RED SNAPPER
When you prepare this delicious "Catch of the Day," be prepared to catch compliments.

Recipes begin on *page 118;*
timings for low-wattage microwave ovens
and conventional directions included.

## REUBEN-STYLE CHICKEN

    2  whole large chicken
       breasts, skinned, boned,
       and halved lengthwise
    4  slices cooked corned beef
    ½  cup deli coleslaw
Paprika
    2  tablespoons finely chopped
       green onion
    1  tablespoon margarine *or* butter
    1  tablespoon all-purpose flour
Dash pepper
    ½  cup milk
    ½  cup shredded Monterey
       Jack cheese with caraway
       seed (2 ounces)

Rinse chicken; pat dry. Place 1 chicken breast half, boned side up, between 2 pieces of clear plastic wrap. Working from center to edges, pound lightly with the flat side of a meat mallet to form a rectangle about ¼ inch thick. Remove plastic wrap. Repeat with remaining chicken.

Place 1 corned beef slice atop *each* chicken breast half. Spread *one-fourth* of the coleslaw onto *each* slice of corned beef. Fold in sides and roll up each breast half, starting from a narrow end. Secure with wooden toothpicks or nonmetallic skewers.

Arrange chicken rolls, seam side down, in a microwave-safe 8-inch round baking dish. Sprinkle with paprika. Cover with vented clear plastic wrap.

Micro-cook on 100% power (high) for 6 to 8 minutes (low-wattage ovens: 7 to 9 minutes) or till chicken is tender and no pink remains, giving the dish a half-turn and rearranging the rolls after 4 minutes. Remove toothpicks. Cover to keep warm.

For sauce, in a 2-cup glass measure combine green onion and margarine or butter. Cook, uncovered, on high for 30 to 40 seconds or till margarine is melted. Stir in flour and pepper. Stir in milk. Cook, uncovered, on high for 2 to 3 minutes or till thickened and bubbly, stirring after every minute till sauce starts to thicken, then stirring every 30 seconds. Stir in cheese. Cook, uncovered, on high about 30 seconds or till cheese is melted, stirring once. Serve sauce over chicken. Makes 4 servings.

*Conventional directions:* Pound and stuff chicken breasts as directed. Place, seam side down, in a 10x6x2-inch baking dish. Sprinkle with paprika. Bake, uncovered, in a 350° oven for 25 to 30 minutes or till tender and no pink remains. Remove toothpicks.

Meanwhile, in a small saucepan cook green onion in hot margarine or butter till tender but not brown. Stir in flour and pepper. Add ⅔ cup milk all at once. Cook and stir till thickened and bubbly. Cook and stir for 1 minute more. Stir in cheese till melted. Serve chicken and sauce as directed.

*Nutrition information per serving:* *372 cal., 48 g pro., 5 g carbo., 17 g fat, 139 mg chol., 499 mg sodium, 422 mg potassium, 1 g dietary fiber. U.S. RDA: 46% vit. A, 19% riboflavin, 84% niacin, 18% calcium, 15% iron.*

## RICE FLORENTINE SALMON

    1  pound fresh *or* frozen
       skinned salmon fillets
    1  tablespoon margarine *or* butter
    1  teaspoon lime *or* lemon juice
    ⅛  teaspoon salt
    ⅛  teaspoon pepper
    1  cup quick-cooking rice
    ¾  cup water
    ½  teaspoon instant chicken
       bouillon granules
    ⅛  teaspoon ground nutmeg
    1  10-ounce package frozen
       chopped spinach, thawed
       and well drained
    ⅓  cup sliced green onion
    2  tablespoons grated
       Parmesan cheese
Lime *or* lemon slices
Green onion tops

Thaw fish, if frozen. (Do not thaw frozen fillets in a low-wattage microwave oven. Instead, thaw in the refrigerator for several hours or overnight.) To thaw fillets in a high-wattage microwave oven, unwrap and place in an 8x8x2-inch microwave-safe baking dish. Cover with vented clear plastic wrap. Cook on 30% power (medium-low) for 6 to 8 minutes, giving the dish a quarter-turn and separating the fish after 3 minutes. Let stand for 10 minutes. The fish should be pliable and cold on the outside, but still slightly icy in the thick center areas. Rinse; pat dry.

In a 1-cup glass measure combine margarine or butter, lime or lemon juice, salt, and pepper. Micro-cook on 100% power (high) for 30 to 40 seconds or till margarine is melted. Set aside.

Meanwhile, in a microwave-safe 8x8x2-inch baking dish combine rice, water, bouillon granules, and nutmeg. Spread evenly in bottom of dish. Cover with vented clear plastic wrap. Cook on high for 2 minutes (low-wattage ovens: 2½ minutes). Stir in spinach, green onion, and cheese; spread evenly in dish.

Arrange salmon fillets on top of rice mixture, with the thicker portions toward the edges of the dish. Turn under any thin portions of fillets to obtain an even thickness of about ½ inch. Drizzle margarine mixture over fish. Cover with vented clear plastic wrap.

Cook on high for 6 to 8 minutes (low-wattage ovens: 7 to 9 minutes) or just till fish flakes with a fork, giving the dish a half-turn after 3 minutes. Garnish with lime or lemon slices and green onion tops. Makes 4 servings.

*Conventional directions:* Thaw fish, if frozen. In a medium saucepan combine water, bouillon granules, and nutmeg. Bring to boiling; stir in rice. Remove from heat. Cover; let stand for 5 minutes or till liquid is absorbed.

Meanwhile, in a small saucepan melt margarine or butter. Stir in lime or lemon juice, salt, and pepper. Set mixture aside.

Stir spinach, green onion, and Parmesan cheese into rice mixture. Spread rice mixture evenly in a greased 8x8x2-inch baking dish.

Arrange salmon fillets atop rice as directed. Drizzle with the margarine mixture. Cover with foil. Bake in a 350° oven for 25 to 30 minutes or just till fish flakes with a fork. Serve as directed.

*Nutrition information per serving:* *359 cal., 28 g pro., 23 g carbo., 16 g fat, 42 mg chol., 299 mg sodium, 730 mg potassium, 2 g dietary fiber. U.S. RDA: 96% vit. A, 22% thiamine, 14% riboflavin, 47% niacin, 27% calcium, 23% iron.*

## APPLE-PROSCIUTTO CHICKEN

  2 **whole large chicken breasts, skinned, boned, and halved lengthwise**
  4 **slices prosciutto *or* boiled ham**
  ½ **cup finely chopped apple**
  ⅛ **teaspoon apple pie spice**
**Apple pie spice**
  2 **tablespoons finely chopped green onion**
  1 **tablespoon margarine *or* butter**
  1 **tablespoon all-purpose flour**
**Dash pepper**
  ½ **cup milk**
  ½ **cup shredded provolone cheese (2 ounces)**
**Hot cooked rice (optional)**

Rinse chicken; pat dry. Place 1 chicken breast half, boned side up, between 2 pieces of clear plastic wrap. Working from center to edges, pound lightly with the flat side of a meat mallet to form a rectangle about ¼ inch thick. Remove plastic wrap. Repeat with remaining chicken.

Place 1 prosciutto or boiled ham slice atop *each* chicken breast half.

In a small bowl combine the apple and the ⅛ teaspoon apple pie spice.

Spoon *one-fourth* of the apple mixture over *each* prosciutto slice. Fold in sides and roll up each breast half, starting from a narrow end. Secure chicken roll with wooden toothpicks or nonmetallic skewers.

Arrange chicken rolls, seam side down, in a microwave-safe 8-inch round baking dish. Sprinkle with additional apple pie spice. Cover with vented clear plastic wrap.

Micro-cook on 100% power (high) for 6 to 8 minutes (low-wattage ovens: 7 to 9 minutes) or till chicken is tender and no pink remains, giving the dish a half-turn and rearranging the rolls after 4 minutes. Remove toothpicks. Cover to keep warm.

For sauce, in a 2-cup glass measure combine green onion and margarine or butter. Cook, uncovered, on high for 30 to 40 seconds or till margarine is melted. Stir in flour and pepper. Stir in milk. Cook, uncovered, on high for 2 to 3 minutes or till thickened and bubbly, stirring after every minute till sauce starts to thicken, then stirring every 30 seconds. Stir in cheese. Cook, uncovered, on high about 30 seconds or till heated through, stirring once. Serve sauce over chicken and, if desired, rice. Makes 4 servings.

***Conventional directions:*** Pound and stuff chicken breasts as directed. Place, seam side down, in a 10x6x2-inch baking dish. Bake, uncovered, in a 350° oven for 25 to 30 minutes or till tender and no pink remains. Remove toothpicks. Meanwhile, in a small saucepan cook onion in margarine or butter till tender but not brown. Stir in flour and pepper. Add ⅔ *cup* milk all at once. Cook and stir till thickened and bubbly; cook and stir for 1 minute more. Stir in cheese till melted. Serve as directed.

***Nutrition information per serving:*** *315 cal., 43 g pro., 6 g carbo., 12 g fat, 116 mg chol., 427 mg sodium, 425 mg potassium, 1 g dietary fiber. U.S. RDA: 15% thiamine, 16% riboflavin, 81% niacin, 17% calcium.*

## TOMATO COD FILLETS

*Be sure to check for doneness at the earliest recommended cooking time. When perfectly cooked, the fish will appear opaque and just flake with a fork—*

  1 **pound fresh *or* frozen skinned cod, monkfish, *or* pollack fillets**
  1 **tablespoon margarine *or* butter**
  1 **teaspoon lemon juice**
  ⅛ **teaspoon salt**
  ⅛ **teaspoon pepper**
  1 **cup quick-cooking rice**
  ¾ **cup water**
  ½ **teaspoon instant chicken bouillon granules**
  ¼ **teaspoon dried basil, crushed**
  2 **medium tomatoes, peeled, seeded, and finely chopped (1½ cups)**
  ⅓ **cup sliced green onion**
  2 **tablespoons grated Parmesan cheese**
**Curly endive**
**Grated Parmesan cheese**
**Lemon wedges (optional)**

Thaw fish, if frozen. (Do not thaw fillets in a low-wattage microwave oven. Instead, thaw in the refrigerator for several hours or overnight.) To thaw fillets in a high-wattage microwave oven, unwrap and place in an 8x8x2-inch microwave-safe baking dish. Cover with vented clear plastic wrap. Cook on 30% power (medium-low) for 6 to 8 minutes, giving the dish a quarter-turn and separating the fish after 3 minutes. Let stand for 10 minutes. The fish should be pliable and cold on the outside, but still slightly icy in the thick center areas. Rinse and pat dry.

In a 1-cup glass measure combine margarine or butter, lemon juice, salt, and pepper. Micro-cook on 100% power (high) for 30 to 40 seconds or till margarine is melted. Set aside.

Meanwhile, in an 8x8x2-inch microwave-safe baking dish combine rice, water, bouillon granules, and basil. Spread evenly in bottom of dish. Cover with vented clear plastic wrap. Cook on high for 2 minutes (low-wattage microwave ovens: 2½ minutes). Stir in tomatoes, green onion, and the 2 tablespoons cheese. Spread evenly in dish.

Arrange fish fillets on top of the rice mixture, with the thicker portions toward the edges of the dish. Turn under any thin portions of fillets to obtain an even thickness of about ½ inch. Drizzle margarine mixture over fish. Cover with vented clear plastic wrap.

Cook on high for 6 to 8 minutes (low-wattage microwave ovens: 7 to 9 minutes) or just till the fish flakes with a fork, giving the dish a half-turn after 3 minutes.

Arrange fillets and rice over curly endive on dinner plates. Sprinkle top of fish lightly with additional Parmesan cheese. If desired, serve fish with lemon wedges. Makes 4 servings.

***Conventional directions:*** Thaw fish, if frozen. In a medium saucepan combine water, bouillon granules, and basil. Bring to boiling; stir in rice. Remove from heat. Cover and let stand for 5 minutes or till liquid is absorbed.

Meanwhile, in a small saucepan melt the margarine or butter. Stir in lemon juice, salt, and pepper. Set aside.

Stir tomatoes, green onion, and 2 tablespoons Parmesan cheese into rice. Spread evenly in a greased 8x8x2-inch baking dish.

Arrange fillets atop rice as directed. Drizzle with margarine mixture. Cover with foil. Bake in a 350° oven for 25 to 30 minutes or just till fish flakes with a fork. Serve as directed.

***Nutrition information per serving:*** *238 cal., 24 g pro., 23 g carbo., 5 g fat, 51 mg chol., 273 mg sodium, 627 mg potassium, 2 g dietary fiber. U.S. RDA: 18% vit. A, 13% vit. C, 16% thiamine, 17% niacin.*

## BACON-MUSHROOM CHICKEN

2 whole large chicken
   breasts, skinned, boned,
   and halved lengthwise
½ cup finely chopped mushrooms
1 tablespoon finely snipped
   parsley
2 tablespoons margarine *or*
   butter, softened
6 slices Canadian-style
   bacon, halved
2 tablespoons finely
   chopped green onion
1 tablespoon margarine *or* butter
1 tablespoon all-purpose flour
Dash pepper
½ cup milk
½ cup shredded cheddar *or*
   American cheese (2 ounces)
4 slices rye bread

Rinse chicken; pat dry. Place 1 chicken breast half, boned side up, between 2 pieces of clear plastic wrap. Working from center to edges, pound lightly with the flat side of a meat mallet to form a rectangle about ¼ inch thick. Remove plastic wrap. Repeat with remaining chicken.

In a small bowl combine mushrooms, parsley, and the 2 tablespoons margarine or butter.

Place 3 bacon halves atop each chicken breast half. Spoon *one-fourth* of the mushroom mixture over bacon on *each* breast half. Fold in sides and roll up each breast half, starting with a narrow end. Secure with wooden toothpicks or nonmetallic skewers.

Arrange chicken rolls, seam side down, in a microwave-safe 8-inch round baking dish. Cover with vented clear plastic wrap.

Micro-cook on 100% power (high) for 6 to 8 minutes (low-wattage ovens: 7 to 9 minutes) or till chicken is tender and no pink remains, giving the dish a half-turn and rearranging the rolls after 4 minutes. Remove toothpicks. Cover to keep warm.

For sauce, in a 2-cup glass measure combine green onion and the 1 tablespoon margarine or butter. Cook, uncovered, on high for 30 to 40 seconds or till margarine is melted. Stir in flour and pepper. Stir in milk. Cook, uncovered, on high for 2 to 3 minutes or till thickened and bubbly, stirring after every minute till sauce starts to thicken,

then stirring every 30 seconds. Stir in cheese; cook, uncovered, on high for 30 seconds or till cheese melts, stirring once.

Slice each chicken roll and place atop a slice of rye bread. Serve sauce over chicken. Makes 4 servings.

*Conventional directions:* Pound and stuff chicken breasts as directed. Place, seam side down, in a 10x6x2-inch baking dish. Bake, uncovered, in a 350° oven for 25 to 30 minutes or till tender and no pink remains. Remove toothpicks. Meanwhile, in a small saucepan cook onion in margarine or butter till tender but not brown. Stir in flour and pepper. Add ⅔ *cup* milk all at once. Cook and stir till thickened and bubbly; cook and stir for 1 minute more. Stir in cheese till melted. Serve as directed.

*Nutrition information per serving:* *467 cal., 50 g pro., 18 g carbo., 21 g fat, 132 mg chol., 915 mg sodium, 563 mg potassium, 2 g dietary fiber. U.S. RDA: 13% vit. A, 10% vit. C, 30% thiamine, 24% riboflavin, 95% niacin, 18% calcium, 14% iron.*

## HERBED PEPPER RED SNAPPER

*Red sweet peppers and dried fines herbes add flavor to this quick entrée—*

1 pound fresh *or* frozen
   skinned red snapper *or*
   orange roughy fillets
1 tablespoon margarine *or* butter
1 teaspoon lemon juice
⅛ teaspoon salt
⅛ teaspoon pepper
1 cup quick-cooking rice
¾ cup water
½ teaspoon instant chicken
   bouillon granules
¼ teaspoon fines herbes
2 small yellow, green, red,
   *or* purple sweet
   peppers, chopped
⅓ cup sliced green onion
2 tablespoons grated
   Parmesan cheese
Sliced green onion tops (optional)
Orange slices (optional)

Thaw fish, if frozen. (Do not thaw fillets in a low-wattage microwave oven. Instead, thaw in the refrigerator for several hours or overnight.) To thaw fillets in a high-wattage microwave oven, unwrap and place in an 8x8x2-inch microwave-safe baking dish. Cover with vented clear plastic wrap. Cook on 30%

power (medium-low) for 6 to 8 minutes, giving the dish a quarter-turn and separating the fish after 3 minutes. Let stand for 10 minutes. The fish should be pliable and cold on the outside, but still slightly icy in the thick center areas. Rinse and pat dry.

In a 1-cup glass measure combine margarine or butter, lemon juice, salt, and pepper. Micro-cook on 100% power (high) for 30 to 40 seconds or till margarine is melted. Set aside.

Meanwhile, in a microwave-safe 8x8x2-inch baking dish combine rice, water, bouillon granules, and fines herbes. Spread mixture evenly in bottom of dish. Cover with vented clear plastic wrap. Cook on high for 2 minutes (low-wattage ovens: 2½ minutes).

Stir in sweet peppers, green onion, and cheese; spread evenly in dish.

Arrange fish fillets on top of rice mixture with thicker portions toward edges of the dish. Turn under any thin portions of fillets to obtain an even thickness of about ½ inch. Drizzle melted margarine mixture over fish. Cover with vented clear plastic wrap.

Cook on high for 6 to 8 minutes (low-wattage ovens: 7 to 9 minutes) or just till fish flakes with a fork, giving the dish a half-turn after 3 minutes. If desired, sprinkle with green onion tops and garnish with oranges. Serves 4.

*Conventional directions:* Thaw fish, if frozen. In a medium saucepan combine water, bouillon granules, and fines herbes. Bring to boiling; stir in rice. Remove rice mixture from heat. Cover and let stand for 5 minutes or till the liquid is absorbed.

Meanwhile, in a small saucepan melt the margarine or butter. Stir in the lemon juice, salt, and pepper. Set mixture aside.

Stir sweet peppers, green onion, and Parmesan cheese into the rice mixture. Spread the mixture evenly in a greased 8x8x2-inch baking dish.

Arrange fillets atop rice as directed. Drizzle margarine mixture over fish. Cover with foil and bake in a 350° oven for 25 to 30 minutes or just till fish flakes with a fork. Serve as directed.

*Nutrition information per serving:* *257 cal., 27 g pro., 23 g carbo., 6 g fat, 45 mg chol., 279 mg sodium, 577 mg potassium, 1 g dietary fiber. U.S. RDA: 58% vit. C, 13% thiamine.*

## TURKEY MOLE

1 pound ground raw turkey
1 stalk celery, sliced (½ cup)
¼ cup chopped onion
1 clove garlic, minced
1 8-ounce can whole kernel
   corn, drained
3 tablespoons all-purpose flour
2 teaspoons unsweetened
   cocoa powder
1½ to 2 teaspoons chili powder
1 teaspoon sugar
¼ teaspoon salt
¼ teaspoon pepper
⅛ teaspoon apple pie spice
1¼ cups beef broth
Tortilla chips
Dairy sour cream
Chopped tomato

In a 1½- or 2-quart microwave-safe casserole crumble turkey. Add celery, onion, and garlic.

Micro-cook, covered, on 100% power (high) for 6 to 8 minutes (low-wattage
ovens: 8 to 10 minutes) or till no pink
remains and onion is tender, stirring
once. Drain off fat.

Stir in corn, flour, cocoa powder,
chili powder, sugar, salt, pepper, and
apple pie spice. Stir in broth.

Cook, uncovered, on high for 6 to 8
minutes (low-wattage ovens: 8 to 10
minutes) or till thickened and bubbly,
stirring every 2 minutes (low-wattage
ovens: stirring after 4 minutes, then after every 2 minutes). Cook for 1 minute
more (low-wattage ovens: 2 minutes).

Place a fourth of the turkey mixture and tortilla chips in *each* of 4 individual casseroles. Top with sour cream
and chopped tomato. If desired, serve
with avocado slices. Serves 4.

***Conventional directions:*** In a
large skillet cook turkey, celery, onion,
and garlic in 1 tablespoon *cooking oil*
till no pink remains and vegetables are
tender. Drain off fat. Stir in corn, flour,
cocoa powder, chili powder, sugar, salt,
pepper, and apple pie spice. Stir in beef
broth. Cook and stir till thickened and
bubbly; cook and stir for 1 minute
more. Serve as directed.

***Nutrition information per serving:***
*339 cal., 29 g pro., 24 g carbo., 14 g fat, 90
mg chol., 688 mg sodium, 484 mg potassium, 2 g dietary fiber. U.S. RDA: 13%
vit. A, 10% thiamine, 17% riboflavin,
31% niacin, 12% calcium, 18% iron.*

## LAMB CURRY

1 pound ground lamb
1 stalk celery, sliced (½ cup)
¼ cup chopped onion
1 clove garlic, minced
¼ cup all-purpose flour
3 to 4 teaspoons curry powder
2 teaspoons instant chicken
   bouillon granules
¼ teaspoon pepper
1 medium apple, cored and
   coarsely chopped (1 cup)
1 cup water
1 cup milk
⅓ cup raisins
Salt
Hot cooked couscous
Sliced kumquat (optional)
Peanuts (optional)
Shaved coconut (optional)

In a 2-quart microwave-safe casserole
crumble lamb. Add celery, onion, and
garlic.

Micro-cook, covered, on 100% power (high) for 5 to 7 minutes (low-wattage
ovens: 7 to 9 minutes) or till no pink
remains and celery and onion are
tender, stirring once. Drain off fat.

Stir in flour, curry powder, bouillon granules, and pepper. Then stir in
apple, water, milk, and raisins.

Cook, uncovered, on high for 8 to
10 minutes (low-wattage ovens: 12 to 14
minutes) or till thickened and bubbly,
stirring after every minute (low-wattage ovens: stirring after 4 minutes,
then every 2 minutes). Cook for 1 minute more (low-wattage ovens: 2 minutes
more). Season to taste with salt.

Serve over couscous. If desired,
garnish with kumquat slices and pass
peanuts and coconut to sprinkle atop.
Makes 4 servings.

***Conventional directions:*** In a
large skillet cook lamb, celery, onion,
and garlic till no pink remains and vegetables are tender. Drain off fat. Stir in
flour, curry powder, bouillon granules,
and pepper. Add apple, water, milk,
and raisins. Cook and stir till thickened
and bubbly; cook and stir for 1 minute
more. Serve as directed.

***Nutrition information per serving:***
*359 cal., 27 g pro., 48 g carbo., 6 g fat, 71
mg chol., 346 mg sodium, 529 mg potassium, 5 g dietary fiber. U.S. RDA: 18%
thiamine, 22% riboflavin, 27% niacin,
12% calcium, 18% iron.*

## BEEF ITALIANO

1 pound lean ground beef
1 stalk celery, sliced (½ cup)
¼ cup finely chopped onion
1 clove garlic, minced
1 tablespoon all-purpose flour
1 teaspoon sugar
½ teaspoon dried Italian seasoning
¼ teaspoon pepper
⅛ teaspoon salt
1 15-ounce can tomato sauce
½ of a red *or* green sweet
   pepper, cut into strips
¼ cup dry red wine
Hot cooked fettuccine
4 sprigs cilantro (optional)
Grated Parmesan cheese

In a 1½-quart microwave-safe casserole crumble beef. Add celery, onion,
and garlic.

Micro-cook, covered, on 100% power (high) for 4 to 6 minutes (low-wattage
ovens: 6 to 7 minutes) or till no pink
remains and onion is tender, stirring
once. Drain off fat.

Stir in flour, sugar, dried Italian
seasoning, pepper, and salt. Add tomato sauce, sweet pepper, and wine.

Cook, uncovered, on high for 5 to 6
minutes (low-wattage ovens: 7 to 9 minutes) or till thickened and bubbly, stirring every 2 minutes (low-wattage
ovens: stirring after 4 minutes, then every 2 minutes). Cook for 1 minute more
(low-wattage ovens: 2 minutes more).

Serve over hot cooked fettuccine
that has been twisted into nests with a
long-tined fork. If desired, garnish with
sprigs of cilantro. Pass grated Parmesan cheese. Makes 4 servings.

***Conventional directions:*** In a
large skillet cook ground beef, celery,
onion, and garlic till no pink remains
and vegetables are tender. Drain off
fat. Stir in flour, sugar, Italian seasoning, pepper, and salt. Add tomato
sauce, sweet pepper, and wine. Cook
and stir till thickened and bubbly; cook
and stir for 1 minute more. Serve meat
mixture as directed.

***Nutrition information per serving:***
*477 cal., 34 g pro., 56 g carbo., 12 g fat, 82
mg chol., 839 mg sodium, 875 mg potassium, 2 g dietary fiber. U.S. RDA: 39%
vit. A, 52% vit. C, 46% thiamine, 30%
riboflavin, 50% niacin, 10% calcium,
34% iron.*

# MELONS!

## GRAND WAYS TO ENJOY THESE LUSCIOUS, JUICY FRUITS

### By Barbara Johnson

**M**elons take the award as one of the season's best buys. These wonderfully juicy and sweet fruits are low in calories and high in vitamins, especially vitamins A and C. Take advantage of the peak melon supply available now for these recipes.

## MELON AND BERRIES A LA CRÈME

*For a fancy presentation, scoop out balls of melon, then hollow out the melon half. Serve the balls in the melon half with crème and blueberries atop—*

- 1 **8-ounce package Neufchâtel cheese, softened***
- ¾ **cup orange *or* lemon yogurt**
- 1 **small melon *or* ½ of a large melon (*except* watermelon), peeled, seeded, and cut into 4 wedges**
- 1 **to 2 tablespoons milk (optional)**

**Fresh blueberries**

For crème, in a small mixer bowl beat Neufchâtel cheese and yogurt till smooth. Cover and chill several hours.

To serve, loosen melon from rind with sharp knife, leaving melon in a wedge shape. Replace melon in rind; cut each melon wedge crosswise into quarters. If necessary, stir milk into crème to thin mixture. Spoon over melon wedges. Sprinkle with blueberries. Makes 4 servings.

***Note:*** To soften Neufchâtel cheese in your microwave oven, unwrap and place on a microwave-safe plate. Microcook, uncovered, on 100% power (high) for 15 to 20 seconds or till softened.

*Nutrition information per serving: 223 cal., 8 g pro., 17 g carbo., 14 g fat, 45 mg chol., 260 mg sodium, 369 mg potassium, 1 g dietary fiber. U.S. RDA: 57% vit. A, 49% vit. C, 12% riboflavin, 12% calcium.*

Pick your favorite melon for these easy, refreshing recipes.

PHOTOGRAPHS: SCOTT LITTLE

## IDENTIFYING DIFFERENT MELON VARIETIES

**Cantaloupe**
This melon has a fragrant orange pulp encased in a raised, netted tan rind.

**Crenshaw**
The gold-skinned crenshaw melon is large (about the size of a bowling ball) and smooth. It has a pale orange pulp.

**Honeydew**
Smooth yellow-green skin and a pale green pulp are trademarks of the honeydew melon.

## MELON MOUSSE

*The delicate flavor of the melon stands out in this pastel dessert. The color will be a pale green or pale orange depending on which variety of melon you choose—*

- 2 **cups cubed melon (*except* watermelon)**
- ½ **cup orange juice**
- 2 **tablespoons sugar**
- 1 **envelope unflavored gelatin**
- ¾ **cup whipping cream**

• • •

**Fresh mint sprigs (optional)**

In a blender container or a food processor bowl combine melon and orange juice. Cover and blend or process till smooth.

In a small saucepan combine sugar and gelatin. Stir in the melon puree. Cook and stir over medium heat till gelatin and sugar are dissolved. Chill till partially set (the consistency of unbeaten egg whites).

In a small mixer bowl beat whipping cream till soft peaks form. Gently fold whipped cream into melon mixture till combined. Spoon into 6 dessert dishes. Cover and chill for 3 to 24 hours or till firm. Top each dessert with a fresh mint sprig just before serving. Makes 6 servings.

*Nutrition information per serving: 151 cal., 2 g pro., 12 g carbo., 11 g fat, 41 mg chol., 17 mg sodium, 227 mg potassium, 1 g dietary fiber. U.S. RDA: 43% vit. A, 51% vit. C.*

## SHOPPING/SERVING TIPS

- Although you'll find some melons year-round, midsummer to early-fall months bring you melons that taste better and cost less.
- Choose melons that smell sweet and feel heavy for their size.
- Melons taste best when served slightly chilled.

THE MAGAZINE FOR AMERICAN FAMILIES

# Better Homes and Gardens

OCTOBER 1988
●$1.50

THE ART OF ARRANGING DRIED FLOWERS

SPRING BLOOMS TO PLANT NOW

**Welcome-Home Rooms**
*Decorating Ideas You'll Love*

**COAST-TO-COAST NEW DREAM HOUSES UNDER $125,000**

**DECORATORS' ALMANAC**
•TREASURES
•TRENDS
•TIPS

**NEW-STYLE ENTERTAINING**
•MENU
•RECIPES

# TASTY TIMESAVING ENTRÉES
## FIX AND FREEZE; HEAT AND EAT

By Joy Taylor

**S**tock your freezer with these delicious make-ahead entrées. Each recipe gives you several single-serving meals to freeze now and enjoy later. You'll have the satisfaction of knowing you have quality, home-made meals at your fingertips.

## CREAMY PORK CHOP DINNER

*Dinner's ready in as little as six minutes when you micro-reheat—*

- 4 pork loin rib chops, cut ½ inch thick (1¼ to 1½ pounds)
- 1 tablespoon cooking oil
- 1 cup sliced fresh mushrooms
- 1 green onion, thinly sliced
- 1¼ cups milk
- 1 tablespoon cornstarch
- ½ teaspoon garlic salt
- ¼ teaspoon dried rosemary, crushed
- ½ of a 3-ounce package cream cheese, cut up
- 2 tablespoons dry white wine
- 1 9-ounce package frozen French-style green beans, thawed and well drained

Season chops with *salt* and *pepper*. In a skillet cook chops in hot oil 8 to 10 minutes on *each* side or till no pink remains. Remove from skillet, reserving drippings; drain chops on paper towels.

For sauce, cook mushrooms and onion in reserved drippings till tender. Stir together milk, cornstarch, garlic salt, rosemary, and ⅛ teaspoon *pepper*; add all at once to mushroom mixture. Cook and stir till thickened and bubbly. Cook and stir 1 minute more. Stir in cream cheese till melted. Remove from heat. Stir in wine. Stir *1 cup* of the sauce into beans. Divide bean mixture among 4 shallow individual baking or au gratin dishes. Top *each* with *one* chop. Spoon remaining sauce atop. Wrap in moisture- and vaporproof wrap; seal, label, and freeze. Makes 4 single-serving entrées.

***Conventional reheating:*** Unwrap entrée(s). Bake, covered, in a 375° oven for 50 to 55 minutes.

**A FLAVORFUL MUSHROOM SAUCE** makes this dinner special.

**ZESTY SALSA** jazzes up corn- and cheese-filled shells.

***Microwave reheating:*** Unwrap *one* entrée. Micro-cook, covered with waxed paper or vented plastic wrap, on 70% power (medium-high) [low-wattage oven: 100% power (high)] for 6 to 8 minutes or till heated through, giving dish a half-turn once.

***Nutrition information per serving:*** *360 cal., 29 g pro., 11 g carbo., 21 g fat, 97 mg chol., 403 mg sodium, 648 mg potassium, 2 g dietary fiber. U.S. RDA: 56% thiamine, 32% riboflavin, 28% niacin.*

## HERBED CHEESE MANICOTTI

- 6 manicotti
- 1 beaten egg
- 1 cup shredded Monterey Jack cheese (4 ounces)
- ¾ cup ricotta cheese
- ½ cup loose-pack frozen whole kernel corn
- 1 2-ounce can mushroom stems and pieces, drained
- 2 tablespoons chopped green pepper
- 1 tablespoon snipped fresh chives
- 1½ cups salsa
- ½ teaspoon garlic powder
- ¼ teaspoon dried Italian seasoning

Cook manicotti according to package directions. Drain. Rinse with cold water. Drain well; set aside.

In a medium mixing bowl combine egg, ½ cup Monterey Jack cheese, all of the ricotta cheese, corn, mushrooms, green pepper, and chives. Spoon about ¼ cup of the cheese mixture into *each* manicotti. Place *2* manicotti in *each* of 3 greased shallow individual au gratin or baking dishes; set aside.

In a small bowl combine salsa, garlic powder, and Italian seasoning. Spoon a *third* of the salsa mixture over manicotti in *each* dish. Sprinkle with remaining cheese. Wrap in moisture- and vaporproof wrap; seal, label, and freeze. Makes 3 single-serving entrées.

***Conventional reheating:*** Unwrap entrée(s). Bake, covered, in a 375° oven for 60 minutes or till heated through.

***Microwave reheating:*** Unwrap *one* entrée. Micro-cook, covered with waxed paper or vented plastic wrap, on 70% power (medium-high) for 9 to 11 minutes or till heated through, giving dish a half-turn once. [Low-wattage ovens: 100% power (high) for 10 to 12 minutes or till heated through, giving dish a half-turn once.]

***Nutrition information per serving:*** *445 cal., 24 g pro., 44 g carbo., 19 g fat, 144 mg chol., 1,184 mg sodium, 555 mg potassium, 3 g dietary fiber. U.S. RDA: 25% vit. A, 26% vit. C, 28% thiamine, 31% riboflavin, 14% niacin, 52% calcium, 17% iron.*

# SHARING WITH FRIENDS

## A NEW-STYLE DINNER PARTY FOR SIX

By Joy Taylor and Barbara Johnson

**MENU**

HORS D'OEUVRES
**Aperitifs**
**Seafood Sampler**

•

SALAD
**Stir-Fried Beef over Warm Greens**

•

LIGHT ENTRÉE
**Chinese Steamer Basket**

•

SWEET FINALE
**Your Just Desserts**
**Coffee**
**Cordials**

Tⁿhe mood is casual, the food is great, and everyone helps with the cooking.

Sharing the work is sharing the fun in today's dinner parties. The food is lighter than in years gone by, quicker to put together, and tastier. Also, everyone gets to take home a few luscious leftovers.

We invite you to share, on the following pages, in such a dinner party. Feast your eyes on the food, and take our ideas for your own. Then invite your friends to join in your best dinner party ever.

Photographs: Perry Struse
Food stylist: Janet Herwig
Field editor: Mary Didio

# THE HORS D'OEUVRES AND SALAD

"For us, friends, food, and fun are a winning trio. With friends in the house and food on the counter, we know it's time for fun."

Share the work and it's a party! Rick and Ann often call friends to come over, cook along, and have a good time. With some planning and a bit of make-ahead, the evening comes off without a hitch. Their friends bring the makings for a couple of the special dishes, and Rick and Ann greet them with an assortment of hors d'oeuvres.

The salad: Stir-Fried Beef over Warm Greens. Gather a striking blend of greens, then wilt ever so slightly with sizzling sirloin and red peppers.

Rick and Ann mastermind the salad as others shape bundles for the next course. Aperitifs and Seafood Sampler—a deep-sea harvest of Shrimp Vinaigrette, oysters on the half shell, and steamed clams and mussels—are set out so all can sip and nibble while they work.

# THE LIGHT ENTREE

*"For us, cooking is as much fun as eating."*

● **CHINESE FLOWER ROLLS**
To make the indentation in each roll, press a chopstick in the center of the top, parallel to the cut edges. Press firmly so edges fan out.

● **HOISIN PORK BUNS**
Bring edges of dough up around filling, stretching dough a little till edges *just* meet. Pinch to seal.

● **CHICKEN POT STICKERS**
Fold dough in half over filling. Pleat one edge of dough to smoothly fit against opposite edge of dough. Pinch edges to seal.

Line dinner plates with variegated ti leaves to serve as the stylish backdrop for Chinese Flower Rolls, Hoisin Pork Buns, and Chicken Pot Stickers. All three delicious bundles will be ready to come out of the steamer basket just as you clear away the salad plates and pour another round of wine.

# THE SWEET FINALE

"As we're relaxing after one of these fabulous meals, someone invariably asks, 'When can we do this again?'"

● **CHOCOLATE HAZELNUT TORTE**
Any dessert worth eating has to be chocolate! With chocolate on the bottom, white chocolate on top, and hazelnuts in between, this is like nutty fudge!

● **SPICED FRUIT DIAMONDS**
This fruit-filled, honey-drenched dessert is created in the image of classic Greek baklava. It's golden, tender, flaky, and fantastic!

● **CRANBERRY MOUSSE**
Ah, mousse—you know it's light, airy, rich. This cranberry version is guaranteed to lift your spirits. Drizzle with a lush raspberry sauce.

Time for Your Just Desserts! Savor a tasting of each of the three luscious desserts along with your choice of fresh-brewed coffee, after-dinner liqueurs, and spirits. (P.S. There's enough of the Chocolate Hazelnut Torte and Spiced Fruit Diamonds for everyone to take some home, too!)

# GETTING IT TOGETHER

"It doesn't take a lot of effort to put one of these dinner parties together because everyone participates."

## WHO DOES WHAT

**Picture yourself enjoying a pleasant evening with your friends and this fabulous dinner. Here are a few suggestions for making these good times roll.**

● This new-style dinner party serves six adults. So that everyone gets in on the planning and cooking, divvy up the recipes and the grocery shopping for the meal.

● The host couple provides the aperitifs and Seafood Sampler plus one of the desserts.

● Another couple volunteers to bring the vegetables, meat, and other makings for the salad course plus another of the desserts.

● The third couple brings what's needed for the Chinese Steamer Basket and Autumn Fruit Platter plus the remaining dessert.

● Each couple contributes a bottle of wine or liqueur.

### BONUS
## THE FEAST LIVES ON

In creating these recipes, we built in extra servings so guests can carry home a selection of classy leftovers to enjoy later. (Pack up the portions and chill at once.) Each couple takes:
2 Hoisin Pork Buns
2 Chinese Flower Rolls
4 Chicken Pot Stickers
Sake Dipping Sauce
Hot 'n' Sour Plum Sauce
2 servings Spiced Fruit Diamonds
2 servings Chocolate Hazelnut Torte

## HOW THE MEAL UNFOLDS

● **Hors d'oeuvres.** Once your guests arrive, head straight to your kitchen, and let the care-free cooking begin! The elegant evening starts with Seafood Sampler that you set out on the kitchen counter or table for nibbling as you go. Offer dry sherry and vermouth for sipping.

● **Salad.** For Stir-Fried Beef over Warm Greens, enlist two friends to chop vegetables, clean the greens, and stir-fry the already marinated beef. The four remaining cooks are in no way jobless: They create the three-tiered Chinese Steamer Basket. Read on!

● **Light entrée.** Filling and shaping these three tasty nibbles as a team builds party esprit de corps. Set up an assembly line, if you like. Start with the Chinese Flower Rolls, move on to the Hoisin Pork Buns, and wind up with the Chicken Pot Stickers. All three are quite easy because the dough and fillings are made ahead. Let the precious bundles steam while you sit down to enjoy the salad.

● **Sweet finale.** This last course is proof positive that your good planning pays off. Because you and your guests made all the sweet treats pre-party, you need only to pull out dessert plates, serve, and enjoy!

## HORS D'OEUVRES
### SEAFOOD SAMPLER
*Make the shrimp, oysters, and dipping sauces ahead. Steam the mussels and clams just before party time—*

**Perfect to munch on while everyone joins in the fun of cooking.**

 1  recipe Shrimp Vinaigrette
12  oysters in shells
 1  recipe Easy Tomato Dipper
 1  recipe Fresh Horseradish Sauce
 ● ● ●
12  clams in shells
12  mussels in shells
 4  quarts cold water
⅓  cup salt
    Lettuce leaves

**AHEAD**

●**Prepare** Shrimp Vinaigrette. Cover and chill.

●**To clean oysters,** scrub the shells under cold running water. For easier shucking, chill before opening.

●**To open oysters,** hold an oyster in an oven mitt with the flat side up. Using a strong-bladed oyster knife with a hand guard, insert the knife tip into the hinge between the shells. Twisting the blade to pry open the oyster, move the blade along the inside of the upper shell to free the muscle from the shell.

*To order a wok, steamer, seafood forks, or springform dessert pan, see page*

# October

## SEAFOOD SAMPLER

*Make the shrimp, oysters, and dipping sauces ahead. Steam the mussels and clams just before party time—*

Shrimp Vinaigrette (see recipe, right)
12 oysters in shells
Easy Tomato Dipper (see recipe, far right)
Fresh Horseradish Sauce (see recipe, far right)
12 clams in shells
12 mussels in shells
4 quarts cold water
Lettuce leaves

Prepare the Shrimp Vinaigrette. Cover and chill.

To clean oysters, scrub the shells under cold running water. For easier shucking, chill before opening.

To open oysters, hold an oyster in an oven mitt with the flat side up. Using a strong-bladed oyster knife with a hand guard, insert the knife tip into the hinge between the shells. Twisting the blade to pry open the oyster, move the blade along the inside of the upper shell to free the muscle from the shell.

Remove and discard the top shell of the oyster. Slide the knife under the oyster to sever muscle from the bottom shell. Discard any bits of shell on the oyster. Replace oyster muscle in the bottom shell for serving on the half shell. Cover and chill.

Prepare Easy Tomato Dipper. Cover and chill.

Prepare grated horseradish mixture for Fresh Horseradish Sauce. Cover and chill.

Scrub clam and mussel shells under cold running water, using a stiff brush. With your fingers, pull out mussel beards visible between shells.

In an 8-quart Dutch oven combine the cold water and ⅓ cup *salt*. Add the clams and the mussels. Soak for 15 minutes; drain and rinse. Discard the water. Repeat this soaking, draining, and rinsing 2 more times.

In the same Dutch oven add water to a depth of ½ inch; bring to boiling. Place the clams and the mussels in a steamer basket; place in the Dutch oven. Steam, covered, about 5 minutes or till shells open. Discard any unopened shells. Cool slightly.

Finish preparing the Fresh Horseradish Sauce.

Arrange Shrimp Vinaigrette, oysters on the half shell, steamed clams, and steamed mussels on lettuce-lined platter. Serve with the Easy Tomato Dipper and Fresh Horseradish Sauce. Makes 6 appetizer servings.

*Nutrition information per serving:* *374 cal., 18 g pro., 27 g carbo., 22 g fat, 117 mg chol., 819 mg sodium, 566 mg potassium, 1 g dietary fiber. U.S. RDA: 17% vit. A, 25% vit. C, 11% riboflavin, 11% niacin, 11% calcium, 49% iron.*

## SHRIMP VINAIGRETTE

*Sun-dried tomatoes enhance the flavor of this exquisite appetizer. They are available both dried and packed in oil. Look for them in the Italian or gourmet section of your grocery store. Either kind will work in this recipe—*

12 ounces fresh *or* frozen jumbo shrimp in shells
⅓ cup salad oil
¼ cup white wine vinegar
2 teaspoons snipped fresh tarragon *or* ¾ teaspoon dried tarragon, crushed
1 teaspoon sugar
1 teaspoon Dijon-style mustard
1 clove garlic, minced
¼ teaspoon salt
2 tablespoons snipped sun-dried tomatoes

Peel and devein shrimp, leaving tails intact. In a large saucepan bring *lightly salted water* to boiling. Add shrimp; return to boiling. Boil gently for 1 to 2 minutes or till the shrimp turn pink. Drain.

Meanwhile, in a small mixing bowl use a wire whisk or a fork to stir together oil, vinegar, tarragon, sugar, mustard, garlic, and salt. Add hot shrimp and tomatoes; toss to coat. Cover and chill in the refrigerator for several hours or overnight.

Use a slotted spoon to transfer the shrimp to a serving platter. Makes 6 appetizer servings.

*Nutrition information per serving:* *158 cal., 8 g pro., 3 g carbo., 13 g fat, 59 mg chol., 173 mg sodium, and 126 mg potassium.*

## EASY TOMATO DIPPER

½ cup chutney
½ cup cocktail sauce
2 tablespoons lemon juice
1 tablespoon finely chopped green onion *or* snipped chives
Several dashes to ¼ teaspoon bottled hot pepper sauce

Place chutney in a medium mixing bowl. With kitchen shears snip any large pieces. Stir in cocktail sauce, lemon juice, green onion, and hot pepper sauce. Cover and chill in the refrigerator for several hours or overnight. Serve with Seafood Sampler. Makes about 1 cup sauce.

*Nutrition information per 2 tablespoons:* *56 cal., 0 g pro., 14 g carbo., 0 g fat, 0 mg chol., 234 mg sodium, 97 mg potassium.*

## FRESH HORSERADISH SAUCE

*Heating the grated horseradish mixture tones down the bite a bit—*

3 to 4 ounces fresh horseradish, peeled and coarsely chopped (½ to ¾ cup)
⅓ cup water
2 tablespoons white-wine Worcestershire sauce
½ teaspoon salt
⅛ teaspoon pepper
½ cup whipping cream
Snipped chives

In a blender container or food processor bowl combine the horseradish, water, Worcestershire sauce, salt, and pepper. Cover; blend or process till finely grated. (The mixture will not be smooth.)

In a small saucepan cook and stir horseradish mixture just till heated through. (*Do not* boil.) Cool. Cover and chill for several hours or overnight.

In a small mixer bowl beat whipping cream with an electric mixer till soft peaks form. Fold whipped cream into horseradish mixture. Sprinkle with chives. Serve with the Seafood Sampler. Makes about 1½ cups sauce.

*Nutrition information per 2 tablespoons:* *42 cal., 0 g pro., 2 g carbo., 4 g fat, 14 mg chol., 122 mg sodium, 48 mg potassium.*

## STIR-FRIED BEEF OVER WARM GREENS

- ¾ **pound boneless beef sirloin steak** *or* **pork tenderloin, cut 1 inch thick**
- 1 **8-ounce bottle (1 cup) oil-and-vinegar salad dressing**
- 2 **tablespoons dry sherry**
- 2 **tablespoons soy sauce**
- 1 **tablespoon brown sugar**
- ½ **teaspoon bottled minced garlic**
- ⅛ **teaspoon ground ginger**
- 12 **cups torn mixed greens**
- 1½ **cups sliced fresh shittake** *or* **straw mushrooms**
- ½ **cup sliced green onions**
- 1 **tablespoon olive oil**
- 1 **large sweet red pepper, cut into thin strips**

Partially freeze meat. Thinly slice across the grain into bite-size strips.

For marinade, in a small bowl stir together salad dressing, sherry, soy sauce, brown sugar, garlic, and ginger.

To marinate meat, place meat in a large plastic bag; set in a deep bowl. Pour marinade over meat; close bag. Marinate in the refrigerator for 6 hours or overnight, turning bag occasionally to evenly distribute marinade.

In a large bowl toss together the greens, mushrooms, and green onions. Divide among 6 dinner plates; set aside.

Drain meat, reserving ⅔ cup of the marinade.

Preheat a wok or large skillet over high heat; add oil. (Add more oil as necessary.) Stir-fry sweet pepper in hot oil about 2 minutes or till crisp-tender. Remove from wok.

Add meat to hot wok. Stir-fry for 2 to 3 minutes or till tender. Add reserved marinade and sweet pepper. Cook and stir till heated through.

To serve, spoon the hot meat mixture over the plates of greens. Serve at once. Makes 6 servings.

***Nutrition information per serving:*** *342 cal., 15 g pro., 16 g carbo., 23 g fat, 32 mg chol., 904 mg sodium, 640 mg potassium, 3 g dietary fiber. U.S. RDA: 88% vit. A, 133% vit. C, 13% thiamine, 16% riboflavin, 19% niacin, 17% iron.*

## HOT 'N' SOUR PLUM SAUCE

*Prepare this spicy plum sauce ahead and serve it chilled with the steamed bundles—*

- 2 **12-ounce jars plum preserves**
- ⅔ **cup red wine vinegar**
- 1 **teaspoon instant chicken bouillon granules**
- 1 **teaspoon ground ginger**
- 1 **teaspoon crushed red pepper**
- 2 **cloves garlic, minced**
- 1 **tablespoon water**
- 2 **teaspoons cornstarch**

Cut up any large pieces of fruit in preserves.

In a small saucepan combine the preserves, vinegar, bouillon granules, ginger, red pepper, and garlic. Bring to boiling; reduce heat. Cover and simmer for 2 minutes. Stir water into cornstarch; add to the hot mixture. Cook and stir till mixture is slightly thickened and bubbly. Cook and stir for 2 minutes more. Remove from the heat; cool. Cover and chill for several hours or overnight. Makes 3 cups sauce.

***Nutrition information per ¼ cup:*** *160 cal., 0 g pro., 41 g carbo., 0 g fat, 0 mg chol., 38 mg sodium, 71 mg potassium.*

## SAKE DIPPING SAUCE

- 1½ **cups chicken broth**
- ⅔ **cup soy sauce**
- ½ **cup sake** *or* **dry sherry**
- 2 **teaspoons sugar**

In a small saucepan combine broth, soy sauce, sake, and sugar. Bring to boiling, stirring till sugar dissolves. Remove from heat; cool. Cover and chill for several hours or overnight.

Reheat sauce while Chinese bundles are steaming. Makes 2½ cups sauce.

***Nutrition information per 3 tablespoons:*** *29 cal., 2 g pro., 3 g carbo., 0 g fat, 0 mg chol., 929 mg sodium, 83 mg potassium.*

## BASIC YEAST DOUGH

*Just one recipe makes the dough for all three bundles: Chinese Flower Rolls, Hoisin Pork Buns, and Chicken Pot Stickers (see recipes, pages 135 and 136). If you chill the dough, punch it down and divide it into thirds just before dinner party time. If you have to transport the dough to the dinner party, be sure to count that time as part of the 30- to 35-minute standing time—*

- 4½ **to 4¾ cups all-purpose flour**
- 1 **package active dry yeast**
- 1½ **cups milk**
- ⅓ **cup cooking oil**
- 3 **tablespoons sugar**

In a large mixer bowl stir together *2 cups* of the all-purpose flour and the active dry yeast.

In a medium saucepan heat the milk, cooking oil, sugar, and ½ teaspoon *salt* just till warm (120° to 130°), stirring constantly. Add to the flour mixture. Beat with an electric mixer on low speed for ½ minute, scraping bowl constantly. Beat for 3 minutes on high speed. Using a spoon, stir in as much of the remaining flour as you can.

On a lightly floured surface knead in enough of the remaining flour to make a moderately stiff dough that is smooth and elastic (6 to 8 minutes total). Shape into a ball. Place in a lightly greased bowl; turn once to grease surface. Cover; chill in the refrigerator overnight. *Or,* cover the dough and let rise in a warm place till nearly double (about 1 hour). Punch dough down; divide into thirds. Cover and let rest for 10 minutes. Use to make Chinese Flower Rolls, Hoisin Pork Buns, and Chicken Pot Stickers.

## CHINESE FLOWER ROLLS

*When checking the steamed bundles for doneness, tilt the lid of the steamer away from you. This will allow the steam to escape without burning you—*

⅓ **recipe Basic Yeast Dough (see recipe, page 134)**
2 **teaspoons sesame oil *or* cooking oil**
1 **tablespoon finely snipped chives**
1 **tablespoon toasted sesame seed**

Let chilled Basic Yeast Dough stand at room temperature for 30 to 35 minutes.

On a lightly floured surface, roll half of the dough into an 8-inch square. Brush *half* of the oil over dough. Sprinkle with *half* of the chives and sesame seed. Roll up jelly-roll style; press long seam to seal. Cut into six 1¼-inch-wide rolls. Using a chopstick, make a deep indentation in the center of the top of each roll parallel to the cut edges. Press firmly till edges slightly fan out (see how-to photo, *below*). Repeat with the remaining dough, oil, chives, and sesame seed.

Cover and chill 6 of the rolls.

Using a 3-tier steamer, remove and grease the top basket. Place the remaining 6 rolls that you didn't chill on the greased basket so the sides do not touch. Cover and let the rolls rise in a warm place till nearly double (about 25 minutes).

Meanwhile, in the steamer bring the water to boiling over high heat. Steam the risen rolls, covered, on the top tier of the steamer about 12 minutes or till rolls spring back when touched. Serve the rolls warm. Repeat rising and steaming with chilled rolls. Makes 12 rolls. If desired, serve with an assortment of fresh fruit such as green or red grapes, carambola (star fruit), kiwi fruit, papaya, plums, and red or green pears.

**Reheating directions:** Wrap bundles in foil. Bake in a 375° oven for 10 minutes or till heated through.

*Nutrition information per roll: 95 cal., 2 g pro., 14 g carbo., 3 g fat, 1 mg chol., 36 mg sodium, 38 mg potassium, 1 g dietary fiber.*

## CHICKEN POT STICKERS

*Steam rather than fry this simplified version of pot stickers. You never have to fret over them sticking to the pot!*

12 **dried mushrooms (¾ cup)**
1 **whole medium chicken breast, skinned, boned, and finely chopped**
¼ **cup chopped green onions**
2 **tablespoons oyster sauce**
1½ **teaspoons cornstarch**
½ **teaspoon grated gingerroot**
⅓ **recipe Basic Yeast Dough (see recipe, page 134)**

In a small bowl soak mushrooms in enough *hot water* to cover for 30 minutes. Rinse and squeeze to drain thoroughly. Remove and discard the stems; finely chop mushrooms. Set aside.

For the filling, in a large mixing bowl stir together the drained and chopped mushrooms, chopped chicken, and chopped green onions. In a small bowl stir together the oyster sauce, cornstarch, and grated gingerroot. Add this mixture to the chicken mixture; mix well. Cover and chill in the refrigerator for up to 24 hours.

Let chilled dough stand at room temperature for 30 to 35 minutes.

Divide the dough into 24 portions. Roll each portion into a ball. On a well-floured surface roll or pat each ball into a 3-inch round. Spoon a *scant tablespoon* of the filling in the center of *each* round.

To shape *each* pot sticker, moisten the edge of the round with water. Fold round in half over filling, pleating 1 edge of the dough to fit smoothly against opposite edge; pinch edges to seal (see photo, *below*). Holding pot sticker sealed side up, press gently against surface to flatten bottom of pot sticker slightly. Cover 12 of the pot stickers; chill in the refrigerator.

Using a 3-tier steamer, remove and lightly grease the bottom rack. Place remaining 12 pot stickers on the greased rack of steamer so they do not touch one another. Cover; steam on bottom tier of steamer about 12 minutes or till chicken is no longer pink. (Cut into a pot sticker to check for doneness.) Repeat, steaming the remaining pot stickers. Makes 24 pot stickers.

If desired, serve with an assortment of fresh fruit, such as green or red grapes, carambola (star fruit), kiwi fruit, papaya, plums, and red or green pears.

**Reheating directions:** Wrap bundles in foil. Bake in a 375° oven for 10 minutes or till heated through.

*Nutrition information per pot sticker: 61 cal., 4 g pro., 8 g carbo., 1 g fat, 7 mg chol., 36 mg sodium, 69 mg potassium.*

## HOISIN PORK BUNS

*Shaping the fancy buns is just as much fun as eating them.*

- ¼ **pound ground pork**
- 2 **tablespoons finely chopped celery**
- 2 **tablespoons hoisin sauce**
- ⅓ **recipe Basic Yeast Dough (see recipe, page 134)**

For filling, in a small skillet cook pork and celery till no pink remains. Drain off fat. Stir in hoisin sauce. Cover and chill for up to 24 hours.

Let chilled dough stand at room temperature for 30 to 35 minutes.

Divide dough into 16 portions. Roll into balls; set *4* of the balls aside. On a lightly floured surface pat *each* of the 12 remaining balls into a 2½-inch circle, making center of circle thicker and edges of circle thinner. Spoon about *1 teaspoon* of the filling in the center of *each* circle. To shape *each* bun, bring edges of dough up around filling to center, stretching dough a little till edges *just* meet, forming a round ball. Pinch to seal (see photo, *below*).

For decorative ropes, divide each of the remaining 4 dough balls into 6 pieces. (You'll have 24 pieces total.) Roll *each* piece into a 3-inch rope. Twist *2* of the ropes together. Place over smooth side of each bun; tuck ends under.

Cover and chill 6 of the buns.

Using a 3-tier steamer, place remaining 6 buns, seam side down, on lightly greased middle rack of steamer so the sides do not touch. Cover and let rise in a warm place till nearly double (12 to 15 minutes).

Meanwhile, in steamer bring water to boiling. Steam buns, covered, on middle tier of steamer about 12 minutes or till buns spring back when touched. Repeat rising and steaming with chilled buns. Serve warm.

If desired, serve with an assortment of fresh fruit, such as green or red grapes, carambola (star fruit), kiwi fruit, papaya, plums, and red or green pears. Makes 12 buns.

**Reheating directions:** Wrap bundles in foil. Bake in a 375° oven for 10 minutes or till heated through.

*Nutrition information per bun:* *103 cal., 4 g pro., 14 g carbo., 3 g fat, 8 mg chol., 63 mg sodium, 72 mg potassium, and 1 g dietary fiber. U.S. RDA: 13% thiamine.*

## CHOCOLATE HAZELNUT TORTE

- ¾ **cup margarine *or* butter**
- 3 **squares (3 ounces) unsweetened chocolate**
- 1½ **cups packed brown sugar**
- 3 **eggs**
- 1 **teaspoon vanilla**
- 1 **cup all-purpose flour**
- ½ **cup coarsely chopped hazelnuts (filberts)**
- 6 **ounces vanilla-flavored confectioners' coating, coarsely chopped**
- 1 **tablespoon shortening**
- 1 **ounce chocolate-flavored confectioners' coating, coarsely chopped**
- ½ **teaspoon shortening**
- **Fresh strawberries (optional)**

Grease and flour the bottom of an 8-inch springform pan; set aside.

In a small saucepan melt margarine and unsweetened chocolate over low heat, stirring constantly. Remove from heat; cool slightly. Stir in brown sugar. Add eggs and vanilla. Lightly beat mixture by hand just till combined. (*Do not* overbeat or torte will rise during baking, then fall and crack.) Stir in flour. Spread mixture in prepared pan. Sprinkle with nuts.

Bake in a 350° oven for 40 to 45 minutes or till a slight imprint remains when touched in the center. Let cool slightly on a wire rack for 5 minutes. Loosen sides of torte with a knife. Remove sides of pan; cool completely.

In a heavy small saucepan melt the vanilla-flavored confectioners' coating and the 1 tablespoon shortening over low heat, stirring constantly. Set torte on a wire rack over waxed paper. Drizzle melted confectioners' coating over torte, spreading as necessary to glaze the top and sides completely.

In the same saucepan melt the chocolate-flavored confectioners' coating and the ½ teaspoon shortening over low heat, stirring constantly. Remove from heat; stir till smooth. Drizzle over top of torte in a random zigzag fashion.

Chill torte in the refrigerator for several hours or overnight.

Bring torte to room temperature.

To serve torte, warm a knife in hot water; dry knife. Use knife to cut torte into wedges, rewarming knife as necessary. Serve torte with strawberries, if desired. Makes 12 servings.

*Nutrition information per serving:* *444 cal., 5 g pro., 47 g carbo., 28 g fat, 204 mg chol., 161 mg sodium, 246 mg potassium, 1 g dietary fiber. U.S. RDA: 14% vit. A, 10% riboflavin, 15% iron.*

## SPICED FRUIT DIAMONDS

    1 cup mixed dried fruit bits
  ½ cup apple juice
  ½ teaspoon ground nutmeg
  ⅔ cup finely chopped pecans
  10 sheets frozen phyllo dough
       (18x12-inch rectangles), thawed
  ½ cup margarine or butter, melted
  ½ cup sugar
    2 tablespoons honey
    2 teaspoons lemon juice
Kumquat flowers (optional)*

In a small saucepan bring fruit bits, apple juice, and nutmeg to boiling; reduce heat. Cover; simmer about 5 minutes or till fruit is plumped and liquid has been absorbed. Remove from heat. Stir in nuts. Cool slightly.

Trim phyllo sheets, if needed, to form 18x12-inch rectangles. Cut phyllo sheets in half crosswise. Cut in half lengthwise. (You should have forty 9x6-inch sheets.) Cover with a damp towel.

Butter bottom of a 10x6x2-inch baking dish. To assemble dessert, layer *thirteen* 9x6-inch sheets of phyllo in dish, brushing *one-third* of margarine or butter between sheets. (Work with *one* 9x6-inch sheet of phyllo at a time; keep remainder covered with damp towel.) Spread *half* of the fruit mixture over phyllo in dish. Repeat with another *thirteen* 9x6-inch sheets of the phyllo, another *third* of the margarine or butter, and remaining fruit mixture. Top with remaining 9x6-inch sheets of the phyllo, brushing *each* with some of the remaining margarine or butter.

Score the top of phyllo into ten 2-inch diamonds. Bake in a 350° oven for 40 to 45 minutes or till deep golden brown.

Meanwhile, in a small saucepan combine sugar, honey, and ½ cup *water*. Bring to boiling. Boil gently, uncovered, for 10 minutes. Remove from heat. Stir in lemon juice; pour over warm pastry. Cut into diamonds along scored lines. Cool. Garnish with kumquat flowers, if desired. Makes about 10 diamonds.

*To make kumquat flowers: Use a sharp knife to cut a crisscross on top of fresh kumquats. Insert knife under each center point; gently pull peel back.

*Nutrition information per diamond:* *249 cal., 2 g pro., 30 g carbo., 37 g fat, 0 mg chol., 166 mg sodium, 182 mg potassium, and 2 g dietary fiber. U.S. RDA: 11% vit. A.*

## CRANBERRY MOUSSE

  ½ cup sugar
    1 envelope unflavored gelatin
  ¼ teaspoon finely shredded
       orange peel
  ½ cup orange juice
    2 cups fresh cranberries
    2 egg whites
    2 tablespoons sugar
  ½ cup whipping cream
Raspberry Sauce
    (see recipe, right)
Fresh mint leaves (optional)

In a medium saucepan combine the ½ cup sugar and gelatin. Stir in orange juice. Cook and stir over medium heat till gelatin is dissolved. Stir in orange peel and cranberries. Bring to boiling; reduce heat. Cover; simmer about 5 minutes or till cranberry skins pop.

Transfer the cranberry-gelatin mixture to a medium mixing bowl. Chill till the mixture is cool and thickened, stirring occasionally. Remove from the refrigerator (mixture will continue to set).

In a small mixer bowl immediately beat egg whites with an electric mixer on medium speed till soft peaks form (tips curl). Gradually add the 2 tablespoons sugar, beating on high speed till stiff peaks form (tips stand straight).

When gelatin mixture is partially set (the consistency of unbeaten egg whites), fold in stiff-beaten egg whites.

In a small mixer bowl beat the whipping cream with an electric mixer on low speed till soft peaks form. Fold into gelatin mixture.

Chill till mixture mounds when spooned. Spoon into a 1-quart glass bowl. Chill for several hours or till firm.

To serve mousse, spoon onto dessert plates; top with Raspberry Sauce. Garnish with mint leaves, if desired. Makes 6 servings.

**Raspberry Sauce:** Sieve one 10-ounce package *frozen raspberries,* thawed; discard seeds. Add *water* to make *1 cup.* In a small saucepan combine raspberry juice, 2 tablespoons *sugar,* and 2 teaspoons *cornstarch.* Cook and stir over medium-high heat till bubbly; cook and stir for 2 minutes more. Stir in 2 teaspoons *vanilla.* Cover; chill.

*Nutrition information per serving:* *251 cal., 3 g pro., 45 g carbo., 8 g fat, 27 mg chol., 27 mg sodium, 147 mg potassium, and 4 g dietary fiber. U.S. RDA: 34% vit. C.*

# MEATLESS MAIN DISH
## READY IN 30 MINUTES!

By Barbara Johnson

**Y**ou'll like this meal—it's healthful, meatless, made in one skillet, and ready in 30 minutes. Your family will like the rich tomato flavor and the satisfying "I'm full" after-dinner feeling.

Round out the meal with warm pita bread and deli coleslaw.

### SAUCY CHEESE AND EGGPLANT SKILLET

*The combination of garbanzo beans, feta cheese, and nuts makes this a protein-rich main dish—*

- 1 **medium eggplant (1 to 1¼ pounds)**
- ¼ **cup water**

• • •

- 1 **15-ounce can garbanzo beans, drained**
- 1½ **teaspoons fennel seed, slightly crushed**
- ½ **teaspoon bottled minced garlic**
- 1 **15½-ounce jar meatless spaghetti sauce**

• • •

- 1 **cup crumbled feta cheese (4 ounces)**
- ¼ **cup sliced pitted ripe *or* Greek olives**
- 2 **tablespoons pine nuts *or* chopped walnuts**

Peel eggplant, if desired. Cut into ½-inch-thick slices; halve slices. In a 10-inch skillet combine the eggplant and water. Bring to boiling; reduce heat.

You'll have plenty of time to sit down to dinner as a family when you serve this hearty but fast-to-fix Saucy Cheese and Eggplant Skillet.

Save a bowl! Stir seasonings into the jar of sauce; pour over mixture in skillet.

Cover and simmer about 10 minutes or till tender. Drain well.

Spread beans over eggplant in skillet. Stir fennel seed and garlic into spaghetti sauce; pour over the eggplant mixture. Bring to boiling; reduce heat. Sprinkle with cheese and olives. Simmer, uncovered, about 3 minutes or till heated through. Sprinkle with nuts. Makes 4 main-dish servings.

*Nutrition information per serving:* *331 cal., 14 g pro., 41 g carbo., 14 g fat, 25 mg chol., 1,139 mg sodium, 851 mg potassium, and 9 g dietary fiber. U.S. RDA: 13% vit. A, 16% thiamine, 20% riboflavin, 11% niacin, 24% calcium, and 18% iron.*

138

# NOVEMBER

# TURKEY ROASTING GUIDE

**U**se these times and tips to roast your holiday bird to juicy perfection.

## How much to buy

For a 12-lb.-or-less bird, buy 1 lb. per serving; more than 12 lb., ¾ lb. per serving. For turkey breast (bone-in), buy ⅓ lb. per serving.

## Frozen turkey

**Refrigerator thawing:** Place wrapped bird on tray in refrigerator 3 to 4 days (24 hours for each 5 pounds).

**Cold-water thawing:** Place wrapped bird in sink of cold water. Change water every 30 minutes. (Allow 30 minutes per pound.)

## Before roasting

Unwrap, free legs and tail, then remove the giblets and neck piece from the cavities. Thoroughly rinse turkey; pat dry. *Don't stuff turkey till you're ready to roast it.*

To stuff the turkey, spoon some stuffing *loosely* into neck cavity. Pull neck skin over stuffing; fasten to back of bird with skewer. Place turkey, neck side down, in large bowl. Loosely spoon stuffing into body cavity; *do not* pack (stuffing would not reach a safe temperature quickly enough). Tuck drumsticks under band of skin across tail or tie legs to tail. Twist wing tips under back.

## Roasting directions

Place turkey, breast side up, on a rack in a shallow roasting pan. Brush with cooking oil. Insert a meat thermometer in center of inside thigh muscle so bulb does not touch the bone.

**Open roasting pan:** Cover turkey *loosely* with foil; leave air space between turkey and foil. Press foil in lightly at end of drumsticks and neck. Roast in a 325° oven, basting occasionally. When turkey is two-thirds done, cut skin or string between legs. Remove foil last 30 to 45 minutes to brown.

**Covered roasting pan:** *Do not* add water. Roast, covered with vent open, in 325° oven 20 to 25 minutes per pound. Uncover; drain, reserving juices. Turn oven to 475°. Roast 20 minutes more or till turkey is brown.

## TURKEY ROASTING TIMES

*Because birds differ in size, shape, and tenderness, use these roasting times as a general guide.*

| Type of Turkey | Ready-to-Cook Weight | Oven Temp. | Guide to Roasting Time |
|---|---|---|---|
| **Stuffed Whole Turkey*** | 6–8 lb. | 325° | 3–3½ hr. |
| | 8–12 lb. | 325° | 3½–4½ hr. |
| | 12–16 lb. | 325° | 4–5 hr. |
| | 16–20 lb. | 325° | 4½–5½ hr. |
| | 20–24 lb. | 325° | 5–6½ hr. |
| **Unstuffed Foil-Wrapped Turkey** | 8–10 lb. | 450° | 1¼–1¾ hr. |
| | 10–12 lb. | 450° | 1¾–2¼ hr. |
| | 12–16 lb. | 450° | 2¼–3 hr. |
| | 16–20 lb. | 450° | 3–3½ hr. |
| | 20–24 lb. | 450° | 3½–4½ hr. |
| **Frozen Stuffed Turkey** | 5–7 lb. | 325° | 4¾–5 hr. |
| | 7–9 lb. | 325° | 5–5½ hr. |
| | 9–11 lb. | 325° | 5½–6 hr. |
| | 11–14 lb. | 325° | 6–6½ hr. |
| | 14–16 lb. | 325° | 6½–7 hr. |
| **Turkey Breast and Portions (bone-in)** | 2–4 lb. | 325° | 1½–2 hr. |
| | 3–5 lb. | 325° | 1½–2½ hr. |
| | 5–7 lb. | 325° | 2–2½ hr. |

**Testing for doneness:** Roast whole turkeys till thermometer registers 180° to 185° (170° for turkey breast—*do not* overcook). Meat should be fork tender, and juices no longer pink when pierced with a fork. (Pierce thigh meat on whole turkeys, breast meat on turkey breasts.) Remove from oven; cover loosely with foil. Let stand 10 to 15 minutes before carving. Stuffing temperature should be 165°.
*Unstuffed turkeys generally require 30 to 45 minutes less total roasting time than stuffed turkeys.*

**Foil-wrapped turkey:** *Do not* stuff turkey roasted this way. (Because the turkey is roasted at a high temperature, the meat will cook before the stuffing reaches a safe temperature.) Wrap *unstuffed* turkey, breast side up, in greased, heavy foil. Place in a large shallow roasting pan. Insert a meat thermometer in thigh muscle through foil. Roast in a 450° oven. Open foil the last 20 to 30 minutes.

**Frozen stuffed turkey:** *Do not* thaw turkey. Remove wrapping and any bags containing gravy, neck, or giblets; place the frozen turkey, breast side up, on a rack in a shallow roasting pan. Brush with cooking oil. Roast in a 325° oven, basting occasionally. Cover loosely with foil to prevent overbrowning, if necessary. After 3 hours, insert a meat thermometer in the center of the inside thigh muscle, so the bulb does not touch the bone. Continue roasting till turkey is done.

**Turkey breast and portions (bone-in):** Thaw turkey, if frozen, as directed. Place turkey, skin side up, on a rack in a shallow roasting pan. Insert a meat thermometer into the center so the bulb does not touch the bone. Brush with cooking oil. Roast, uncovered, in a 325° oven, basting occasionally. Cover turkey loosely with foil to prevent overbrowning, if necessary. ▦

# FESTIVE FOODS FOR HOLIDAY ENTERTAINING

## So Special, So Elegant, So Easy to Fix

By Barbara Goldman

### FRESH FRUIT AMARETTI TRIFLE ▲

● *No cooking necessary! Just assemble and chill.*

Appealingly simple, this new rendition of a traditional trifle blends a touch of nostalgia with a touch of class. Layer crushed Italian macaroons with fresh fruit and a yogurt-sour-cream sauce—then chill. Delicious! What a fantastic way to entertain graciously during the holiday season.

## DESSERTS

## POACHED FRUIT ▲ IN ZINFANDEL

● *Create an outstanding make-ahead fruit dessert in less than 30 minutes!*

Luscious enough for special occasions—easy enough for any time! But don't take our word for it, try it yourself. Plump dried figs and cherries in boiling water, add oranges, then chill in a subtly spiced wine syrup. For easy, elegant serving, spoon into goblets, and add a cookie, mint sprig, and whimsical twist of orange.

## HOLIDAY ICE-CREAM ▶ BOMBE

● *Spectacularly dramatic, surprisingly easy!*

Here's a chance to indulge your guests with a holiday dessert fantasy of three ice creams: pistachio, vanilla laced with candied fruit, and chocolate. Complement with a heavenly chocolate sauce.

## ◀ APRICOT-MACADAMIA COOKIES

● *Easy as pie—start with refrigerated piecrust.*

Start a new holiday tradition: dainty cookies with a tart-sweet filling. Drizzle with brandy-spiked icing.

## APPETIZERS

## EXOTIC MUSHROOM ▲ STRUDEL

● *A party-stopper of an appetizer, made easy with purchased phyllo dough.*

It sounds extraordinary, looks extraordinary, and tastes extraordinary! But thawed sheets of phyllo make this savory strudel easy to assemble. And the special mushrooms are available in most supermarkets. For extra flair, arrange strudel slices over lemon leaves from your florist.

## MEDITERRANEAN ▶ VEGETABLE APPETIZER

● *Just open jars, marinate, arrange—and serve!*

Transfer sun-dried tomatoes, artichokes, baby corn, and olives from jars into a bowl and chill to blend flavors. Arrange with fresh Belgian endive and sprouts.

## ◀ STEAMED MUSSELS VINAIGRETTE

● *Never prepared mussels? This way's a cinch!*

And you'll love the succulent flavor of the New Zealand green-lipped variety.

## BREADS

### PIZZA PINWHEEL◄ CRESCENTS

● *Hot roll mix cuts precious preparation time.*

Stir up the dough in a jiffy while the sausage and vegetables brown. Then roll out, fill, and assemble into two crescent-shaped loaves. The loaves will rise in 20 minutes, bake in 25. And if you think preparation is fast, just watch how quickly the rolls disappear!

### COILED SAFFRON FRUIT BREAD ▶

● *Use quick-rise yeast in a dazzling one-rise bread.*

Take a respite from the holiday whirl with a cup of tea and a slice of glorious-looking, scrumptious-tasting fruit-swirled bread.

### ◄ HARVEST CHOCOLATE BREAD

● *A unique stir-together bread for coffee or dessert!*

This spicy sweet potato loaf hides a surprise chocolate center.

SNACKS

## ZESTY ITALIAN ▲ PEASANT BREAD

● *Super good, super simple, super any time—from brunch to late at night!*

1   16-ounce package Boboli (Italian bread shell)* *or* 1 recipe Make-Your-Own Italian Bread Shell (see recipe, *page* 155)

● ● ●

1   to 2 tablespoons olive *or* cooking oil
1   clove garlic, minced
⅛   teaspoon pepper
1   medium tomato, peeled, seeded, and chopped

¼   cup crumbled Gorgonzola cheese *or* blue cheese
1   tablespoon snipped fresh rosemary, oregano, *or* basil *or* 1 teaspoon dried rosemary, oregano, *or* basil, crushed
Fresh rosemary, oregano, *or* basil (optional)

●**Place** Boboli or Make-Your-Own Italian Bread Shell on a lightly greased baking sheet.
●**In a small bowl stir** together oil, garlic, and pepper. Brush generously over the bread.

●**Sprinkle** tomato, cheese, and desired snipped herb over bread.
●**Bake** in 400° oven 10 to 15 minutes or till warm and cheese melts. Cut into 12 wedges. Top with whole herb. Serve hot. Serves 12.

  *Look for Boboli (*BO-bo-lee*), a round, flat prebaked bread, in refrigerator cases in certain supermarkets and specialty food shops.

***Nutrition information per serving:*** *129 cal., 4 g pro., 19 g carbo., 4 g fat, 5 mg chol., 228 mg sodium, 57 mg potassium, and 1 g dietary fiber. U.S. RDA: 10% thiamine.*

***Red Onion and Tomato Peasant Bread:*** Prepare Zesty Italian Peasant Bread as directed at *left, except* layer ½ of a *red onion*, thinly sliced, over the bread. Top with the chopped tomato. Omit the Gorgonzola or blue cheese, and instead sprinkle 2 tablespoons grated *Parmesan cheese* and the desired snipped herb over the bread. Bake as directed in the recipe at *left*.

# DRINKS

## ◀ SPARKLING CRANBERRY APERITIF

● *Make the holidays bubbly with a frothy concoction of sparkling water, cranberry sauce, and liqueur.*

1½ cups lemon- *or* lime-flavored carbonated water, chilled
1 8-ounce can jellied cranberry sauce, chilled
¼ cup cranberry, raspberry, *or* orange liqueur, chilled
1 tablespoon sugar
Cracked ice (optional)

● **In blender container** or food processor bowl combine *half* of the carbonated water, all of the cranberry sauce, liqueur, and sugar. Cover and blend or process till smooth, scraping down sides of the container or bowl once or twice, if necessary.

● **Pour** cranberry mixture into 4 long-stem glasses. Add ice, if desired. Fill glasses with the remaining carbonated water. Makes 4 (5-ounce) servings.

*Nutrition information per serving: 145 cal., 0 g pro., 37 g carbo., 0 g fat, 0 mg chol., 16 mg sodium, 15 mg potassium, and 1 g dietary fiber.*

## ◀ CHOCOLATE CAFÉ AU LAIT

● *Create the perfect ending to a holiday evening with this divine mocha beverage-dessert.*

½ cup whipping cream
2 tablespoons sugar
1 teaspoon vanilla
• • •
1 ounce German sweet chocolate, grated (about ¼ cup)
• • •
2 cups hot brewed coffee
Pieces of milk chocolate lace candy *or* chocolate curls (optional)

● **In a small mixer bowl** beat whipping cream, sugar, and vanilla with an electric mixer on low speed till soft peaks form. Fold in the grated German sweet chocolate.

● **Pour** the hot brewed coffee into 4 coffee cups. Pipe or spoon a *fourth* of the whipped cream mixture over coffee in each cup. Top with milk chocolate lace candy or chocolate curls. Serve at once. Makes 4 (6-ounce) servings.

*Nutrition information per serving: 166 cal., 1 g pro., 11 g carbo., 14 g fat, 41 mg chol., 15 mg sodium, 85 mg potassium, and 1 g dietary fiber.*

---

## HOLIDAY SIPPERS

● **CHAMPAGNE AND SPARKLING WINES**
Holiday time is the perfect time to bring on the bubbly. Because the field is overcrowded, the price is likely to be right.

● **SPARKLING WATERS**
Concerns for safety and fitness are making celebrations, at any time of the year, less alcoholic. Serve these as they are, or blended with juices and/or liqueurs or wines.

● **QUALITY WINES**
The popularity of jug wines has faded. Currently, premium chardonnays, zinfandels, and Australian and Spanish wines are big. Economically speaking, lower-cost jug wines are perfect for holiday parties. But hot, they're not!

## ENTERTAINING TIPS

● **ENJOY!**
To enjoy your own party, plan only what you can accomplish easily. If time is at a premium, extend homemade offerings with deli or bakery items. Or, host a potluck or co-op party, so that friends can help out by bringing some of the food.

● **DON'T OVERSPEND**
It's the impression, not the cost, that counts. Just a few personal touches contribute style. Make guests feel special: That's what they'll remember the most.

● **INVITE WISELY**
The right mix of people is as important as the right mix of food and drinks. Invite guests with common—or wide-ranging—interests, and choose a good blend of listeners and talkers.

● **STAGE THE MENU**
Plan a menu with which you're comfortable—with interesting, contrasting food colors and textures. Presentation is important. When food looks great, it even seems to taste better. Make one dish splashy; then let other foods play important, but supporting, roles.

## FRESH-FRUIT AMARETTI TRIFLE

*Look for amaretti (Italian macaroons) in specialty stores. Or, substitute toasted crumb mixture (at right). Try halved orange slices for some of the fruit. Pictured on page 139—*

1½ **cups coarsely crushed amaretti** *or* **amarettini (about 30 amaretti** *or* **95 amarettini)***
3 **medium pears, cored and sliced**
2 **tablespoons lemon juice**
5 **kiwi fruit, peeled, sliced, and halved**
1½ **cups seedless red** *or* **green grapes**
2 **8-ounce cartons vanilla yogurt**
1 **8-ounce carton dairy sour cream**
**Amarettini** *or* **crushed amaretti (optional)**

In a 2-quart glass serving bowl, a souf-flé dish, or 8 individual soufflé dishes sprinkle ¾ cup of the crushed amaretti or amarettini.

Dip pear slices in lemon juice to prevent browning. Arrange *half* of the pear slices, kiwi slices, and grapes over amaretti layer.

In a small mixing bowl combine yogurt and sour cream. Spoon *half* of the yogurt mixture over the fruit layer (see photo, below). Repeat layers with remaining ¾ cup amaretti, fruit, and yogurt mixture.

Serve immediately or cover and chill up to 1 hour. Garnish top with amarettini or crushed amaretti, if desired. Makes 8 servings.

***Note:*** As a substitute for the crushed amaretti or amarettini, combine 3 cups *soft bread crumbs*, ¼ cup melted *margarine or butter*, ¼ cup finely chopped *almonds*, and 3 tablespoons *sugar*. Spread in a 13x9x2-inch baking pan. Bake in a 375° oven for 12 to 15 minutes or till lightly toasted, stirring once or twice. Continue as directed, *except* stir ¼ teaspoon *almond extract* into the yogurt mixture.

***Nutrition information per serving:*** *432 cal., 10 g pro., 63 g carbo., 17 g fat, 17 mg chol., 400 mg sodium, 540 mg potassium, 3 g dietary fiber. U.S. RDA: 12% vit. A, 72% vit. C, 15% thiamine, 23% riboflavin, 12% niacin, 21% calcium, 12% iron.*

## HOLIDAY ICE-CREAM BOMBE

*If you don't have a mold, use a freezer-proof bowl lined with plastic wrap. Wrap makes unmolding a snap—*

3 **cups pistachio ice cream** *or* **mint chocolate chip ice cream**
3 **cups vanilla ice cream**
⅓ **cup diced mixed candied fruits and peels**
1 **quart chocolate** *or* **chocolate fudge ice cream**
**Pistachio nuts (optional)**
**Chocolate Leaves (optional) (see recipe, right)**
1 **recipe Chocolate Sauce (see recipe, right)**

In a chilled mixing bowl stir pistachio ice cream just to soften. Spread evenly in the bottom of a 2-quart mold. Freeze for 30 minutes.

Meanwhile, in a chilled mixing bowl stir vanilla ice cream just to soften. Stir in candied fruits and peels. Spread evenly over pistachio ice-cream layer. Freeze for 30 minutes.

In a chilled mixing bowl stir chocolate ice cream just to soften. Spread evenly over vanilla ice-cream layer. Cover and freeze several hours or up to one month.

To serve, wrap a hot damp towel around mold for several seconds. Center an upside-down serving platter over the mold. Holding tightly, invert the plate and mold. Lift off the mold. Garnish with pistachio nuts and Chocolate Leaves, if desired. Serve at once with Chocolate Sauce. Makes 10 servings.

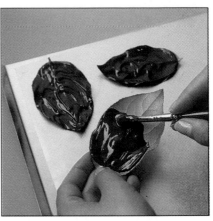

*Chocolate Leaves:* In a heavy saucepan cook 2 squares (2 ounces) *semisweet chocolate* over low heat, stirring constantly till the chocolate begins to melt. Immediately remove the chocolate from the heat and stir till smooth. With a small paintbrush, brush melted chocolate on the underside of nontoxic fresh leaves (such as lemon, mint, or ivy), building up layers of chocolate so garnish will be sturdy (see photo, above). Wipe off chocolate that may have run onto the front of the leaves. Place on a baking sheet lined with waxed paper; chill or freeze till hardened. Just before using, carefully peel the fresh leaves away from the chocolate leaves.

*Chocolate Sauce:* In a small saucepan combine 8 squares (8 ounces) cut-up *semisweet chocolate* and ⅔ cup *light cream.* Cook over medium-low heat till slightly thickened and bubbly. Remove from heat. Stir in 1 teaspoon *vanilla.* Serve warm. Makes 1 cup.

***Nutrition information per serving:*** *434 cal., 6 g pro., 50 g carbo., 26 g fat, 70 mg chol., 140 mg sodium, 357 mg potassium, 3 g dietary fiber. U.S. RDA: 13% vit. A, 22% riboflavin, 20% calcium.*

## POACHED FRUIT
## IN ZINFANDEL

*Dried red cherries contribute a sweet-tart flavor to this deliciously spiked fruit combination—*

 8 **dried Calimyrna figs**
 2 **cups water**
 ½ **cup dried tart red cherries**
    *or* **light raisins**
 2 **oranges**
 1½ **cups white zinfandel wine**
 ⅔ **cup sugar**
 ¼ **cup orange liqueur**
 10 **cardamom pods**
**Cookies (optional)**
**Mint sprigs (optional)**
**Orange peel curls (optional)**
**Whipped cream (optional)**

Remove stems from figs. In a medium saucepan combine the figs, water, and cherries or raisins. Bring to boiling. Remove from heat and let stand for 15 minutes. Drain.

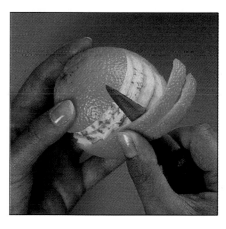

Using a sharp knife, remove peel and bitter white membrane from oranges in strips (see photo, above). Reserve peel for garnish, if desired. Cut oranges crosswise in ½-inch-thick slices. Then cut *each* slice in half.

In a large bowl combine fig and cherry mixture and orange slices.

In a medium saucepan combine the wine, sugar, and orange liqueur. Break pods to release seeds (you should have ½ teaspoon seed). Tie cardamom

seed in cheesecloth; add to wine mixture. Cook and stir to dissolve sugar. Bring to boiling; reduce heat. Cover and simmer for 5 minutes. Remove from heat. Remove and discard cardamom bag.

Pour hot syrup over fruit, stirring gently to coat fruit. Cool slightly. Chill, covered, for several hours or overnight.

To serve, divide the fruit mixture among 4 individual wine goblets or dessert dishes. Pour the remaining syrup over fruit mixture in dishes. Garnish with a cookie, mint sprig, and orange peel curl, if desired. Serve with whipped cream, if desired. Serves 4.

***Nutrition information per serving:*** *426 cal., 3 g pro., 95 g carbo., 1 g fat, 0 mg chol., 7 mg sodium, 524 mg potassium, 4 g dietary fiber. U.S. RDA: 60% vit. C.*

## APRICOT-MACADAMIA
## COOKIES

*It's easy! Tuck a four-ingredient nutty fruit filling inside fancy shapes of ready-made piecrust. Pictured on page 139—*

 1 **15-ounce package folded,**
    **refrigerated, unbaked piecrusts**
    **(2 crusts)**
 1 **6-ounce (1 cup) package**
    **dried apricots**
 ½ **cup macadamia nuts** *or*
    **slivered almonds**
 ½ **cup sugar**
 2 **tablespoons water**
**Milk**
**Sugar**
 1 **recipe Apricot Brandy Icing**
    **(optional), (see recipe, right)**
**Macadamia nuts** *or* **almonds,**
    **finely chopped and toasted**
    **(optional)**

Let the piecrusts stand at room temperature as directed on the package.

Meanwhile, in a food processor bowl place the apricots and the ½ cup macadamia nuts or almonds. Cover and

process the apricots and nuts until they are very finely chopped. (Or, you can run the apricots and the nuts through the fine blade of a food grinder.)

In a small saucepan combine the apricot mixture, the ½ cup sugar, and water. Cook and stir over low heat till mixture is heated through. Cool to room temperature.

Meanwhile, carefully unfold *one* of the piecrusts on a lightly floured surface and press together any fold lines. Using a lightly floured rolling pin, roll the crust till ⅛ inch thick. Cut into 2½-inch rounds with a scalloped cookie cutter. Place the cutout rounds 1 inch apart on an ungreased cookie sheet. Repeat with the remaining piecrust. If desired, using a sharp knife or hors d'oeuvre cutter, cut slits or designs on *half* of *each* dough round.

To fill cookies, spoon a scant *1 teaspoon* apricot-macadamia filling on *half* of *each* round. Moisten edge of *each* round with water. Fold other half of round over filling; press edges together to seal.

Bake in a 375° oven for 7 minutes. Remove from oven; brush cookies with milk. Sprinkle with sugar. Return the cookies to oven and bake 2 to 4 minutes more or till light golden brown. Cool for 1 minute on cookie sheet; transfer cookies to wire racks. Cool completely.

To decorate cookies, dip rounded edges of cooled cookies in Apricot Brandy Icing. If desired, dip iced edges in toasted nuts. Drizzle remaining icing over tops of cookies. Makes 34 cookies.

*Apricot Brandy Icing:* In a small mixing bowl combine 1 cup sifted *powdered sugar* and enough *apricot brandy* (1 to 2 tablespoons) to make icing of pouring consistency.

***Nutrition information per cookie:*** *115 cal., 1 g pro., 13 g carbo., 7 g fat, 0 mg chol., 51 mg sodium, 96 mg potassium, 1 g dietary fiber.*

*Cookie Sandwiches:* Prepare recipe as directed, *except* cut dough with a 2-inch scalloped cookie cutter. Transfer *half* of the rounds to an ungreased baking sheet. Spoon a scant *1 teaspoon* of filling onto the center of *each* round. Brush edges of rounds with water. Top with the remaining rounds and lightly press edges together to seal. Bake as directed, *except* after brushing cookies with milk and sprinkling with sugar, return to oven and bake about 4 minutes more or till light golden brown. Decorate cookies as desired. Makes 26.

## EXOTIC MUSHROOM STRUDEL

*You'll find the exotic mushrooms in many supermarkets and in Oriental food shops—*

- 8 ounces fresh shiitake, oyster, *or* wood ear mushrooms
- 8 ounces fresh button mushrooms
- 6 green onions, sliced
- 3 tablespoons margarine *or* butter
- 3 tablespoons dry white wine
- 2 tablespoons diced pimiento
- 2 tablespoons snipped parsley
- ¼ teaspoon dried sage, crushed
- ¼ teaspoon pepper
- ⅛ teaspoon dried thyme, crushed
- 1 egg yolk
- 6 sheets frozen phyllo dough (18x12-inch rectangles), thawed
- ¼ cup margarine *or* butter, melted
- 2 tablespoons fine dry bread crumbs
- **Assorted fresh mushrooms (optional)**
- **Lemon leaves (optional)**

Remove any of the woody stems from the mushrooms; discard. Coarsely chop mushrooms. (You should have about 2 cups of shiitake, oyster, or wood ear mushrooms and about 3 cups of button mushrooms.)

In a 10-inch skillet cook mushrooms and onions in the 3 tablespoons margarine or butter for 4 to 5 minutes or till tender. Add wine and cook on high for 2 to 3 minutes or till liquid has evaporated. Remove from heat. Stir in pimiento, parsley, sage, pepper, and thyme. Cool about 10 minutes.

In a blender container or food processor bowl place *half* of the mushroom mixture and egg yolk. Cover and blend or process till finely chopped. Combine the chopped mushroom mixture with the remaining mushroom mixture.

Cut the sheets of phyllo dough in half crosswise. (You should end up with twelve 12x9-inch sheets.) Cover the phyllo sheets with a damp towel. Layer *six* half-sheets of the phyllo on a large ungreased baking sheet, brushing some of the ¼ cup melted margarine or butter between the sheets. (Remove 1 sheet of the phyllo at a time and keep the remaining sheets of phyllo covered.) Sprinkle *half* of the dry bread crumbs down the length of *one side* of phyllo to within 3 inches of long edge and 1½ inches of short edges.

Spoon *half* of the mushroom mixture over bread crumbs (see photo, above). Fold short edges of phyllo toward center; roll jelly-roll style from long side nearest filling. Brush roll with melted margarine. Cut diagonal slits about 1 inch apart to, *but not through,* mushroom mixture.

Repeat with the remaining phyllo, margarine, bread crumbs, and mushroom mixture to make a second roll.

Bake in 400° oven 15 to 18 minutes or till golden. Cool 5 minutes. With a serrated knife, cut rolls completely through at diagonal slits. Arrange slices on a serving platter lined with lemon leaves. Garnish with the additional mushrooms, if desired. Makes 2 strudels (12 to 16 appetizer servings).

*Nutrition information per serving:* 102 cal., 2 g pro., 8 g carbo., 7 g fat, 23 mg chol., 117 mg sodium, 123 mg potassium, 1 g dietary fiber.

## STEAMED MUSSELS VINAIGRETTE

*The New Zealand green-lipped mussels pictured on page 144 exhibit a distinctive, luminous green color. The mussels are available in specialty seafood shops; they take just a few minutes more to cook than the smaller mussels. Other mussel varieties may be substituted in this recipe. No matter what variety you use, buy a few extra to allow for those that don't open during cooking—*

- 1 pound mussels, scrubbed
- 3 quarts cold water
- 6 tablespoons salt
- 1 medium green pepper, finely chopped (½ cup)
- 3 cloves garlic, minced
- 2 tablespoons margarine *or* butter
- ½ cup dry white wine
- 1 medium tomato, seeded and chopped
- 2 tablespoons snipped fresh basil *or* 1½ teaspoons dried basil, crushed
- 1 teaspoon snipped cilantro *or* 1 tablespoon snipped parsley
- **Sliced French bread**

Remove beards from mussels (see photo, below). In a large bowl or kettle combine *1 quart* of the cold water and *2 tablespoons* of the salt; add mussels. Soak the mussels for 15 minutes; drain and rinse. Discard water. Repeat soaking, draining, and rinsing twice.

In a 3-quart saucepan cook green pepper and garlic in margarine or butter till almost crisp-tender. Stir in wine, tomato, and basil. Add mussels. Bring to boiling; reduce heat. Cover and simmer for 3 to 4 minutes or till mussels just open. Remove from heat. Discard mussels that do not open.

Using a slotted spoon, transfer mussel mixture to a large serving bowl. Cover and set aside.

If necessary, simmer the sauce, uncovered, till it has been reduced to 1½ cups. Pour the sauce over the mussels. Sprinkle with cilantro or parsley. Serve with French bread. Makes 3 or 4 appetizer servings.

*Nutrition information per serving:* 162 cal., 7 g pro., 8 g carbo., 9 g fat, 22 mg chol., 931 mg sodium, 314 mg potassium, 1 g dietary fiber. U.S. RDA: 22% vit. A, 71% vit. C, 14% iron.

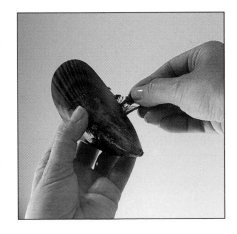

## MEDITERRANEAN VEGETABLE APPETIZER

- 8 ounces sun-dried tomatoes packed in olive oil
- 1 13¾-ounce jar marinated artichoke hearts
- 1 10-ounce jar whole baby corn, drained
- ½ cup sliced pitted ripe olives, drained
- 1 teaspoon capers, drained

Belgian endive leaves
Alfalfa sprouts *or* mixed fresh sprouts (optional)

To prepare vegetables for marinating, drain tomatoes, reserving *2 tablespoons* of the oil. Snip or chop tomatoes and place in a shallow nonmetallic bowl with the reserved oil. Add the *undrained* artichoke hearts, baby corn, olives, and capers.

Cover and chill the marinating mixture for several hours or overnight, stirring occasionally.

Just before serving, drain vegetable mixture. Line a serving platter with Belgian endive leaves; spoon vegetable mixture in the center. Garnish with fresh sprouts, if desired. Makes about 8 appetizer servings.

***Nutrition information per serving:*** *54 cal., 2 g pro., 8 g carbo., 2 g fat, 0 mg chol., 156 mg sodium, 185 mg potassium, and 2 g dietary fiber. U.S. RDA: 14% vitamin C.*

## PIZZA PINWHEEL CRESCENT

- 1 16-ounce package hot roll mix
- 1 pound bulk sweet *or* hot Italian sausage
- 1 cup finely chopped green *or* sweet red pepper
- ½ cup chopped onion
- 1 cup shredded mozzarella cheese (4 ounces)
- 2 tablespoons snipped parsley
- 1 teaspoon dried Italian seasoning
- 1 egg white
- 1 tablespoon water

Sesame seed (optional)

Prepare hot roll mix according to package directions through the kneading step. Cover and let rest.

Meanwhile, for sausage filling, in a skillet cook sausage, green pepper, and onion till sausage is brown and vegetables are tender; drain well. Stir in cheese, parsley, and Italian seasoning.

To shape each loaf, divide dough in half. On a lightly floured surface roll

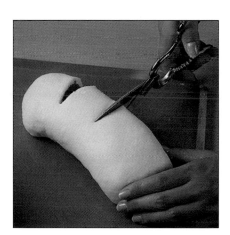

*one* portion of the dough into a 10x8-inch rectangle. Spoon *half* of the sausage filling over the dough to within 1 inch of all edges. Beginning at one long edge, roll up the dough jelly-roll style. Moisten and pinch ends and edges to seal. Repeat with the remaining dough and filling to make a second loaf.

Place each loaf, seam side down, on a greased baking sheet; form into a crescent shape. Using kitchen scissors, snip each crescent-shaped loaf in three places, from outer edge three-fourths of the way to the center (see photo, below left).

Cover and let rise in a warm place about 20 minutes or till nearly doubled.

Meanwhile, in a small bowl stir together the egg white and the water. Just before baking, brush the egg white mixture over the top of each of the loaves. Sprinkle the loaves with sesame seed, if desired.

Bake in a 375° oven for 25 minutes or till bread is golden brown. Serve bread warm. Cut into slices to serve. Makes 2 loaves (8 slices per loaf).

If desired, cool bread just till room temperature. Wrap, label, and freeze bread in moisture- and vapor-proof wrap. To serve, thaw the bread, unopened, in the refrigerator for at least 6 hours. Place the foil-wrapped bread in a 350° oven for 30 to 40 minutes or till bread is warmed through.

***Nutrition information per slice:*** *168 cal., 8 g pro., 22 g carbo., 5 g fat, 14 mg chol., 354 mg sodium, 119 mg potassium, 2 g dietary fiber. U.S. RDA: 15% vit. C, 19% thiamine, 13% riboflavin, 8% niacin.*

## COILED SAFFRON FRUIT BREAD

*A hint of saffron contributes a golden tinge to this spiral-shaped loaf. Simply crush the feather-fine threads of saffron in your hand—*

    5 to 6 cups all-purpose flour
    ⅓ cup sugar
    2 packages quick-rising active
      dry yeast
    1 teaspoon salt
    ½ teaspoon ground nutmeg
    ⅛ teaspoon thread saffron,
      crushed, *or* dash ground saffron
    1¾ cups milk
    ¾ cup margarine *or* butter
    1 cup light raisins
    ½ cup dark raisins
    1 tablespoon finely shredded
      orange peel
    1 egg
    ¼ cup margarine *or* butter, melted
    1 egg
    1 tablespoon milk

In a large mixer bowl stir together *2 cups* of the flour, sugar, yeast, salt, nutmeg, and saffron.

In a medium saucepan heat the 1¾ cups milk, the ¾ cup margarine or butter, raisins, and orange peel just till warm (120° to 130°), stirring constantly to melt the margarine or butter.

Stir the raisin mixture into the flour mixture; add one egg. Beat with an electric mixer on low speed for 30 seconds, scraping the sides of the bowl constantly. Beat with mixer on high speed for 3 minutes. Using a spoon, stir in as much of the remaining flour as you can.

Turn dough out onto a lightly floured surface. Knead in enough of the remaining flour to make a moderately stiff dough that is smooth and elastic (5 to 8 minutes total). Divide the dough in half; shape each portion of dough into a ball. Cover and let rest for 10 minutes.

To shape each loaf, roll *one* portion of the dough into a 16x12-inch rectangle. Cut the dough lengthwise into *six* 2-inch-wide strips. Brush the strips with *half* of the melted margarine or butter. Roll up *one* of the strips very loosely and place it, cut side up, in the

center of a lightly greased 9x1½-inch round baking pan. Coil the remaining dough strips very loosely around the rolled center strip. Repeat cutting and rolling with remaining dough and brushing with melted margarine to make a second loaf.

Cover; let rise in a warm place till double (20 to 30 minutes). Combine remaining egg and the 1 tablespoon milk. Brush mixture over loaves.

Bake in a 350° oven about 35 minutes or till bread is golden. (Cover bread loosely with foil the last 10 to 15 minutes to prevent overbrowning.) Remove from oven. Cool on wire racks.

If desired, seal bread in a moisture- and vaporproof wrap or in an airtight container and freeze for up to 8 months. Before serving, let the bread stand at room temperature for at least 5 hours to thaw. Makes 2 loaves (12 slices per loaf).

**Nutrition information per slice:** *218 cal., 4 g pro., 31 g carbo., 9 g fat, 24 mg chol., 195 mg sodium, 143 mg potassium, 2 g dietary fiber. U.S. RDA: 13% thiamine, 12% riboflavin.*

## HARVEST CHOCOLATE BREAD

*Sweet potatoes and chocolate combine to create a unique, yummy flavor—*

    2 cups all-purpose flour
    1 tablespoon baking powder
    1 teaspoon ground cinnamon
    ½ teaspoon baking soda
    ½ teaspoon ground ginger
    ¼ teaspoon salt
    ¼ teaspoon ground cloves
    2 eggs

    1 8-ounce can vacuum-packed
      sweet potatoes, mashed, *or*
      1 cup mashed cooked sweet
      potatoes
    ⅔ cup sugar
    ½ cup cooking oil
    ½ cup milk
    1 teaspoon vanilla
    ½ cup coarsely chopped walnuts
      *or* pecans
    2 squares (2 ounces) semisweet
      chocolate, melted and cooled
    1 recipe Powdered Sugar Glaze
      (see recipe, below)
    1 square (1 ounce) semisweet
      chocolate, melted and cooled
    1 to 2 teaspoons hot water

In a medium mixing bowl stir together flour, baking powder, cinnamon, soda, ginger, salt, and cloves. Set aside.

In a large mixing bowl beat together eggs, sweet potatoes, sugar, oil, milk, and vanilla. Add flour mixture and nuts, mixing well. (Batter will be stiff.) Stir the 2 ounces melted chocolate into *1 cup* of the batter.

To layer batter, place *half* of the remaining plain batter in a greased and lightly floured 9x5x3-inch loaf pan. (Or, place *half* of the remaining plain batter into two greased and lightly floured 7½x3½x2-inch loaf pans.) Spoon chocolate batter over top of plain batter in pan (see photo, below left). Then spoon remaining plain batter over chocolate layer.

Bake in a 350° oven about 55 minutes or till a wooden toothpick inserted near the center comes out clean. (Allow about 40 minutes for 7½x3½x2-inch loaf pans.) Cool the loaf in the pan for 10 minutes. Remove from pan; cool completely on a wire rack.

Pipe about *half* of the Powdered Sugar Glaze over the loaf. To remaining glaze stir in the 1 ounce melted chocolate; add enough hot water to make glaze of drizzling consistency. Pipe the chocolate glaze beside the Powdered Sugar Glaze. Garnish with chocolate-dipped walnuts, if desired. Makes 1 loaf (about 12 slices).

*Powdered Sugar Glaze:* In a small mixing bowl combine 1 cup sifted *powdered sugar* and 1 to 2 tablespoons *water* till of drizzling consistency.

**Nutrition information per slice:** *368 cal., 5 g pro., 53 g carbo., 16 g fat, 46 mg chol., 191 mg sodium, 158 mg potassium, 3 g dietary fiber. U.S. RDA: 32% vit. A, 11% thiamine.*

## MAKE-YOUR-OWN ITALIAN BREAD SHELL

*Take your pick! Instead of the purchased Boboli, you can prepare this easy shell for the Zesty Italian Peasant Bread. The recipe for this bread begins on page 148—*

1 **16-ounce loaf frozen white bread dough, thawed**
¼ **cup finely shredded mozzarella cheese (1 ounce)**

On a lightly floured surface form the thawed bread dough into a ball. Cover and let rest for 5 minutes. Roll the dough into a 14-inch circle, allowing the dough to rest if necessary.

Transfer dough to a greased 12-inch pizza pan, folding extra dough over top edge of crust. Sprinkle with the shredded cheese.

Bake in a 400° oven for 15 minutes or till brown and crusty. Cool to room temperature. Makes one 10-inch Italian bread shell (12 servings).

*Nutrition information per serving:* *108 cal., 4 g pro., 16 g carbo., 2 g fat, 1 mg chol., 236 mg sodium, 25 mg potassium. U.S. RDA: 10% thiamine.*

# KNOW YOUR APPLES

## SEVEN VARIETIES

**Red Delicious:** Named when a nurseryman in 1894 exclaimed, "My that's delicious!" Sweet and juicy. Best for snacking; poor for baking. Available year-round.

**Golden Delicious:** No kin to Red Delicious. Slightly elongated; sweet, juicy. All-purpose apple—great for snacking, cooking, and baking. Available September to June.

**Red Rome (Rome Beauty):** Named for an apple-growing area in Ohio, not Italy. Slightly tart. Best for baking. Available October to August.

**Winesap:** Granddaddy of American apples. Winelike flavor. All-purpose apple. Available November to July.

**Granny Smith:** Mrs. Maria Smith nurtured first seedling in mid 1800s. Mildly tart. Best for snacking; good for baking. Available year-round.

**McIntosh:** First apple tree planted by John McIntosh about 1811. Two-toned red and green. All-purpose apple. Available September to June.

**Jonathan:** Deep red; mildly tart, rich flavor. Versatile apple—excellent for snacking and baking. Available September to April.

---

## APPLE ARITHMETIC

**1 pound apples** = 4 small OR 3 medium OR 2 large apples

**1 pound apples** = 3 cups diced OR 2¾ cups sliced apples

**1 bushel apples** = 126 medium apples OR 18 to 20 quarts of canned or frozen apple slices OR 16 to 20 quarts of applesauce

**2 pounds apples** = one 9-inch apple pie

**A word about nutrition.** The apple is relatively low in calories with about 80 calories per apple. It's an excellent snack food that supplies vitamins and minerals without adding any fat.

# CROCKERY COOKER MEALS
## COME HOME TO A SIMMERING STEW

By Joy Taylor

**O**ne of the small joys in this world is knowing that dinner is ready when you walk in the door after a busy day. Let it happen with help from your crockery cooker.

**COMFORTING STEW—** perfect for a cozy family meal before a warming fire.

## CHICKEN AND SAUSAGE CASSOULET

*An easy, delicious version of the classic French bean stew called cassoulet—*

- 3 **medium carrots, cut into ½-inch pieces (1 cup)**
- 1 **medium onion, chopped (½ cup)**
- ⅓ **cup water**
- 1 **6-ounce can tomato paste**
- ½ **cup dry red wine**
- 1 **teaspoon garlic powder**
- ½ **teaspoon dried thyme, crushed**
- ⅛ **teaspoon ground cloves**
- 2 **bay leaves**
- 2 **15-ounce can navy beans, drained**
- 4 **boneless, skinless chicken breast halves, frozen individually**
- ½ **pound fully cooked polish sausage, sliced ¼ inch thick**

● In a small saucepan combine the carrot, onion, and water. Bring to boiling; reduce heat. Simmer, covered, 5 minutes. Transfer to a 3½- or 4-quart crockery cooker. Stir in tomato paste, wine, and seasonings. Add beans.

**ACCOMPANY BOWLFULS OF CHICKEN AND SAUSAGE CASSOULET** with a crisp lettuce salad, crusty bread, and an ice-cold glass of milk.

**USE FROZEN CHICKEN PIECES** so the chicken cooks tender, but not overdone.

● **Place frozen chicken atop** bean mixture. Place sausage atop chicken. Cover; cook on low-heat setting for 9 to 10 hours or high-heat setting for 5½ to 6 hours. *(Do not cook for less time; this long cooking time is necessary when starting with frozen chicken pieces.)*

● **Before serving,** remove bay leaves and skim off fat. Makes 4 servings.

*Nutrition information per serving:* *626 cal., 56 g pro., 46 g carbo., 22 g fat, 136 mg chol., 948 mg sodium, 1,628 mg potassium, 15 g dietary fiber. U.S. RDA: 325% vit. A, 29% vit. C, 46% thiamine, 25% riboflavin, 102% niacin, 42% iron.*

# SERVE A DELICIOUS, NO-FUSS AFTER-WORK MEAL

Crockery cooker meals do require a bit of upfront work. But you can bypass morning rush by doing some or all of the preparation for this recipe the night or day before.

## HARVEST DINNER

*An old-fashioned pot roast dinner seasoned with a touch of cinnamon. If you don't want to fix the gravy, just spoon the juices over the meat—*

- 1 1½- to 2-pound boneless beef chuck pot roast
- 2 tablespoons cooking oil
- 1 medium onion, thinly sliced
- 3 medium sweet potatoes, peeled and quartered (1 pound)
- ⅔ cup beef broth
- ¾ teaspoon celery salt
- ¼ teaspoon salt
- ¼ teaspoon ground cinnamon
- ¼ teaspoon pepper
- 1 tablespoon cornstarch
- 2 tablespoons cold water
  Apple wedges (optional)

● **Trim fat from roast.** In a 10-inch skillet brown roast on all sides in hot oil. Drain well. If desired, wrap meat in foil and chill overnight.

● **In a 3½- to 4-quart crockery cooker** place first the onion then the sweet potatoes. Place roast atop vegetables. (Cut roast, if necessary, to fit.) Combine beef broth, celery salt, salt, cinnamon, and pepper. Pour over all. Cover; cook on low-heat setting for 10 to 12 hours or high-heat setting for 4 to 5 hours.

● **To serve,** transfer roast and vegetables to platter, reserving juices. Skim fat from juices. Measure *1 cup* of the juices. For gravy, in a small saucepan stir cornstarch into water; add the 1 cup juices. Cook and stir till thickened and bubbly. Cook and stir 2 minutes more. Serve gravy with roast and vegetables. Garnish platter with apples. Makes 6 servings.

*Nutrition information per serving: 283 cal., 24 g pro., 18 g carbo., 12 g fat, 69 mg chol., 441 mg sodium, 353 mg potassium, 2 g dietary fiber. U.S. RDA: 261% vit. A, 19% vit. C, 16% riboflavin, 21% niacin, 19% iron.*

**EVEN WHEN YOU'RE GONE ALL DAY,** you and your family can enjoy a home cooked beef dinner brimming with fresh sweet potatoes.

**THE NIGHT BEFORE:** Brown the roast then wrap in foil and chill.

## HEAD STARTS

● **The night before:**
1. Brown the meat, drain well, and wrap in foil. Chill.
2. Chop and measure vegetables. Place in separate bowls or layer as recipe directs in the crockery liner if it is removable. Cover; chill.
3. Combine broth and seasonings; cover and chill.

● **To use an automatic timer:**
Before you leave the house, place the *chilled* food in the cooker. Plug the cooker into the timer, set the timer, and turn on the cooker. *Do not let the food stand more than two hours at room temperature before the cooker switches on.*

PHOTOGRAPH (left): SCOTT LITTLE. FOOD STYLIST: JANET HERWIG. PHOTOGRAPH (right): SUSAN SCHELLING. FOOD STYLIST: STEVIE BASS.

# DIET AND HEALTH

## BEST-BET THANKSGIVING DINNER

*A great-tasting, lightened-up feast—with all the traditional flavors!*

By Barbara Goldman

### TRADITIONAL MENU
Adds up to: 2,173 cal., 110 g fat, 414 mg chol., 2,099 mg sodium

### HEALTH HINTS
*Reduce fat, cholesterol, sodium, and calories; retain all the flavor!*

### LIGHTENED MENU
Adds up to: 1,109 cal., 13 g fat, 122 mg chol., 890 mg sodium

---

● **Roast turkey (white and dark)**
*6 ounces turkey: 289 cal., 8 g fat, 130 mg chol., 120 mg sodium*

● **Choose white meat** *without the skin for lower fat and cholesterol. Forgo self-basting birds with extra fat.*

● **Roast turkey (white only)**
*6 ounces turkey: 266 cal., 5 g fat, 118 mg chol., 106 mg sodium*

---

● **Turkey gravy**
*¼ cup: 76 cal., 7 g fat, 7 mg chol., 0 mg sodium*

● **Skim all fat from juices** *before thickening gravy. Add flavor with herbs instead of salt.*

● **Fat-free turkey gravy**
*¼ cup: 14 cal., 0 g fat, 0 mg chol., 0 mg sodium*

---

● **Bread stuffing**
*⅔ cup: 290 cal., 17 g fat, 43 mg chol., 713 mg sodium*

● **Replace** *one-fourth of the bread with cut-up vegetables, using only about 1 tablespoon margarine to sauté.*

● **Vegetable-bread stuffing**
*⅔ cup: 193 cal., 4 g fat, 2 mg chol., 398 mg sodium*

---

● **Oven candied sweet potatoes**
*¾ cup: 236 cal., 6 g fat, 16 mg chol., 216 mg sodium*

● **Combine** *apple and sweet potato slices with apple juice, omit margarine. For microwave recipe, see page 159.*

● **Spiced-apple sweet potatoes**
*¾ cup: 105 cal., 0 g fat, 0 mg chol., 9 mg sodium*

---

● **Creamy molded fruit salad**
*¾ cup: 246 cal., 15 g fat, 94 mg chol., 102 mg sodium*

● **Serve fresh fruit** *splashed with champagne in place of fruit gelatin with cream cheese and sour cream.*

● **Champagne fruit salad**
*¾ cup: 42 cal., 0 g fat, 0 mg chol., 3 mg sodium*

---

● **Broccoli-onion casserole**
*¾ cup: 184 cal., 13 g fat, 36 mg chol., 334 mg sodium*

● **Steam vegetables,** *then toss with almonds, lemon juice, and a dab of margarine. Eliminate cheese and sauces.*

● **Tomato-broccoli amandine**
*¾ cup: 45 cal., 1 g fat, 2 mg chol., 61 mg sodium*

---

● **Cranberry sauce**
*½ cup: 210 cal., 0 g fat, 0 mg chol., 40 mg sodium*

● **Grind cranberries** *with oranges, apples, or peaches; sprinkle with just enough sugar to cut the tartness.*

● **Fruity cranberry sauce**
*½ cup: 94 cal., 0 g fat, o mg chol., 1 mg sodium*

---

● **Dinner roll, butter**
*1 roll, 1 pat butter: 192 cal., 11 g fat, 22 mg chol., 275 mg sodium*

● **Give a fiber boost** *with whole grain rolls. Serve with 1 teaspoon fruit preserves rather than butter.*

● **Whole wheat roll, preserves**
*1 roll, 1 teaspoon fruit preserves: 108 cal., 1 g fat, 0 mg chol., 197 mg sodium*

---

● **Pumpkin pie, whipped cream**
*⅛ pie: 450 cal., 33 g fat, 66 mg chol., 299 mg sodium*

● **Make pumpkin filling** *with less sugar, skim milk; substitute baked meringue for crust. For recipe, see page 159.*

● **Pumpkin chiffon meringue**
*1 individual meringue: 142 cal., 2 g fat, 0 mg chol., 115 mg sodium*

## PUMPKIN CHIFFON MERINGUES

*It's hard to believe, but one luscious dessert adds up to only 142 calories—*

- 1 recipe Meringue Shells (see recipe, right)
- 1 cup canned pumpkin
- 1 teaspoon pumpkin pie spice
- ¼ teaspoon salt
- 1 envelope unflavored gelatin
- ¾ cup water
- 2 tablespoons sugar
- 2 egg whites
- 2 tablespoons sugar
- 1 1.4-ounce envelope whipped dessert topping mix
- ½ cup skim milk

Prepare Meringue Shells.

For filling, in a large mixing bowl stir together pumpkin, pumpkin pie spice, and salt; set aside.

In a small saucepan combine gelatin and water. Let stand 5 minutes. Stir in 2 tablespoons of sugar. Cook and stir over medium heat till gelatin is dissolved. Cool 10 minutes.

Stir the cooled gelatin mixture into the pumpkin mixture. Chill in the freezer about 15 minutes or till the mixture is slightly thickened, stirring occasionally. Remove mixture from freezer (gelatin mixture will continue to set).

In a small mixing bowl immediately begin beating egg whites with electric mixer on medium speed till soft peaks form (tips curl). Gradually add 2 tablespoons sugar, beating with electric mixer on high speed till stiff peaks form (tips stand straight). When gelatin mixture is partially set (consistency of unbeaten egg whites), fold in stiff-beaten egg whites. Wash bowl and beaters thoroughly.

In the same small mixing bowl prepare dessert topping according to package directions, *except* use the ½ cup skim milk. Reserve ½ *cup* of the whipped topping for each serving. Fold remaining whipped topping into gelatin mixture. Cover and chill the mixture till it mounds when spooned. Spoon into meringue shells.

Cover and chill in the refrigerator for at least 3 hours or till set.* Before serving, stir reserved topping and dollop on each meringue. Serves 8.

***Note:** The Pumpkin Chiffon Meringues may be made the day ahead and stored, covered, in the refrigerator.*

***Nutrition information per serving:** 142 cal., 4 g pro., 28 g carbo., 2 g fat, 0 mg chol., 115 mg sodium, 127 mg potassium. U.S. RDA: 137% vit. A.*

## MERINGUE SHELLS

*The egg whites will beat up more quickly and to a greater volume if they are at room temperature—*

- 3 egg whites
- ½ teaspoon vanilla
- ¼ teaspoon cream of tartar
- ¾ cup sugar

Cover a baking sheet with brown paper. Draw eight 3-inch circles on paper, leaving 1 inch between each.

In a small mixing bowl beat egg whites, vanilla, and cream of tartar with an electric mixer on medium speed till soft peaks form (tips curl). Gradually add sugar, beating on high speed till stiff peaks form (tips stand straight) and sugar is almost dissolved. Immediately pipe or spoon beaten egg-white mixture into a shell shape—building edges up high—in each circle on the paper-lined baking sheet.

Bake in a 300° oven for 30 minutes. Turn off the oven and let the meringue shells dry with oven door closed for at least 1 hour. Peel off paper. Makes 8 meringue shells.

## SPICED-APPLE SWEET POTATOES

*You can micro-cook this tasty sweet potato side dish in less than 20 minutes—*

- 4 medium sweet potatoes, peeled and cut into ¼-inch-thick slices (5 cups)
- 3 firm medium cooking apples peeled, cored, and cut into wedges (3 cups)
- ½ cup apple juice *or* apple cider
- 1 teaspoon cornstarch
- ¾ teaspoon ground cinnamon

In a 2-quart casserole combine sweet potatoes, apples, and ¼ *cup* of the apple juice or cider. Micro-cook, uncovered, on 100% power (high) for 14 to 16 minutes or till potatoes and apples are crisp-tender, stirring twice.

In a small bowl stir together remaining apple juice, cornstarch, and cinnamon. Stir into potato mixture. Cook, covered, on high for 2 to 3 minutes or till vegetables are glazed and heated through, stirring twice. Makes 8 servings.

***Nutrition information per serving:** 105 cal., 1 g pro., 25 g carbo., 0 g fat, 0 mg chol., 9 mg sodium, 206 mg potassium, 3 g dietary fiber. U.S. RDA: 261% vit. A, 28% vit. C.*

# HOLIDAY TIP
# TURKEY SHOPPING

**E**ven though prices per pound are higher than last Thanksgiving, turkey is still a good buy.

### ● Fresh turkey
Buy it a maximum of two days before roasting. Take the turkey right home to your refrigerator.

### ● Fresh stuffed turkey
Avoid buying a fresh turkey that's been stuffed but not cooked. Raw turkey should be stuffed only *right before* cooking. Otherwise, bacteria can multiply, causing food-borne illness.

### ● Roasted stuffed turkey
If you decide to purchase a stuffed turkey that's been completely roasted from a store or restaurant, plan to pick it up *just before* dinnertime. Make sure the turkey is hot! Then, take it home and eat right away.

### ● Frozen turkey
Look over the frozen turkey you choose to make sure the packaging is free from tears and frost. Store the turkey in your freezer up to 12 months. After 12 months, the turkey is still safe, but will begin deteriorating in quality. Buy frozen turkey at least 3 to 4 days before serving to allow for thawing.

### ● Smoked turkey
Even though smoked turkey is fully cooked, it needs refrigeration. Keep unopened turkey in your refrigerator up to 2 weeks. Or, wrap unopened turkey in moisture- and vaporproof wrap; seal, label, and freeze up to 2 months.

### ● Mail-order turkey
Many companies sell different forms of turkey through mail-order catalogs. Be sure turkey you purchase this way, or that is sent as a gift, is still cold upon delivery. To keep the turkey cold, it is typically shipped in a plastic foam container with dry ice or an ice pack. Try to arrange shipment so that someone can immediately put the turkey in a refrigerator upon delivery.

# HOW TO MAKE
# SENSATIONAL CHEESE SAUCE

A velvety cheese sauce to spoon over hot vegetables.

## CHOOSE-A-CHEESE SAUCE
- 1 green onion, thinly sliced
- 1 tablespoon margarine *or* butter
- 1 tablespoon all-purpose flour
- ⅔ cup milk
- ½ cup shredded Bel Paese®, Gruyère, Jarlsberg, Swiss, *or* cheddar cheese (2 ounces)
- 1 tablespoon diced pimiento
- 1 tablespoon dry white wine *or* 1 teaspoon lemon juice

In a 1-quart saucepan cook onion in hot margarine or butter about 2 minutes or till tender. Stir in flour and dash *ground white pepper*. Add milk. Cook and stir over medium heat till thickened and bubbly. Cook and stir 1 minute more. Reduce heat to low. Stir in cheese just till melted. Remove from heat at once; stir in remaining ingredients. If mixture is thick, stir in 1 to 2 tablespoons additional *milk*. Makes 1 cup.

*Nutrition information per tablespoon:* 28 cal., 1 g pro., 1 g carbo., 2 g fat, 6 mg chol., 22 mg sodium.

---

### 4 TRICKS FOR A PERFECT CHEESE SAUCE
● Low heat and short cooking are two secrets of a perfect cheese sauce. Add cheese toward the end of cooking, then cook over low heat *only* till cheese starts to melt. If you cook natural cheese longer, it separates, becoming tough.
● Accurate measuring pays off handsomely in a sauce that's of just the right consistency. Use this easy guide: Two ounces natural or process cheese equals ½ cup when shredded.
● No more lumps! Stir the flour and butter together completely so all the flour is coated with fat. Then, add the milk all at once and stir well.
● Give your sauce premium taste by getting rid of the starchy taste of uncooked flour. Before adding cheese, cook your sauce an extra minute after it thickens and bubbles.

# SHARE THE HOLIDAY SPIRIT!

By Barbara Johnson

*Sharing is the heart of Christmas. Sharing love, sharing gifts, sharing traditions, and, of course, sharing food. From cookies, candies, and breads bedecked for gift giving to appetizers and special menus for festive gatherings, here are recipes perfect for sharing the cheer of the season with the ones you love.*

## GIVE YOUR HOMEMADE GIFTS

The special people in your life deserve equally special Christmas presents—like these unique food gifts you can handcraft right in your own kitchen. To take a closer look at each of these classy, gourmet-style ideas, see the map, opposite.

# December

## LEMON POPPY SEED BREAD

*For gift-giving, wrap each loaf in clear plastic wrap and tie with a ribbon—*

1¾ **cups all-purpose flour**
⅔ **cup sugar**
1 **tablespoon finely shredded lemon peel**
1½ **teaspoons baking powder**
1 **teaspoon poppy seed**
**Dash salt**
1 **egg**
¾ **cup milk**
¼ **cup cooking oil**
1 **tablespoon lemon juice**
**Lemon Icing**
**Finely shredded lemon peel**

Grease the bottoms of four 4½x2½x1½-inch individual loaf pans. Set aside.

In a large bowl stir together flour, sugar, the 1 tablespoon lemon peel, baking powder, poppy seed, and salt.

In a small mixing bowl combine egg, milk, oil, and lemon juice. Add to flour mixture, stirring just till moistened. Pour batter into prepared pans.

Bake in a 400° oven for 25 to 30 minutes or till golden brown and a toothpick inserted in the center comes out clean. Cool in the pans for 10 minutes. Remove from the pans; place on a wire rack over waxed paper. Cool the loaves completely.

Drizzle Lemon Icing over loaves. Sprinkle with additional lemon peel. Let the icing dry till firm. Makes 4 small loaves (8 slices each).

*Lemon Icing:* Combine 1 cup sifted *powdered sugar* and enough *lemon juice* (4 to 5 teaspoons) to make an icing of drizzling consistency. Tint *half* of the icing with green food coloring, if desired. Makes ⅓ cup.

***Nutrition information per slice:*** *78 cal., 1 g pro., 13 g carbo., 2 g fat, 9 mg chol., 23 mg sodium, 20 mg potassium.*

## HOMEMADE FOOD GIFTS
1. Chocolate Hazelnut Sauce
2. Cherry-Apple Jam
3. Cranberry-Cinnamon Vinegar
4. Lemon Poppy Seed Bread
5. Fiery Marinated Olives
6. Peach-Fig Relish
7. Dark Hazelnut Toffee
8. Chocolate Cashew Butter

## CHERRY-APPLE JAM

*To add a personal touch, label the jars and decorate the lids with seasonal fabric and ribbon—*

1 **16-ounce package frozen unsweetened pitted tart red cherries**
1 **medium apple, cored and finely chopped (1 cup)**
¼ **cup lemon juice**
1 **1¾-ounce package regular powdered fruit pectin**
5 **cups sugar**

Finely chop frozen cherries, reserving juices. You should have *3 cups* chopped fruit.

In an 8- or 10-quart kettle or Dutch oven combine chopped cherries, reserved juices, apple, and lemon juice. Add pectin; mix well. Bring mixture to a full rolling boil. Stir in sugar. Bring again to full rolling boil, stirring often. Boil hard, uncovered, 1 minute. Remove from heat; quickly skim off foam with a metal spoon.

Ladle into hot clean half-pint jars, leaving a ¼-inch headspace. Wipe jar rims; adjust lids. Process in boiling water bath for 15 minutes (start this timing when the water boils). Makes about 5 half-pints.

***Nutrition information per 2 teaspoons:*** *36 cal., 0 g pro., 9 g carbo., 0 g fat, 0 mg chol., 0 mg sodium, and 7 mg potassium.*

## CHOCOLATE HAZELNUT SAUCE

    3  squares (3 ounces) semisweet
       chocolate
    ¼  cup margarine or butter
    1  5-ounce can (⅔ cup) evaporated
       milk
    ½  cup sugar
    3  tablespoons hazelnut liqueur

In a heavy, medium saucepan melt the semisweet chocolate and margarine or butter over low heat, stirring frequently. Stir in the evaporated milk and sugar. Cook and stir over medium heat about 5 minutes or till the mixture is slightly thickened and bubbly. Remove from the heat. Add the hazelnut liqueur; stir till mixture is smooth. Cool slightly.

Pour sauce into a pint jar. Cover and chill up to 1 month.

To serve, in a medium saucepan cook and stir over low heat till heated through. Or, transfer the sauce to a microwave-safe bowl and micro-cook on 100% power (high) about 1 minute or till heated through. Serve sauce over ice cream or pound cake. Makes about 1½ cups sauce.

**Nutrition information per 2 tablespoons:** *132 cal., 1 g pro., 17 g carbo., 7 g fat, 4 mg chol., 60 mg sodium, 67 mg potassium.*

## FIERY MARINATED OLIVES

*Be sure to chill the olives for the specified time before serving so they take on the delicious combination of flavors in the marinade—*

    2  3-ounce jars almond-stuffed
       olives, drained
    ⅓  cup salad oil
    ¼  cup water
    3  tablespoons lime juice
    1  tablespoon fresh, snipped or
       freeze-dried cilantro
    1  tablespoon crushed red pepper
    1  teaspoon cumin seed
    1  clove garlic, minced

In a small saucepan combine all ingredients. Bring to boiling; reduce heat. Simmer, covered, 5 minutes. Remove from heat. Cool to room temperature.

Use slotted spoon to transfer olives to 2 screw-top half-pint jars. Pour cooking liquid equally over olives in jars.

Cover and chill in the refrigerator for 4 to 7 days before serving. Store in the refrigerator up to 3 weeks. Makes 2 half-pint jars.

**Nutrition information per olive:** *23 cal., 1 g pro., 1 g carbo., 2 g fat, 0 mg chol., 96 mg sodium, 22 mg potassium.*

## CRANBERRY-CINNAMON VINEGAR

*Brimming with fresh cranberry flavor, this pleasantly tart and spicy vinegar adds pizzazz to salads, sauces, and marinades. Gift wrap a bottle for your favorite host——*

    6  inches stick cinnamon
    1½ cups fresh cranberries
    2  cups cider vinegar
    1  cup dry red wine
    ¼  cup sugar

Place cinnamon in a clean 1-quart jar. Set aside.

In a colander thoroughly rinse the cranberries with cold water; drain well. In a stainless steel or enamel saucepan bring the rinsed and drained cranberries, cider vinegar, dry red wine, and sugar to boiling. Boil gently, uncovered, for 3 minutes.

Pour hot cranberry mixture over cinnamon in jar. Cover; let stand in a cool, dark place for 1 week.

Line a sieve or colander with fine-woven cloth or a cup-shaped coffee filter. Pour mixture through sieve or colander and let drain into a bowl.

Transfer strained liquid to 3 clean half-pint bottles or jars. Cover tightly with a glass, plastic, or cork lid. Store up to 6 months. Makes 3 half-pint jars.

**Nutrition information per tablespoon:** *11 cal., 0 g pro., 2 g carbo., 0 g fat, 0 mg chol., 0 mg sodium, 17 mg potassium.*

## PEACH-FIG RELISH

*This tasty relish goes well with pork, veal, chicken, and turkey—*

    2  29-ounce cans peach slices
    1  5½-ounce can peach or apricot
       nectar
    ½  teaspoon finely shredded lemon
       peel
    ¼  cup lemon juice
    1  teaspoon ground cardamom
    3  cups chopped, dried light figs
       (1 pound)
    1  tablespoon peach brandy or
       brandy

Drain peach slices, reserving ½ cup syrup. Coarsely chop peach slices.

In a large saucepan combine the chopped peaches, reserved syrup, nectar, lemon peel, lemon juice, and cardamom. Bring to boiling. Boil gently, uncovered, 5 minutes. Stir in figs and brandy. Cook for 2 minutes more, stirring occasionally.

Ladle hot relish mixture into hot, clean half-pint jars, leaving a ½-inch headspace. Wipe jar rims; adjust lids. Process in a boiling water bath for 15 minutes (start timing when the water boils). Makes about 8 half-pint jars.

**Nutrition information per tablespoon:** *16 cal., 0 g pro., 4 g carbo., 0 g fat, 0 mg chol., 1 mg sodium, 43 mg potassium, 1 g dietary fiber.*

## DARK HAZELNUT TOFFEE

*Use butter instead of margarine to keep the fat from separating out onto the surface of the candy—*

- ¾ **cup coarsely chopped hazelnuts (filberts)**
- 1 **cup butter**
- 1¼ **cups packed brown sugar**
- 3 **tablespoons water**
- 1 **tablespoon dark corn syrup**
- ¾ **cup milk chocolate pieces**
- ¼ **cup finely chopped hazelnuts (filberts)**

Line a 13x9x2-inch baking pan with foil, extending the foil over the edges of the pan. Sprinkle the ¾ cup hazelnuts on the bottom of the foil-lined pan. Set the pan aside.

Butter the sides of a heavy 2-quart saucepan. In the saucepan melt the 1 cup butter over low heat. Stir in brown sugar, water, and syrup. Cook over medium-high heat to boiling, stirring constantly with a wooden spoon to dissolve sugar. (This should take about 4 minutes.) Avoid splashing mixture on sides of pan. Carefully clip candy thermometer to side of pan.

Cook over medium heat, stirring frequently, till thermometer registers 290° (soft-crack stage). Mixture should boil at a moderate, steady rate over the entire surface. (Reaching the soft-crack stage should take about 15 minutes. Watch carefully after candy mixture reaches 280°.)

Remove pan from heat; remove thermometer. Immediately pour mixture into prepared pan. Let stand 2 to 3 minutes or till surface is firm. Sprinkle with chocolate pieces; let stand 1 to 2 minutes. When softened, spread chocolate pieces evenly over toffee mixture.

Sprinkle with the ¼ cup hazelnuts; press nuts lightly into melted chocolate. Chill till firm. Lift candy out of pan; break into pieces. Store in a tightly covered container. Makes about 1½ pounds (48 pieces).

***Nutrition information per piece:*** *85 cal., 1 g pro., 8 g carbo., 6 g fat, 11 mg chol., 44 mg sodium, 42 mg potassium.*

## CHOCOLATE CASHEW BUTTER

*Create this nut spread in just 20 minutes. For gift-giving, layer the spread with additional cashews in a crock—*

- 1½ **cups cashews**
- ¼ **cup margarine *or* butter, softened**
- ¼ **cup semisweet chocolate pieces**
- 1 **teaspoon instant coffee crystals**
- 1 **teaspoon water**

Place nuts in a blender container or food processor bowl. Cover and blend or process till finely ground. Add *half* of the margarine or butter. Cover and blend or process about 3 minutes more or till mixture is spreadable. Stop and scrape down sides of container or bowl as necessary. Transfer the nut mixture to a small mixing bowl.

Meanwhile, in a small saucepan heat remaining margarine or butter and chocolate pieces over low heat, stirring constantly till melted. Dissolve coffee crystals in water. Stir chocolate mixture and coffee into nut mixture.

To store, chill, covered, up to 3 months. To serve, let stand at room temperature for 1 hour. Makes about 1 cup butter.

***Nutrition information per tablespoon:*** *114 cal., 2 g pro., 6 g carbo., 10 g fat, 0 mg chol., 36 mg sodium, 86 mg potassium, 1 g dietary fiber.*

# HOLIDAY PARTIES
## ON AN EVERYDAY BUDGET

**Y**ou may find dollar signs dancing through your head now that the holiday party season is here. Don't fret. It is possible to gather friends and family for a little good cheer without overspending.

### Set the style

● **Think small.** Obviously, the smaller your gathering and the less food you buy, the smaller your food bill. Don't feel you have to outdo every other hostess this time of year.

● **Go potluck.** Today, it's a very acceptable way to entertain. (Some guests actually feel guilty if they don't bring something!) Not only is this a money saver, it's the best timesaver, too.

● **Consider an oriental meal.** For a dinner party, a stir-fry meal stretches the meat (usually the most expensive portion of a meal). Enhance the stir-fry with one or two "exotic" vegetables.

● **Plan a soup party.** Friends love the informality of a homemade soup and bread party; you'll like the reasonable prices on these scratch foods.

● **Serve brunch.** Popular brunch foods such as egg dishes and coffee cakes can run considerably less than dinner menus. Also, people drink less or not at all at brunch.

● **Plan a party activity.** Focus your party on an activity (tree trimming or caroling) so there's more to do than eat.

### Menu notes

● **Dramatize one food.** Make one super-fantastic dish—guests focus their attention on that and overlook the simple dishes.

● **Be flexible.** Don't lock yourself into a rigid menu. When you grocery shop and spot store specials, be willing to alter your menu. For example, decide on the type of fish to buy when you're at the fish counter, not beforehand.

● **Think seasonal.** Avoid higher-cost out-of-season produce.

# BAKE A BATCH OF
# COOKIES

*C*ookie baking at Christmas is a tradition as dear to our hearts as the story of old Saint Nick. This year, as you and your kids share the baking of your family's favorite cookies, give some of our new ideas a try, too. They're clever, fun, festive, and great tasting!

**Christmas Cookie Ornaments**

Easy as 1-2-3: Slice, bake, decorate. The cookies double as ornaments and treats at a tree-trimming party!

**Chocolate Ginger Cutouts**
*Give gingerbread a chocolate twist—*

**Pistachio-Almond Tartlets**
*Marvelous tastes come in tiny bites—*

**Meringue Kisses**
*Hide a candy kiss inside—*

**White Christmas Crinkles**
*They magically crinkle as they bake—*

**Chocolate Macadamia Bars**
*Dust with fresh-fallen "snow"—*

**Meringue Cookie Gems**
*The jam glistens like stained glass—*

## CHRISTMAS COOKIE ORNAMENTS

*Kids will love to help shape and decorate these colorful tree ornaments. For best results, use only butter and bake the cookies in batches according to size—*

    3  cups all-purpose flour
    1  teaspoon baking powder
 1½  cups butter
 1½  cups sugar
    1  egg
 1½  teaspoons vanilla
  30  drops red food coloring *or* red
       food-coloring paste (about ¼
       teaspoon)
    3  to 5 drops oil of cinnamon
Several drops green food
       coloring
   ¼  teaspoon peppermint extract *or*
       5 drops oil of peppermint
Decorating Icing
Shoestring licorice *or* thin ribbon

In a medium mixing bowl combine flour and baking powder.

In a large mixer bowl beat butter with an electric mixer on medium speed 30 seconds or till softened. Add sugar and beat till fluffy. Add egg and vanilla; beat well. Add flour mixture and beat well.

Divide the dough into 4 equal portions. Stir red food coloring and oil of cinnamon into *2 portions* of the dough, stir green food coloring and peppermint extract into *1 portion* of the dough, and leave remaining dough plain. If necessary, chill the dough about 1 hour or till easy to handle.

On a lightly floured surface roll red dough into a rope, 3 inches in diameter. Roll plain dough into a rope, 2 inches in diameter. Roll green dough into a rope, 1½ inches in diameter.

Wrap each rope of dough in waxed paper or clear plastic wrap. Freeze 1 hour or chill several hours or overnight till firm enough to slice.

Unwrap and reshape each rope of dough as necessary to form an even roll. Cut each rope into ¼-inch-thick slices. Place slices 2 inches apart on an ungreased cookie sheet.

Bake in a 350° oven 8 to 10 minutes for smaller cookies or 10 to 12 minutes for larger cookies or till edges are very light brown. Immediately, with the end of a straw or tip of a paring knife, make a hole in the top of *each* cookie for hanging. Remove and cool on a wire rack.

To decorate, pipe Decorating Icing onto cookies with a decorating bag and writing and/or leaf tip, imitating holly leaves and berries, writing names, or making other designs. Let icing dry till firm. Stack a red, then plain, then green cookie. Thread licorice or ribbon through holes and tie ends together. Makes about 18 cookie ornaments.

*Decorating Icing:* Combine 1 cup sifted *powdered sugar* and enough *milk* (about 1 to 2 tablespoons) to make an icing of piping consistency. Tint with one or two drops red or green food coloring, if desired. Makes ⅓ cup.

**Nutrition information per cookie ornament:** *240 cal., 2 g pro., 32 g carbo., 12 g fat, 43 mg chol., 141 mg sodium, 23 mg potassium.*

## CHOCOLATE GINGER CUTOUTS

    3  cups all-purpose flour
   ½  cup unsweetened cocoa powder
    1  teaspoon baking soda
   ¾  teaspoon ground ginger
   ½  teaspoon baking powder
   ½  teaspoon ground cinnamon
   ¼  teaspoon salt
   ¼  teaspoon ground cloves
   ⅔  cup shortening
   ½  cup sugar
    1  egg
   ½  cup dark corn syrup
   ¼  cup milk
    1  egg white
    1  tablespoon water
    3  recipes Decorating Icing

In a medium mixing bowl combine flour, cocoa powder, baking soda, ginger, baking powder, cinnamon, salt, and cloves.

In a large mixer bowl beat shortening with an electric mixer on medium speed for 30 seconds. Add sugar and beat till fluffy. Add whole egg, corn syrup, and milk; beat well. Beat in flour mixture, stirring in last part with a wooden spoon till well mixed.

Divide dough in half. Cover and chill about 1 hour or till easy to handle.

On a lightly floured surface roll each portion of dough ⅛ inch thick. Cut with 3- to 4-inch cookie cutters. Place on a greased cookie sheet.

Combine the egg white and water; brush on cookie cutouts.

Bake in a 375° oven 5 to 7 minutes or till slightly puffed and set. Cool on cookie sheet 1 minute. Remove and cool

thoroughly on a wire rack. Pipe on Decorating Icing with a decorating bag and writing tip. Makes about 48 cookies.

*Decorating Icing:* Combine 1 cup sifted *powdered sugar* and enough *milk* (about 1 to 2 tablespoons) to make an icing of piping consistency. Tint with one or two drops red or green food coloring, if desired. Makes ⅓ cup.

**Nutrition information per cookie:** *100 cal., 1 g pro., 17 g carbo., 3 g fat, 6 mg chol., 50 mg sodium, 20 mg potassium.*

## WHITE CHRISTMAS CRINKLES

    4  ounces white baking bar with
       cocoa butter
    2  cups all-purpose flour
   ½  teaspoon baking soda
   ¼  teaspoon salt
   ⅓  cup margarine *or* butter
    1  cup sugar
    1  egg
   ¼  cup buttermilk *or* sour milk*
    1  teaspoon vanilla
Sugar
   ½  cup semisweet chocolate pieces
    2  teaspoons shortening
Striped, round, hard peppermint
       candies, chopped

Melt baking bar over low heat, stirring constantly. Set aside.

In a small mixing bowl combine flour, baking soda, and salt.

In a small mixer bowl beat margarine or butter with electric mixer on medium speed 30 seconds. Add the 1 cup sugar and beat till well combined. Beat in melted baking bar, egg, buttermilk, and vanilla. Add flour mixture; beat till well mixed. Cover; chill dough at least 1 hour or till easy to handle.

Shape dough into 1-inch balls; roll in additional sugar. Place 2 inches apart on an ungreased cookie sheet.

Bake in a 375° oven about 10 minutes or till bottoms are light brown. Remove and cool on a wire rack.

Meanwhile, in a small saucepan cook and stir the semisweet chocolate pieces and shortening over low heat till melted; drizzle over cookies. Sprinkle cookies with chopped peppermint candies. Makes 48 cookies.

**\*To make sour milk:** Combine ¾ teaspoon *lemon juice* or *vinegar* and enough *milk* to make ¼ cup.

**Nutrition information per cookie:** *76 cal., 1 g pro., 12 g carbo., 3 g fat, 6 mg chol., 44 mg sodium, 22 mg potassium.*

## MERINGUE KISSES AND MERINGUE COOKIE GEMS

*This recipe makes two cookies: kisses and cookie gems. Look for the cream mints for the kisses at department store candy counters and candy or food gift shops—*

- ½ **cup margarine** *or* **butter**
- ½ **cup sugar**
- 1 **tablespoon milk**
- ½ **teaspoon vanilla**
- 1¼ **cups all-purpose flour**
- 2 **egg whites**
- ½ **teaspoon vanilla**
- ¼ **teaspoon cream of tartar**
- ½ **cup sugar**
- ⅓ **cup preserves (cherry, apricot, peach, pineapple, raspberry** *or* **strawberry)** *or* **jelly (mint-flavored, apple, crab apple, currant,** *or* **plum)**
- 12 **pastel cream mints** *or* **chocolate kisses (about 3 ounces)**
- **Green** *or* **red colored sugar**

For cookie dough, in small mixer bowl beat margarine or butter with electric mixer on medium speed till softened. Add ½ cup sugar; beat till fluffy. Add milk and ½ teaspoon vanilla; beat well. Stir in flour.

On waxed paper or clear plastic wrap shape dough into an 8-inch rope. Wrap and freeze 1 hour or chill several hours or overnight. Wash small mixer bowl and beaters.

For meringue, in the small mixer bowl beat egg whites, ½ teaspoon vanilla, and cream of tartar on medium speed till soft peaks form (tips curl). Gradually add ½ cup sugar, beating on high till stiff peaks form (tips stand straight).

For meringue cookie gems, unwrap and reshape cookie dough as necessary to form an even roll. Cut dough into ¼-inch-thick slices; place slices 1 inch apart on an ungreased cookie sheet.

Spoon meringue into a decorating bag fitted with a small star tip. Pipe meringue around outside of *each* cookie. Spoon about ½ *teaspoon* of preserves or jelly into center of *each* cookie.

Bake in a 325° oven about 22 minutes or till meringue just starts to brown. Let stand 1 minute. Remove from cookie sheet; cool on a wire rack.

Meanwhile, for meringue kisses, on a lightly greased cookie sheet pipe *some* of the remaining meringue into 12 rounds, *each* about 1¼ inches in diameter. Press a mint or chocolate kiss into each meringue round. Pipe meringue around each kiss in concentric circles, starting at base and working toward top, till kiss is completely covered. Sprinkle with colored sugar.

Bake in a 325° oven for 20 to 25 minutes or till light brown on the edges. Immediately remove from cookie sheet and cool on a wire rack. Makes about 12 kisses and 30 gem cookies.

***Nutrition information per kiss:** 35 cal., 0 g pro., 9 g carbo., 0 g fat, 0 mg chol., 17 mg sodium, 3 mg potassium.*

***Nutrition information per gem cookie:** 74 cal., 1 g pro., 11 g carbo., 3 g fat, 0 mg chol., 39 mg sodium, 13 mg potassium.*

## CHOCOLATE MACADAMIA BARS

- 1 **6-ounce package semisweet chocolate pieces**
- 2 **squares (2 ounces) unsweetened chocolate**
- 2 **tablespoons margarine** *or* **butter**
- ⅔ **cup sugar**
- 2 **eggs**
- 1 **teaspoon vanilla**
- ¼ **cup all-purpose flour**
- ¼ **teaspoon baking powder**
- **Dash salt**
- 1 **cup chopped macadamia nuts** *or* **pecans**
- 2 **ounces white baking bar with cocoa butter, chopped**
- **Powdered sugar**

In a medium saucepan heat chocolate pieces, unsweetened chocolate, and margarine or butter over low heat till melted, stirring constantly. Remove from heat; cool 10 minutes. Stir in sugar. Add eggs and vanilla; beat by hand till combined. Stir in flour, baking powder, and salt. Fold in nuts and white baking bar. Spread batter in a greased 9x9x2-inch baking pan.

Bake in a 350° oven for 30 minutes. Cool completely on a wire rack. Sift powdered sugar over top. Cut into bars. Makes 24 bars.

***Nutrition information per bar:** 143 cal., 2 g pro., 14 g carbo., 10 g fat, 23 mg chol., 28 mg sodium, 75 mg potassium.*

## PISTACHIO-ALMOND TARTLETS

- ½ **cup margarine** *or* **butter**
- 1 **3-ounce package cream cheese, softened**
- 1 **cup all-purpose flour**
- 1 **egg**
- ½ **cup sugar**
- ½ **of an 8-ounce can (½ cup) almond paste, crumbled**
- ¼ **cup coarsely chopped pistachios** *or* **almonds**
- ¼ **cup currant** *or* **red raspberry jelly (optional)**
- **Finely chopped pistachios** *or* **almonds (optional)**

For crust, in a small mixer bowl beat margarine or butter and cream cheese with an electric mixer on medium speed till softened. Stir in flour. Cover and chill about 1 hour or till dough is easy to handle.

Form chilled dough into a ball. Divide dough into 24 equal portions; roll each portion into a ball. Place each ball in an ungreased 1¾-inch muffin cup. Press dough evenly against bottom and up sides of cup. Cover and set aside.

For filling, in a small mixer bowl combine egg, sugar, and almond paste; beat till almost smooth. Stir in the coarsely chopped nuts. Fill *each* dough-lined muffin cup with a rounded *teaspoon* of the filling.

Bake in a 325° oven for 25 to 30 minutes or till tops are light brown. Cool slightly in pan. Remove from pans and cool completely on wire racks.

Store, tightly covered, at room temperature up to 1 week. Or, freeze in a moisture- and vaporproof freezer container up to 12 months.

To serve, thaw tartlets (if frozen), covered, at room temperature. In a small saucepan melt jelly over low heat. Drizzle jelly over each tartlet; top with the finely chopped nuts. Makes 24 tartlets.

***Nutrition information per tartlet:** 111 cal., 2 g pro., 11 g carbo., 7 g fat, 4 mg chol., 59 mg sodium, 58 mg potassium, 1 g dietary fiber.*

**Spinach and Pepperoni Quiche**
*Use refrigerated rolls for the crust—*

**Golden Onion Braid**
*Bake ahead; rewarm to serve—*

**Two-Cheese Shrimp Tarts**
*Fill made-ahead tart shells; bake—*

**Dijon-Sausage Pâté**
*Creamy, smooth, yet no baking—*

**Parmesan-Walnut Bread**
*Freeze ahead to serve anytime—*

# HOST A HOLIDAY OPEN HOUSE

*Getting together with good friends is as comforting as a hot toddy on a crisp winter's eve. And, with the recipes shown here, it's also easy. Make most of the recipes for this splendid appetizer buffet ahead; add the finishing touches just before party time.*

**Hot Buttered Cranberry Toddy**

**Mocha Rum Nog**

Warm, creamy, soothing—ring in the holidays with these spirited beverages.

## GOLDEN ONION BRAID

```
3 to 3¼ cups all-purpose flour
1 package quick-rising active dry
     yeast
¾ cup milk
2 tablespoons sugar
2 tablespoons margarine or butter
1 teaspoon salt
1 egg
1 egg white
1⅔ cups chopped onion
2 tablespoons margarine or butter
1 teaspoon dried basil, crushed
1 teaspoon paprika
1 egg yolk
1 tablespoon water
```

In a small mixer bowl combine *1¼ cups* of the flour and the yeast.

In a small saucepan heat milk, sugar, 2 tablespoons margarine or butter, and salt just till warm (120° to 130°) and margarine is almost melted, stirring constantly.

Add milk mixture, egg, and egg white to flour mixture. Beat with an electric mixer on low speed for 30 seconds, scraping bowl constantly. Beat on high speed for 3 minutes. Using a wooden spoon stir in as much of the remaining flour as you can.

Turn dough out onto a lightly floured surface. Knead in enough of the remaining flour to make a moderately stiff dough that is smooth and elastic (6 to 8 minutes total). Shape the dough into a ball. Cover; let rest 10 minutes.

Meanwhile, in a 10-inch skillet cook onion in 2 tablespoons margarine or butter till tender but not brown. Stir in basil and paprika. Cool slightly.

Roll dough into a 15x9-inch rectangle, stopping to let dough relax, as necessary. Cut into three 15x3-inch strips. Spread *each* strip with a *third* of the onion mixture to within ½ inch of *each* edge. Combine egg yolk and water; brush *some* of the egg yolk mixture around edges of *each* dough strip. Fold *each* strip in half lengthwise; seal the side and ends.

On a greased baking sheet lay strips, seam side down, side by side. Braid strips loosely, beginning in the middle and working toward the ends. Pinch ends together and tuck under braid. Cover; let rise till nearly double (about 15 minutes). Brush with remaining egg yolk mixture.

Bake in a 375° oven for 20 to 25 minutes or till golden. Test by tapping the top with your finger. A hollow sound means the loaf is done. Cool on a wire rack. Serve at room temperature. To reheat, wrap in foil and place in a 350° oven for 15 minutes or till heated through. Makes 1 loaf, 20 servings.

*Nutrition information per serving:* *118 cal., 3 g pro., 17 g carbo., 4 g fat, 28 mg chol., 145 mg sodium, 73 mg potassium, 1 g dietary fiber. U.S. RDA: 10% thiamine.*

## DIJON-SAUSAGE PÂTÉ

*Chicken livers give this easy pâté a delicate flavor—beef livers, a more robust flavor. If you like, use half of each for a perfect blend—*

```
½ pound bulk pork sausage
1 small onion, chopped (⅓ cup)
½ pound chicken or beef livers
⅓ cup milk
1 tablespoon Dijon-style mustard
1 8-ounce package cream cheese,
     softened
¼ teaspoon fines herbes
⅛ teaspoon garlic powder
Parsley sprigs (optional)
Pimiento cutouts (optional)*
Mustard Pita Wedges
```

In a 10-inch skillet cook sausage and onion till meat is brown and onion is tender; remove with a slotted spoon.

In same skillet cook livers in drippings over medium heat for 5 to 8 minutes or till no longer pink. Drain off any fat or juices. Cool slightly.

In a blender container or food processor bowl combine the cooked livers, milk, and mustard. Cover and blend or process well. Add the sausage mixture, cream cheese, fines herbes, and garlic powder; blend or process till smooth, stopping to scrape sides of container or bowl as necessary.

Line a 3-cup decorative mold with plastic wrap; spoon mixture into mold. Cover; chill several hours or overnight.

To serve, unmold onto a serving plate; discard plastic wrap. Garnish pâté with parsley and pimiento cutouts and serve with Mustard Pita Wedges. Makes 3 cups (18 servings).

***To make pimiento cutouts:** Use a small hors d'oeuvre cutter or end of a decorating tip to cut small decorative shapes from *whole pimientos.*

*Mustard Pita Wedges:* Cut 3 large *pita bread rounds* or six 6- to 7-inch *flour tortillas* into 6 wedges. Gently tear or cut pita wedges in half crosswise to make single layers. In a small mixing bowl combine ¼ cup *margarine* or *butter*, melted; 1 tablespoon *Dijon-style mustard;* and ⅛ teaspoon *onion powder*. Brush *one* side of *each* pita or tortilla wedge with the margarine mixture. Arrange wedges, brushed side up, in a single layer on a baking sheet. Bake in a 350° oven for 10 to 15 minutes or till crisp and golden. Cool. Store in a tightly covered container. Makes 36 wedges.

*Nutrition information per serving with 2 pita wedges:* *125 cal., 5 g pro., 4 g carbo., 10 g fat, 74 mg chol., 205 mg sodium, 80 mg potassium. U.S. RDA: 58% vit. A, 18% riboflavin.*

## MOCHA RUM NOG

```
1 quart dairy eggnog
1 quart chocolate-flavored milk
1 cup whipping cream
⅓ cup rum
⅓ cup crème de cacao or coffee
     liqueur
1 tablespoon instant coffee
     crystals
Shaved chocolate (optional)
```

In saucepan combine eggnog, milk, ½ cup of the whipping cream, rum, crème de cacao or coffee liqueur, and coffee crystals. Heat through. *Do not boil.* Pour into heatproof carafe or pot.

Beat remaining whipping cream to soft peaks. Dollop over each serving. Sprinkle with shaved chocolate. Makes about 10 (7-ounce) servings.

*Nonalcoholic version:* Prepare Mocha Rum Nog as directed, *except* omit rum and crème de cacao or coffee liqueur. Add an additional *1 cup* chocolate-flavored milk and use *1 to 2 tablespoons* instant coffee crystals.

*Nutrition information per serving (alcoholic version):* *333 cal., 7 g pro., 31 g carbo., 18 g fat, 99 mg chol., 122 mg sodium, and 356 mg potassium. U.S. RDA: 18% vit. A, 22% riboflavin, and 26% calcium.*

*Nutrition information per serving (nonalcoholic version):* *304 cal., 8 g pro., 27 g carbo., 19 g fat, 100 mg chol., 137 mg sodium, and 396 mg potassium. U.S. RDA: 19% vit. A, 25% niacin, and 28% calcium.*

## SPINACH AND PEPPERONI QUICHE

1 large red sweet pepper, coarsely chopped
1 tablespoon cooking oil
1 package (8) refrigerated crescent rolls
4 beaten eggs
½ of a 10-ounce package frozen chopped spinach, thawed and well-drained
1 cup shredded Monterey Jack cheese (4 ounces)
2 ounces sliced pepperoni, cut into strips (¼ cup)
¼ cup light cream *or* milk
2 tablespoons grated Parmesan cheese
Tomato roses (optional)*

In a medium skillet cook sweet pepper in hot oil till crisp-tender; drain.

Separate crescent rolls into triangles. Press rolls over bottom and ¾ inch up sides of a 9- or 9½-inch tart pan or quiche dish, pressing dough together well at the perforations.

In a medium mixing bowl combine sweet pepper, eggs, spinach, Monterey Jack cheese, pepperoni, light cream or milk, Parmesan cheese, and ⅛ teaspoon *pepper*. Pour into crust-lined pan.

Bake in a 350° oven about 30 minutes or till set. Top with tomato roses. Cut the quiche into wedges and serve warm. Makes 12 servings.

**\*To make a tomato rose:** Use a sharp paring knife to cut a shallow circle from the bottom of a tomato, but don't sever it completely. Continue cutting a continuous narrow spiral around the sides of the tomato, tapering the strip at the end. Curl the strip onto the base in the shape of a rose.

*Nutrition information per serving: 178 cal., 7 g pro., 10 g carbo., 12 g fat, 108 mg chol., 420 mg sodium, 139 mg potassium, 1 g dietary fiber. U.S. RDA: 35% vit. A, 31% vit. C, 10% riboflavin, 11% calcium.*

## HOT BUTTERED CRANBERRY TODDY

6 cups cranberry juice cocktail
2 cups water
½ cup sugar
3 1-inch-long strips lemon peel
¼ cup lemon juice
3 inches stick cinnamon
1 teaspoon whole cloves
⅓ cup bourbon, rum, *or* orange juice
2 tablespoons butter

In a 4-quart saucepan or Dutch oven combine cranberry juice cocktail, water, sugar, and lemon juice.

Tie lemon peel, stick cinnamon, and cloves in a 6-inch square piece of cheesecloth.

Add spice bag to saucepan. Bring just to boiling; reduce heat. Simmer, covered, 10 minutes. Discard spice bag. Add bourbon, rum, or orange juice and butter. Stir till butter melts.

Transfer to a heatproof serving carafe or pot. Serve with a lemon peel strip and cinnamon stick in each cup. Makes about 10 (7-ounce) servings.

*Nutrition information per serving: 169 cal., 0 g pro., 33 g carbo., 2 g fat, 6 mg chol., 30 mg sodium, 45 mg potassium. U.S. RDA: 78% vit. C.*

## TWO-CHEESE SHRIMP TARTS

⅓ cup semisoft cheese with garlic and herbs *or* one 3-ounce package cream cheese with chives
⅓ cup margarine *or* butter
1 cup all-purpose flour
1 egg yolk
1 cup ricotta cheese
1 tablespoon milk
2 teaspoons finely snipped fresh dill *or* ½ teaspoon dried dillweed
¼ teaspoon salt
1 6-ounce package frozen, peeled, cooked shrimp, thawed and drained
Fresh dill sprigs (optional)
Chopped pimiento (optional)

For pastry, in a small mixing bowl let semisoft cheese or cream cheese and margarine or butter soften at room temperature; stir together. Stir in the flour. Divide into 12 pieces. Place *one* piece in the center of a seasoned 2½-inch sandbakkelser mold.* Press pastry evenly and thinly over bottom and up sides of mold. Repeat with remaining pastry. Place molds on a jelly-roll pan or cookie sheet.

Bake in a 375° oven for 15 minutes or till light brown around edges. Cool. Using a toothpick, carefully loosen and remove pastry from molds. Pack carefully in an airtight container. (Or, re-

turn pastry shells to jelly-roll pan and cover with foil.) Seal, label, and freeze for up to 2 months.

For filling, in a medium mixing bowl stir together egg yolk, ricotta cheese, milk, snipped dill, and salt.

Reserve 12 shrimp; wrap and chill. Chop remaining shrimp. Stir chopped shrimp into ricotta mixture. Cover and chill up to 24 hours.

To serve, place frozen pastry shells on an ungreased baking sheet. Spoon about *2 tablespoons* of the filling into *each* pastry mold.

Bake in a 375° oven for 20 to 25 minutes or till set. Cool for 5 to 10 minutes. Top with reserved shrimp, dill sprigs, and/or pimiento. Makes 12.

**\*To season the sandbakkelser molds:** Grease inside of molds with shortening. Heat molds in a 300° oven 30 minutes. Cool. Wipe out the excess shortening. After use, rinse molds with water and wipe out with paper towels. No further seasoning is needed.

*Nutrition information per tart: 156 cal., 7 g pro., 9 g carbo., 10 g fat, 65 mg chol., 184 mg sodium, 77 mg potassium.*

## PARMESAN-WALNUT BREAD

3 cups all-purpose flour
⅔ cup sugar
½ cup grated Parmesan cheese
4 teaspoons baking powder
½ teaspoon salt
1 beaten egg
1¾ cups milk
⅓ cup walnut oil *or* cooking oil
1 cup chopped walnuts

In a large mixing bowl combine flour, sugar, cheese, baking powder, and salt.

In a small mixing bowl stir together egg, milk, and oil; add to flour mixture, stirring just till combined. Stir in ¾ *cup* of the nuts. Turn into a greased 9x5x3-inch loaf pan. Sprinkle the remaining nuts over the top.

Bake in a 350° oven about 1 hour or till a toothpick inserted in center comes out clean. Cool in pan for 10 minutes. Remove loaf from the pan; cool completely on a wire rack. Wrap and store overnight before slicing. Makes 1 loaf (18 servings).

*Nutrition information per serving: 209 cal., 5 g pro., 25 g carbo., 10 g fat, 18 mg chol., 189 mg sodium, 77 mg potassium, 1 g dietary fiber. U.S. RDA: 11% thiamine, 10% calcium.*

# SHARE A HANUKKAH FEAST

*At* least one night during the eight-day Hanukkah festival many Jewish families gather for a dinner party like the one pictured here. Musts on the evening's menu include such traditional foods as potato latkes, applesauce, and fried sweet-syrup-dipped pastries.

As each night of Hanukkah falls, celebrating Jewish families light another candle on the menorah.

**MENU**

**Sweet 'n' Sour
Brisket**

●

**Winter Vegetable
Medley**

●

**Calico Potato Latkes
with Applesauce**

●

**Citrus-Avocado Salad**

●

**Koeksisters
(Braided Pastries)**

175

## WINTER VEGETABLE MEDLEY

*On the sixth night of Hanukkah, Moroc-can Jews traditionally serve a dish like this one that features couscous (a grain-like pasta) and vegetables—*

- 1 **cup chicken broth**
- 1 **medium carrot, sliced**
- 1 **small onion, chopped**
- 1 **small butternut squash (1 pound), peeled and cut into ½-inch cubes (about 3½ cups)**
- 1 **medium zucchini, quartered lengthwise and sliced in ½-inch slices (about 1½ cups)**
- ½ **cup raisins**
- ¼ **teaspoon salt**
- ¼ **teaspoon ground cinnamon**
- ⅛ **teaspoon ground ginger**
- ⅛ **teaspoon ground turmeric**
- ½ **cup couscous**
- 1 **medium tomato, peeled, seeded, and chopped**

In a 3-quart saucepan bring broth, sliced carrot, and chopped onion to boiling; reduce heat. Cover and simmer for 5 minutes.

Stir in squash, zucchini, raisins, salt, cinnamon, ginger, turmeric, and dash *pepper*. Return to boiling; cover and simmer for 5 minutes or till vegetables are tender. Remove from heat. Stir in couscous and tomato.

Cover and let stand for 5 minutes. Fluff with a fork before serving. Makes 10 to 12 servings.

***Nutrition information per serving:*** *73 cal., 2 g pro., 17 g carbo., 0 g fat, 0 mg chol., 137 mg sodium, 292 mg potassium, 2 g dietary fiber. U.S. RDA: 103% vit. A, 14% vit. C.*

## CALICO POTATO LATKES WITH APPLESAUCE

*Potato latkes are simply potato pan-cakes. This version has green onion and carrot for added color and flavor—*

- 3 **medium potatoes (about 1 pound)**
- 3 **slightly beaten eggs**
- ½ **cup all-purpose flour**
- ½ **cup shredded carrot**
- ¼ **cup thinly sliced green onion**
- ½ **teaspoon salt**
- ¼ **teaspoon garlic powder**
- ¼ **teaspoon pepper**
- **Vegetable oil for shallow frying**
- **Chunk-style applesauce (optional)**

Peel potatoes. Coarsely shred, placing potatoes in cold water as you work to prevent darkening. Drain the potatoes well. Pat dry with paper towels.

In a large mixing bowl stir together drained potatoes, eggs, flour, shredded carrot, green onion, salt, garlic powder, and pepper.

In a 12-inch skillet heat *1 table-spoon* oil over medium heat. For each latke, drop *1 slightly rounded table-spoon* of the potato mixture into the hot oil, spreading gently to about a 2½-inch circle. Fry, 4 to 5 at a time, for 2 to 3 minutes or till edges are crisp; turn. Fry 2 to 3 minutes more or till golden brown. Drain on paper towels; cover and keep warm. Repeat, adding more oil as necessary.

Serve with applesauce. Makes 24.

**To make latkes ahead:** Prepare, fry, and drain latkes on paper towels as directed. Cover and chill. To reheat, place in a single layer on an ungreased baking sheet. Bake, uncovered, in a 400° oven for 10 to 12 minutes or till heated through and crisp.

***Nutrition information per latke:*** *55 cal., 1 g pro., 6 g carbo., 3 g fat, 34 mg chol., 56 mg sodium, 114 mg potassium, 1 g dietary fiber. U.S. RDA: 14% vit. A.*

## CITRUS-AVOCADO SALAD

*Tossing the avocado slices in the citrus juices prevents them from darkening—*

- ½ **cup white wine vinegar**
- ⅓ **cup olive oil *or* salad oil**
- 4 **teaspoons sugar**
- ⅛ **teaspoon salt**
- **Dash pepper**
- 3 **large oranges**
- 2 **large grapefruit**
- 2 **medium avocados, halved, seeded, and peeled**
- **Lettuce leaves**
- ⅓ **cup pomegranate seeds**

For dressing, in a screw-top jar combine vinegar, oil, sugar, salt, and pepper. Cover and shake well.

Peel and section the oranges and grapefruit over a bowl, catching juices. Slice avocados into bowl with juices. Toss to coat avocados.

To serve, arrange oranges, grape-fruit, and avocados on a lettuce-lined platter. Sprinkle with the pomegranate seeds. Shake dressing and drizzle over fruit. Makes 10 to 12 servings.

***Nutrition information per serving:*** *183 cal., 2 g pro., 15 g carbo., 14 g fat, 0 mg chol., 32 mg sodium, 440 mg potassium, 6 g dietary fiber. U.S. RDA: 69% vit. C.*

## KOEKSISTERS
## (BRAIDED PASTRIES)

*The braided shape of these tiny, cake-like pastries (pronounced KO uk sis turs) mimics challah bread—*

- ¾ cup sugar
- 1 tablespoon honey
- 2 teaspoons lemon juice
- ¼ teaspoon ground cardamom *or* cinnamon
- 1⅓ cups all-purpose *or* unbleached flour
- 1 teaspoon baking powder
- ¼ cup vegetable shortening
- 1 slightly beaten egg yolk
- ½ teaspoon vanilla
- Vegetable oil for deep frying
- Pearl sugar (optional)

For syrup, in medium saucepan combine sugar, honey, lemon juice, cardamom, and ⅓ cup *water*. Bring mixture to boiling; reduce heat. Boil gently, uncovered, for 10 minutes. Remove from heat. Cool; cover and chill.

In a medium mixing bowl combine flour and baking powder. Cut in shortening till mixture resembles fine crumbs. Stir together egg yolk, vanilla, and ⅓ cup *water*. Add to flour mixture. Stir till mixture forms a ball.

Turn out onto a lightly floured surface. Knead lightly till dough is smooth and pliable (about 1½ minutes). Cover and let rest for 20 minutes.

On a lightly floured surface roll the dough into a 10x6-inch rectangle. Halve lengthwise, forming two 10x3-inch strips. Cut each strip crosswise into ten 3x1-inch strips.

For each pastry, cut *one* 3x1-inch strip lengthwise into 3 narrow strips, cutting to within ¼ inch of one end. Braid these narrows strips and pinch together at the end to secure.

In a large saucepan heat oil to 375°. Fry pastries, a few at a time, about 1 minute per side or till golden brown. Drain on paper towels. While hot, dip in cooled syrup, coating well. Drain on wire rack. Repeat dipping in syrup, if desired. Sprinkle with pearl sugar. Serve the same day. Makes 20.

*Nutrition information per serving of pastry: 100 cal., 1 g pro., 15 g carbo., 4 g fat, 14 mg chol., 16 mg sodium, 11 mg potassium.*

## SWEET 'N' SOUR BRISKET

- 1 3- to 4-pound fresh beef brisket *or* boneless beef chuck pot roast
- ½ cup vinegar
- ½ cup apple juice
- ½ cup chili sauce
- 2 tablespoons brown sugar
- 1 teaspoon salt
- ¼ teaspoon pepper
- 2 medium onions, sliced
- 1 cup sliced celery with leaves
- 3 small cooking apples, cored and cut into wedges
- 2 tablespoons cornstarch
- ¼ cup cold water

Trim fat from meat; discard fat.

For marinade, in a small mixing bowl stir together vinegar, apple juice, chili sauce, brown sugar, salt, and pepper till sugar and salt are dissolved.

Place an extra large plastic bag in a large bowl. Place meat in bag; pour marinade over meat. Close bag. Chill for 12 to 24 hours, turning bag occasionally to redistribute marinade.

Remove meat from bag, reserving marinade. Place meat in a 3-quart casserole or 13x9x2-inch baking dish. Top with onions and celery. Pour reserved marinade over all.

Cover and roast in a 325° oven about 3 hours or till meat is very tender. Add apple to dish the last 10 minutes.

Remove meat, vegetables, and apples to a serving platter, reserving juices; cover and keep warm.

For gravy, strain reserved juices; measure 2½ cups. In a medium saucepan stir cornstarch into water. Add reserved juices. Cook and stir till slightly thickened and bubbly. Cook and stir 2 minutes more.

To serve, thinly slice meat; pass gravy. Makes 10 to 12 servings.

*Nutrition information per serving: 318 cal., 31 g pro., 18 g carbo., 13 g fat, 95 mg chol., 483 mg sodium, 507 mg potassium, 2 g dietary fiber. U.S. RDA: 15% riboflavin, 21% niacin, 19% iron.*

## COST-SAVING TRICKS
## FOR HOLIDAY RECIPES

**Make** seafood dip with half shrimp and half surimi (crab-flavored fish).

**For a rice pilaf,** use a mixture of half wild rice and half brown rice; they require about the same cooking time and the same amount of liquid.

**Reconstitute** frozen apple juice concentrate with sparkling water for a nonalcoholic bubbly.

**Popcorn** is probably the least expensive munchie around. Make it special: serve in a festive basket.

**Serve** just a few exotic fruits with in-season apples and pears.

**Brew** whole spices (such as cinnamon, vanilla bean, allspice) with coffee instead of buying the higher-priced specialty coffees.

# SERVE A FESTIVE DINNER

*Christmas dinner sure has changed over the years. Oh, there's still the tradition of turkey and all the trimmings. But, today's meals are easy on the cook, glamorous on the table, and sensible for good health—all things on the top of your Christmas wish list!*

Classy, elegant, and luscious—wine-poached pears and tangy cranberry sauce tucked in a delicate, rich pastry.

MENU

Brown-Rice-Stuffed
Turkey Breast
•
Orange-Sauced
Broccoli and Peppers
•
Tropical Fruit with
Sour Cream Dressing
•
Herbed Pumpkin
Rosettes
•
Cranberry Pear Tart

## CRANBERRY PEAR TART

*Choose Bartlett, Comice, Anjou, or Bosc pear varieties for this enticing dessert—*

**Rich Pastry**
- ⅔ cup dry red *or* white wine
- ¼ cup sugar
- 2 tablespoons margarine *or* butter
- ⅛ teaspoon ground nutmeg
- 3 medium pears, peeled, halved, and cored
- 2 teaspoons cornstarch
- 1 tablespoon cold water

**Cranberry Sauce Topping**
- ¼ cup chopped pecans

**Fresh mint sprigs (optional)**

Prepare Rich Pastry.

In a 10-inch skillet combine wine, sugar, margarine or butter, nutmeg, and ⅓ cup *water*. Heat mixture to melt margarine.

Carefully add pear halves to skillet. Simmer, covered, 10 to 12 minutes or till pears are tender, turning once.

Using a slotted spoon, remove the pears, reserving the liquid in the skillet. When cool enough to handle, fan pears by making 6 lengthwise cuts from the large end to but *not through* the stem end.

For glaze, measure ⅔ *cup* of the reserved liquid in skillet; discard any remaining liquid. Return reserved liquid to skillet. Stir cornstarch into cold water; add to reserved liquid. Cook and stir till thickened and bubbly. Cook and stir 2 minutes more. Remove from heat. Cool slightly.

Arrange fanned pears in bottom of Rich Pastry, leaving a 1-inch space along edges. Spoon glaze over top. Chill. Prepare Cranberry Sauce Topping. Spoon around the edge of the tart to form a border. Sprinkle with pecans. Chill 2 to 3 hours more. Top with mint. Makes 6 servings.

*Rich Pastry:* In a medium mixing bowl stir together 1½ cups *all-purpose flour*, 2 tablespoons *sugar,* and ¼ teaspoon *salt;* cut in ½ cup *margarine* or *butter* and 3 tablespoons *shortening* till pieces are the size of fine crumbs. Combine 1 beaten *egg yolk* and 3 tablespoons *ice water.* Gradually add to flour mixture, mixing well. Using fingers, knead lightly to form a ball. Cover; chill ½ to 1 hour or till easy to handle.

On a lightly floured surface roll pastry into a 13½x10½-inch rectangle. Transfer to an 11½x8½x1-inch tart pan with a removable bottom or a 12x7½x2-inch baking dish. Press pastry into fluted sides of tart pan or up sides of baking dish; trim edges. Prick pastry. Line pastry in baking dish with foil. Bake in a 375° oven for 15 to 17 minutes or till pastry is light brown. Remove foil after 8 minutes. Cool completely on a wire rack.

*Cranberry Sauce Topping:* In a small saucepan combine 1 cup *cranberries,* ½ cup *sugar,* and 2 tablespoons *water.* Bring to boiling, stirring to dissolve sugar. Boil rapidly for 2 minutes or till cranberries pop. Remove from heat. Cool thoroughly.

***Nutrition information per serving:*** *571 cal., 5 g pro., 69 g carbo., 30 g fat, 45 mg chol., 317 mg sodium, 186 mg potassium, 3 g dietary fiber. U.S. RDA: 17% vit. A, 18% thiamine, 11% riboflavin, 11% iron.*

## BROWN-RICE-STUFFED TURKEY BREAST

*Ask your butcher to remove the bone from the turkey breast. Or, to remove it yourself, use a sharp knife and cut along one side of the turkey breast next to the bone. Gently pull the meat away from the bone—*

- ¾ cup sliced celery
- ¾ cup chopped onion
- 2 tablespoons margarine *or* butter
- ¾ cup regular brown rice
- 2 teaspoons curry powder
- ½ teaspoon dried thyme, crushed
- 1½ cups chicken broth
- ½ cup coarsely chopped walnuts
- ¼ cup snipped parsley
- 1 2½- to 3-pound turkey breast half with bone
- ¼ cup apple jelly

In a medium saucepan cook celery and onion in hot margarine or butter till tender but not brown. Add brown rice, curry powder, and thyme. Cook and stir for 1 minute. Stir in chicken broth. Bring to boiling; reduce heat. Cover and simmer for 40 to 50 minutes or till rice is tender and liquid is absorbed. Stir in walnuts and parsley. Cover and chill up to 48 hours.

Meanwhile, remove bone from turkey; discard bone. Rinse turkey; pat dry. Butterfly turkey breast by slicing horizontally to cutting surface from thick side to within 1 inch of the opposite side. Fold top portion back. Place turkey, skin side down, between two pieces of plastic wrap. With the flat side of a meat mallet, pound turkey to a 12-inch square, about ¾ inch thick. Remove and discard plastic wrap.

Spoon rice mixture over turkey. Roll up, starting from the side without skin underneath. Tie in at least 6 places with string. Place turkey on a rack in a shallow baking pan.

Roast in a 350° oven for 1 to 1¼ hours or till a thermometer inserted in center of turkey registers 170°, brushing with jelly the last 10 minutes of roasting. Let turkey stand, covered, 10 minutes. Remove string from turkey. Carve into 18 slices. Makes 6 servings.

***Nutrition information per serving:*** *417 cal., 45 g pro., 32 g carbo., 12 g fat, 110 mg chol., 324 mg sodium, 651 mg potassium, 2 g dietary fiber. U.S. RDA: 13% thiamine, 14% riboflavin, 60% niacin, 20% iron.*

## ORANGE-SAUCED BROCCOLI AND PEPPERS

*Another time, serve this tangy sauce on steamed green beans—*

- 1 pound broccoli
- 1 medium red *or* yellow sweet pepper
- 2 tablespoons finely chopped onion
- 1 clove garlic, minced
- 1 tablespoon margarine *or* butter
- 1½ teaspoons cornstarch
- ⅔ cup orange juice
- 2 teaspoons Dijon-style mustard

Cut broccoli stalks lengthwise into uniform spears. Cut pepper into 1-inch pieces.

In a medium saucepan cook broccoli and pepper in a small amount of lightly salted boiling water for 8 to 10 minutes or till broccoli is crisp-tender. Drain; keep warm.

Meanwhile, for sauce, in a small saucepan cook onion and garlic in hot margarine or butter till onion is tender. Stir in cornstarch. Add orange juice and mustard. Cook and stir till mixture is thickened and bubbly. Cook and stir 2 minutes more. Spoon sauce over broccoli and pepper. Makes 6 servings.

**Microwave directions:** Cut up broccoli and pepper as directed. Place in an 8x8x2-inch microwave-safe baking dish. Add 2 tablespoons *water*. Cover with vented clear plastic wrap. Cook on 100% power (high) for 6 to 8 minutes or till broccoli is crisp-tender, rearranging broccoli and pepper once. Let stand, covered, while preparing sauce.

For sauce, in a 2-cup glass measure cook onion, garlic, and margarine or butter on high for 1½ minutes. Stir in cornstarch, ½ *cup* of the orange juice, and mustard. Cook, uncovered, on high for 1 to 2 minutes or till mixture is thickened and bubbly, stirring every 30 seconds. Drain vegetables. Serve as directed *above*.

***Nutrition information per serving:*** *61 cal., 3 g pro., 9 g carbo., 2 g fat, 0 mg chol., 114 mg sodium, 347 mg potassium, 3 g dietary fiber. U.S. RDA: 48% vit. A, 139% vit. C.*

## TROPICAL FRUIT WITH SOUR CREAM DRESSING

- 1 8¼-ounce can pineapple chunks
- ½ cup dairy sour cream
- ¼ cup mayonnaise *or* salad dressing
- ½ teaspoon shredded lime peel
- 1 teaspoon lime juice
- ⅛ teaspoon ground mace *or* nutmeg
- 2 oranges *or* 3 tangelos
- 1 cup seedless red grapes, halved
- Bibb *or* Boston lettuce leaves
- ⅓ cup toasted coconut
- Lime slices, quartered (optional)

Drain pineapple, reserving *1 tablespoon* of the juice. Set pineapple aside.

For dressing, stir together reserved juice, sour cream, mayonnaise, lime peel, lime juice, and mace. Cover and chill.

Peel and section oranges or tangelos. Evenly divide pineapple, orange sections, and grapes among lettuce-lined individual salad plates. Spoon dressing over top. Sprinkle *each* salad with *some* of the coconut. Serve with lime. Makes 6 servings.

***Nutrition information per serving:*** *187 cal., 2 g pro., 17 g carbo., 14 g fat, 14 mg chol., 66 mg sodium, 258 mg potassium, 2 g dietary fiber. U.S. RDA: 48% vit. C.*

## HERBED PUMPKIN ROSETTES

*A shortcut to holiday baking—savory rolls that start with hot roll mix—*

- 1 16-ounce package hot roll mix
- ¾ cup canned pumpkin
- ½ cup water
- ¼ cup sugar
- ¼ cup margarine *or* butter
- 2 eggs
- ½ cup all-purpose flour
- 2 tablespoons margarine *or* butter, melted
- ¼ teaspoon dried rosemary, finely crushed
- ¼ teaspoon dried basil, crushed

In a large mixing bowl stir together the flour and yeast from the package of hot roll mix.

In a medium saucepan heat and stir pumpkin, water, sugar, and the ¼ cup margarine or butter till warm (120° to 125°). Add pumpkin mixture and eggs to yeast mixture; mix well. Stir in as much of the ½ cup flour as possible.

Turn out onto a lightly floured surface. Knead in remaining flour (about 3 minutes). Cover and let rest 5 minutes.

Divide dough into 20 pieces. On a lightly floured surface roll each piece into a 12-inch rope. Tie each rope in a loose knot, leaving two long ends. Tuck top end under roll. Bring bottom end up; tuck into center of roll.

Place 2 to 3 inches apart on lightly greased baking sheets. Brush with the 2 tablespoons margarine or butter. Combine rosemary and basil; sprinkle over rolls. Cover; let rise till nearly double (about 20 minutes).

Bake in a 375° oven for 12 to 15 minutes or till rolls are golden brown. Makes 20 rolls.

***Nutrition information per roll:*** *144 cal., 4 g pro., 23 g carbo., 4 g fat, 27 mg chol., 204 mg sodium, 62 mg potassium, 1 g dietary fiber. U.S. RDA: 44% vit. A, 12% thiamine.*

## MENU

**Phyllo Roll
With Cranberry Sauce**

•

**Orange Streusel
Muffins**

•

**Honey-Lime
Fruit Compote**

•

**White Grape
Spritzers**

*Steven*

# WAKE UP TO A HOLIDAY BRUNCH

*Oh, the magic of Christmas morning! There are presents to open, stockings to empty, new toys to play with, and a special family brunch to share. This hearty menu is completely made ahead; just heat and serve. It's a marvelous meal that'll long be a fond family memory.*

Golden and flaky—Phyllo Roll with Cranberry Sauce is full of cheddar cheese, smoked ham, and vegetables.

## PHYLLO ROLL WITH CRANBERRY SAUCE

⅓ cup chopped celery
⅓ cup chopped green pepper
¼ cup sliced green onion
1½ teaspoons cooking oil
1½ cups diced fully cooked ham (7 ounces)
1 4-ounce can mushroom stems and pieces, drained
½ cup shredded cheddar *or* Monterey Jack cheese (2 ounces)
1 tablespoon all-purpose flour
¼ teaspoon pepper
⅓ cup unsalted margarine *or* butter, melted
1 tablespoon fine dry bread crumbs
8 sheets frozen phyllo dough (18x14-inch rectangles), thawed
1 beaten egg white
Cranberry Sauce

In a large saucepan cook celery, green pepper, and onion in hot oil till tender. Remove from heat. Drain well. Stir in ham, mushrooms, cheese, flour, and pepper.

Lightly brush *some* of the margarine or butter and sprinkle ½ teaspoon of the bread crumbs between *each* phyllo sheet, stacking sheets. Brush top sheet with egg white.

Mound the ham mixture on stack of phyllo dough parallel to and about 3 inches from one of the short edges. Fold the 3-inch edge of dough over the ham mixture. Fold in about 1½ inches on the long sides, then roll up from the short side with the ham mixture. Make shallow cuts in diagonal crisscross fashion across the top.

Place roll in a 13x9x2-inch baking pan. Brush with more of the margarine or butter. Cover; chill up to 24 hours.

To serve, uncover; bake in a 400° oven 25 to 30 minutes or till golden and heated through. Slice and serve with Cranberry Sauce. Makes 4 servings.

*Cranberry Sauce:* In a small saucepan combine ½ cup *cranberry-apple drink* and 1 tablespoon *cornstarch.* Add one 8-ounce can *jellied cranberry sauce* and dash *ground cloves.* Cook and stir till thickened and bubbly; cook and stir 2 minutes more. Stir in 1 tablespoon *margarine* or *butter* till melted. Makes about 1⅓ cups sauce.

**Nutrition information per serving:** *495 cal., 17 g pro., 45 g carbo., 28 g fat, 41 mg chol., 975 mg sodium, 324 mg potassium, 2 g dietary fiber. U.S. RDA: 20% vit. A, 49% vit. C, 34% thiamine, 16% riboflavin, 17% niacin, 13% calcium, 12% iron.*

## ORANGE STREUSEL MUFFINS

1¾ cups all-purpose flour
¼ cup sugar
2½ teaspoons baking powder
½ teaspoon salt
1 beaten egg
¾ cup milk
⅓ cup cooking oil
¼ cup orange marmalade
Streusel Topper

Grease 2½-inch muffin cups or line with paper bake cups. Set aside.

For batter, in a medium mixing bowl stir together flour, sugar, baking powder, and salt. Make a well in the center.

In a small mixing bowl combine egg, milk, and oil. Add egg mixture all at once to flour mixture, stirring just till moistened. Batter should be slightly lumpy. Spoon about *1 tablespoon* of the batter into *each* prepared cup. Top *each* with about *1 teaspoon* of the marmalade. Spoon another *1 tablespoon* of the batter atop marmalade in each cup. Sprinkle with Streusel Topper.

Bake in a 400° oven 20 to 25 minutes or till golden. Remove from pans. Serve at once. *Or,* cool on a wire rack. Wrap muffins in moisture- and vapor-proof wrap. Seal, label, and freeze up to 6 months. To serve, wrap frozen muffins in foil. Reheat the muffins in a 400° oven for 20 minutes or till warm. Makes 12 muffins.

*Streusel Topper:* In a small mixing bowl combine 2 tablespoons *all-purpose flour,* 2 tablespoons *brown sugar,* 1 tablespoon softened *margarine* or *butter,* and 1 teaspoon *ground cinnamon.* Stir in 2 tablespoons chopped *pecans.*

**Nutrition information per muffin:** *206 cal., 3 g pro., 27 g carbo., 10 g fat, 24 mg chol., 179 mg sodium, 65 mg potassium, 1 g dietary fiber. U.S. RDA: 10% thiamine.*

## HONEY-LIME FRUIT COMPOTE

1 lime
2 tablespoons sugar
2 tablespoons honey
1 small red apple, cored and cut into bite-size chunks
1 small green apple, cored and cut into bite-size chunks
2 kiwi fruit, peeled, quartered lengthwise, and sliced
½ cup seedless red *and/or* green grapes, halved
Fresh mint sprigs (optional)

Finely shred ¼ *teaspoon* lime peel; set aside. Juice lime (you should have *3 to 4 tablespoons*).

In a medium bowl combine lime peel, lime juice, sugar, and honey; stir to dissolve sugar. Stir in apples, kiwi fruit, and grapes. Cover; chill up to 12 hours. Top each serving with a mint sprig. Makes 4 servings.

**Nutrition information per serving:** *128 cal., 1 g pro., 34 g carbo., 0 g fat, 0 mg chol., 3 mg sodium, 247 mg potassium, 3 g dietary fiber. U.S. RDA: 60% vit. C.*

## WHITE GRAPE SPRITZERS

Fruit Ice Cubes
2 cups unsweetened white *or* red grape juice, chilled
2 cups lemon-lime carbonated beverage *or* champagne, chilled

Prepare Fruit Ice Cubes.

In each of 4 wineglasses, combine ½ *cup* of the grape juice and ½ *cup* of the carbonated beverage or champagne. Add Fruit Ice Cubes. Makes 4 (8-ounce) servings.

*Fruit Ice Cubes:* Place *strawberries,* or *star fruit* or peeled *kiwi fruit* slices in ice cube trays. Add water. Freeze.

**Nutrition information per serving:** *124 cal., 0 g pro., 32 g carbo., 0 g fat, 0 mg chol., 3 mg sodium, 56 mg potassium, 1 g dietary fiber. U.S. RDA: 67% vit. C.*

# DIET AND HEALTH

## LIGHT HOLIDAY SIPPING
### *The facts on carbonated waters*

Sparkling refreshers:
There is a nutrition difference.

By Barbara Goldman

### A new holiday twist: health-conscious sipping

• **The setting:** A friendly holiday party, complete with appetizers and beverages galore.

• **Your selection:** A light, nonalcoholic beverage, perhaps tonic with a twist, or one of the trendy new seltzers.

• **A fact:** You may not be getting the healthful drink you think you are; some of these carbonated beverages are high in calories and contain sodium.

### How to know what you're drinking

You're off to a good start when you read the list of ingredients on the label. Many seltzers and sparkling waters, whether plain or flavored, *are* calorie free and sodium free or low in sodium. But before you select a light-colored sparkler at a party or from the grocer's shelf, make sure you know what's in it. Don't assume that a clear, sparkling drink located in a section with bottled waters is calorie free.

A flavored seltzer may read "all natural" and "no sucrose," yet contain high-fructose corn syrup—a sugar-based sweetener that is derived from corn rather than cane—with just as many calories as colas and other sugared soft drinks!

### APPROXIMATE CALORIES IN SPARKLING WATERS AND CARBONATED BEVERAGES

| Beverage | Approx. Calories Per 6-Ounce Serving |
|---|---|
| Sparkling water/seltzers (unsweetened, plain or flavored) | 0 |
| Club soda | 0 |
| Tonic water | 60–70 |
| Sweetened seltzers (sugar and sugar-based) | 70–85 |
| Assorted soft drinks (orange soda, root beer, colas, lemon-lime) | 70–95 |

### What's what among sparkling waters?

• **Sparkling water:** any water that is carbonated (made bubbly) by dissolved carbon-dioxide gas that occurs naturally in subsurface water or that has been added later.

• **Sparkling mineral water:** any kind of carbonated water that has minerals dissolved in it, naturally or otherwise. Most are very low in sodium, but a few prove to be the exceptions.

• **Seltzer:** There's no clear definition of a seltzer. "Seltzer" on a label used to infer salt-free, calorie-free, filtered carbonated water without added minerals or mineral salts. Many—flavored and unflavored—conform to this description. Others contain sugar-based sweeteners and some, noncaloric sweeteners.

• **Club soda:** filtered, carbonated water, typically tap, to which minerals and mineral salts have been added. These additives provide a distinctive taste that makes club soda popular as a mixer. Although calorie free, club soda is usually higher in sodium than other sparkling waters.

• **Tonic water:** a carbonated soft drink often used as a mixer. Although tonic water is sweetened similarly to other soft drinks, its sweetness is masked by the taste of quinine.

# FRITTERS! FINE FINGER FOOD
## TRENDY TIDBITS YOU CAN MAKE AT HOME
By Joy Taylor

**G**lance at some hot-spot menus and you're likely to find a new entry: Fritters! These tasty morsels are simple to make at home, especially if you follow our easy instructions.

## COCONUT SHRIMP FRITTERS

1½ pounds fresh large shrimp in shells
¼ cup dry sherry
2 tablespoons soy sauce
1 tablespoon curry powder
2 teaspoons sesame oil
1 teaspoon grated gingerroot
Cooking oil for deep frying
1 egg yolk
1 cup ice cold water
2 egg whites
1 cup all-purpose flour
¾ cup shredded coconut
2 tablespoons cornstarch
½ cup cornstarch

Peel and devein shrimp, leaving tails intact; place in a shallow dish. In a small bowl combine sherry, soy sauce, curry powder, sesame oil, and gingerroot; pour over shrimp. Marinate in the refrigerator for 1 to 2 hours. In a large saucepan or deep fryer heat 4 inches oil to 400°.

Drain shrimp, reserving marinade. For batter, in a small bowl combine the reserved marinade with the yolk and water; set aside. In a large mixer bowl beat the egg whites with an electric mixer on high speed till stiff peaks form (tips stand straight). Combine the flour, coconut, and 2 tablespoons cornstarch; stir in the egg yolk mixture just till moistened. Fold in the egg whites. Do not allow batter to stand more than 10 minutes before using.

Coat shrimp using the ½ cup cornstarch; dip in batter. Fry, 3 or 4 at a time, for 1½ to 2 minutes or till golden, turning after 1 minute. Drain on paper towels. Serve hot. Makes about 35.

*Nutrition information per fritter: 71 cal., 3 g pro., 6 g carbo., 3 g fat, 30 mg chol., 83 mg sodium, 52 mg potassium.*

**COCONUT SHRIMP FRITTERS**

**ALMOND FRITTERS**

### FRITTER KNOW-HOW
**Folding the egg whites into the batter:** Gently fold the stiffly beaten egg whites into the flour-egg-yolk mixture to produce a light batter.

**Adding the fritters to the hot oil:** Carefully drop 3 or 4 of the fritters into the hot oil at a time. Frying a few at a time helps keep the temperature of the oil constant.

## ALMOND FRITTERS WITH HONEY CINNAMON CREAM

*Serve these sweet and nutty fritters for brunch or dessert—*
½ cup all-purpose flour
½ cup ground toasted almonds
2 tablespoons sugar
1 teaspoon baking powder
Dash salt
• • •
1 slightly beaten egg yolk
⅓ cup light cream *or* milk
1 tablespoon margarine *or* butter, melted and cooled
Few drops almond extract
1 egg white at room temperature
• • •
Cooking oil for deep frying
1 recipe Honey Cinnamon Cream

For batter, in a medium mixing bowl thoroughly stir together the all-purpose flour, almonds, sugar, baking powder, and salt. In a small mixing bowl combine egg yolk, light cream or milk, margarine or butter, and almond extract. Add the egg yolk mixture all at once to flour mixture, stirring just till combined.

In a small mixer bowl beat egg white with an electric mixer on high speed till stiff peaks form (tips stand straight). Fold into the batter. In a large saucepan or deep fryer heat 4 inches cooking oil to 375°. Drop batter by teaspoonfuls into hot oil; fry, 3 or 4 at a time, for 2½ to 3 minutes or till fritters are golden, turning after 1½ minutes. Drain on paper towels. Serve hot with Honey Cinnamon Cream for dipping. Makes 18 fritters.

*Honey Cinnamon Cream:* In a small chilled mixing bowl beat ¼ cup *whipping cream* till soft peaks form. Fold in ¼ cup *dairy sour cream*, 1 teaspoon *honey*, ¼ teaspoon *ground cinnamon*, and dash *ground nutmeg*. Cover and chill for up to 1 hour before serving.

*Nutrition information per fritter with cream: 90 cal., 1 g pro., 5 g carbo., 7 g fat, 24 mg chol., 40 mg sodium, 37 mg potassium.*

# MOUSSE MAGIC
## FIVE FINE DESSERTS FROM ONE BASIC RECIPE

**M**aster our basic white mousse recipe, and with a touch of the magic wand (a wooden spoon will do) you can create any of these five spectacular desserts.

## WHITE MOUSSE

*White baking bars with cocoa butter are found in the baking section of your supermarket. Read the ingredient list to determine if the product contains cocoa butter—*

- ¼ **cup sugar**
- 1 **envelope unflavored gelatin**
- 1 **cup cold water**
- 3 **ounces white baking bar with cocoa butter, chopped**
- 3 **beaten egg yolks**
- 1 **cup whipping cream**
- 3 **egg whites**
- 1 **teaspoon vanilla**

In a medium saucepan combine sugar and gelatin. Add water and baking bar. Cook and stir over medium heat till mixture is boiling and gelatin is dissolved. Stir about *1 cup* of the hot mixture into egg yolks; return all to saucepan. Cook and stir just till mixture bubbles. Transfer to a large mixing bowl. Chill till the consistency of unbeaten egg whites (about 45 minutes), stirring occasionally.

Meanwhile, in a chilled bowl beat whipping cream till stiff peaks form. Chill till ready to use.

In a large mixer bowl beat egg whites and vanilla till stiff peaks form (tips stand straight). Stir a small amount of beaten egg white into gelatin mixture; fold in remaining whites. Fold whipped cream into egg white mixture. Spoon into dessert cups; chill 2 hours or till serving time. Makes 8 servings.

*Nutrition information per serving:* 217 cal., 4 g pro., 14 g carbo., 16 g fat, 145 mg chol., 43 mg sodium, 78 mg potassium, 0 g dietary fiber. U.S. RDA: 11% vit. A.

**ONE BASIC RECIPE** is all it takes to prepare (clockwise from left): Mousse and Berry Parfaits, Mousse Torte, White Mousse, Mocha Mousse Pie, and Mint Mousse Soufflé.

## MOCHA MOUSSE PIE

Prepare White Mousse as directed *except omit* vanilla and *add* 2 to 3 tablespoons *coffee liqueur* and 1 tablespoon *crème de cacao* to gelatin and egg yolk mixture after transferring to bowl.

Pour mousse into a *chocolate-flavored crumb pie shell.* Cover and chill 5 hours or overnight. Top with *whipped cream* and *chocolate curls.* Serves 8.

*Nutrition information per serving:* 383 cal., 6 g pro., 31 g carbo., 27 g fat, 157 mg chol., 136 mg sodium, 116 mg potassium, 0 g dietary fiber. U.S. RDA: 18% vit. A, 11% riboflavin.

## MOUSSE TORTE

Prepare and bake one package 2-layer-size regular *deep chocolate cake mix* according to package directions in two 9-inch cake pans. Cool cake on wire racks. Wash cake pans.

Prepare White Mousse as directed. Line bottoms and sides of three 9-inch cake pans with foil. Spread *one-fourth* of the mousse (about 1¼ cups) in *each* pan; chill 1 hour or till firm. Leave remaining mousse at room temperature.

Split cake layers in half horizontally to form 4 layers. Place a cake layer on serving plate. Lift foil with mousse from pan and invert atop cake layer; gently peel foil off mousse. Repeat with remaining chilled mousse and cake.

Spread the room temperature mousse on top of stacked cake layers, letting the mousse flow over the edges. Sprinkle with *grated chocolate.* Chill for at least 1 hour before serving. Makes 8 to 10 servings.

*Nutrition information per serving:* 602 cal., 10 g pro., 67 g carbo., 35 g fat, 248 mg chol., 365 mg sodium, 185 mg potassium, and 1 g dietary fiber. U.S. RDA: 13% vit. A, 12% thiamine, 18% riboflavin, 12% calcium, 13% iron.

## MOUSSE AND BERRY PARFAITS

Prepare White Mousse as directed, *except* add 1 teaspoon finely shredded *orange peel* and ¼ cup *orange juice* to gelatin and egg yolk mixture after transferring to bowl.

Alternately layer mousse and 3 cups sliced fresh *strawberries* in 6 to 8 parfait glasses, ending with mousse. Chill for at least 2 hours. To serve, top with *strawberries.* Makes 6 to 8 servings.

*Nutrition information per serving:* 332 cal., 7 g pro., 28 g carbo., 22 g fat, 193 mg chol., 59 mg sodium, 336 mg potassium, 3 g dietary fiber. U.S. RDA: 16% vit. A, 128% vit. C, 15% riboflavin.

## MINT MOUSSE SOUFFLÉ

Prepare White Mousse as directed *except* fold in ¾ cup finely chopped *chocolate mint wafers* and 4 to 6 drops *green food coloring* after folding in the whipped cream. Pour into a 1-quart soufflé dish with greased collar attached. Cover and chill at least 3 hours.

To serve, remove collar and press ¼ cup *chocolate mint wafer curls* onto top edge of soufflé. Makes 8 servings.

*Nutrition information per serving:* 304 cal., 5 g pro., 31 g carbo., 19 g fat, 145 mg chol., 83 mg sodium, 97 mg potassium, 0 g dietary fiber. U.S. RDA: 11% vit. A.

# INDEX

# D-F

# Index

# Index

## T-Z

## Microwave Wattage

All microwave recipes were tested in countertop microwave ovens that provide 600 to 700 watts of cooking power. The cooking times are approximate because microwave ovens vary by manufacturer.

## Nutrition Analysis

Some nutrient information is given by gram weight per serving. The United States Recommended Daily Allowances (U.S. RDAs) for selected vitamins and minerals are given in the recipes when the value exceeds 10 percent. The U.S. RDAs tell the amounts of certain nutrients necessary to meet the dietary needs of most healthy people.

To obtain the nutrition analysis of each recipe, the following guidelines were used:
● When ingredient options appear in a recipe, the analysis was calculated using the first ingredient choice.
● Optional ingredients were omitted in the analyses.
● The nutrition analyses for recipes calling for fresh ingredients were calculated using the measurements for raw fruits, vegetables, and meats.
● If a recipe gives optional serving sizes (such as "Makes 6 to 8 servings"), the nutrition analysis was calculated using the first choice.

Have BETTER HOMES AND GARDENS® magazine delivered to your door. For information, write to:
MR. ROBERT AUSTIN
P.O. BOX 4536
DES MOINES, IA 50336